TOURISM IN THE NEW EUROPE:

PERSPECTIVES ON SME POLICIES AND PRACTICES

ADVANCES IN TOURISM RESEARCH

Series Editor: **Professor Stephen J. Page**
University of Stirling, UK
s.j.page@stir.ac.uk

Advances in Tourism Research series publishes monographs and edited volumes that comprise state-of-the-art research findings, written and edited by leading researchers working in the wider field of tourism studies. The series has been designed to provide a cutting edge focus for researchers interested in tourism, particularly the management issues now facing decision-makers, policy analysts and the public sector. The audience is much wider than just academics and each book seeks to make a significant contribution to the literature in the field of study by not only reviewing the state of knowledge relating to each topic but also questioning some of the prevailing assumptions and research paradigms which currently exist in tourism research. The series also aims to provide a platform for further studies in each area by highlighting key research agendas, which will stimulate further debate and interest in the expanding area of tourism research. The series is always willing to consider new ideas for innovative and scholarly books, inquiries should be made directly to the Series Editor.

Published:

Benchmarking National Tourism Organisations and Agencies
LENNON, SMITH, COCKEREL & TREW

Extreme Tourism: Lessons from the World's Cold Water Islands
BALDACCHINO

Tourism Local Systems and Networking
LAZZERETTI & PETRILLO

Progress in Tourism Marketing
KOZAK & ANDREU

Indigenous Tourism
RYAN & AICKEN

An International Handbook of Tourism Education
AIREY & TRIBE

Tourism in Turbulent Times
WILKS, PENDERGAST & LEGGAT

Taking Tourism to the Limits
RYAN, PAGE & AICKEN

Tourism and Social Identities
BURNS & NOVELLI

Forthcoming:

Micro-clusters & Networks – The Growth of Tourism
MICHAEL

Tourism and Politics
BURNS & NOVELLI

Hospitality: A Social Lens
LASHLEY, LYNCH & MORRISON

For other titles in the series visit: www.elsevier.com/locate/series/aitr

Related Elsevier Journals — sample copies available on request
Annals of Tourism Research
International Journal of Hospitality Management
Tourism Management

TOURISM IN THE NEW EUROPE:

PERSPECTIVES ON SME POLICIES AND PRACTICES

EDITED BY

RHODRI THOMAS

UK Centre for Events Management, Leeds Metropolitan University, UK

MARCJANNA AUGUSTYN

Hull University Business School @ Scarborough, UK

ELSEVIER

Amsterdam • Boston • Heidelberg • London • New York • Oxford
Paris • San Diego • San Francisco • Singapore • Sydney • Tokyo

Elsevier
The Boulevard, Langford Lane, Kidlington, Oxford OX5 1GB, UK
Radarweg 29, PO Box 211, 1000 AE Amsterdam, The Netherlands

First edition 2007

Notice
No responsibility is assumed by the publisher for any injury and/or damage to persons or property as a matter of products liability, negligence or otherwise, or from any use or operation of any methods, products, instructions or ideas contained in the material herein. Because of rapid advances in the medical sciences, in particular, independent verification of diagnoses and drug dosages should be made

British Library Cataloguing in Publication Data
A catalogue record for this book is available from the British Library

Library of Congress Cataloging-in-Publication Data
A catalog record for this book is available from the Library of Congress

ISBN-13: 978-0-08-044706-3
ISBN-10: 0-08-044706-6 ✔

For information on all Elsevier publications
visit our website at books.elsevier.com

Printed and bound in The Netherlands

07 08 09 10 11 10 9 8 7 6 5 4 3 2 1

Working together to grow
libraries in developing countries

www.elsevier.com | www.bookaid.org | www.sabre.org

ELSEVIER   BOOK AID International   Sabre Foundation

Contents

List of Figures

List of Tables

CONTRIBUTORS

Volkan Altıntaş Centre for European Integration Studies-ZEI(C), Walter-Flex str. 3, 53113 Bonn, Germany

Marcjanna Augustyn Hull University Business School @ Scarborough, UK

Sibel Mehter Aykın Faculty of Economics and Administrative Sciences, Akdeniz University, Turkey

Vladimír Baláž Institute for Forecasting, Slovak Academy of Science, Šancová 56, 81105 Bratislava, Slovak Republic

Mario Castellanos-Verdugo Department of Business Administration and Marketing, University of Seville, Spain

Crispin Dale School of Sport, Performing Arts and Leisure, University of Wolverhampton, Walsall, UK

Marian Gúčik Department of Tourism and Hospitality, Matej Bel University, Banská Bystrica, Slovak Republic

Hans Holmengen Department of Tourism and Applied Social Sciences, Lillehammer University College, Norway

Janusz Klisinski Faculty of Management, University of Technology, Czestochowa, Poland

Raija Komppula Department of Business and Economics, University of Joensuu, Finland

Sonja Sibila Lebe Department of Tourism, Faculty of Economics and Business, University of Maribor and Tourism Section of the Scientific Institute for Regional Development, Slovenia

David Leslie Caledonian Business School, Glasgow Caledonian University, Scotland, UK

Vanda Maráková Department of Tourism and Hospitality, Matej Bel University, Banská Bystrica, Slovak Republic

Barbara Marciszewska Academy of Physical Education and Sport, Gdansk, and Maritime Academy, Gdynia, Poland

Harry Matlay University of Central England Business School, Birmingham, UK

Ziene Mottiar School of Hospitality Management and Tourism, Dublin Institute of Technology, Dublin, Ireland

Mª de los Ángeles Oviedo-García Department of Business Administration and Marketing, University of Seville, Spain

John Pheby Luton Business School, University of Luton, UK

Neil Robinson School of Leisure, Hospitality & Food Management, University of Salford, UK

Theresa Ryan School of Hospitality Management and Tourism, Dublin Institute of Technology, Dublin, Ireland

Viktoria Saprunova OOO "VQ" Consulting, Moscow, Russia (formerly at Moscow Lomonossov State University)

Ivana Šípková Department of Tourism and Hospitality, Matej Bel University, Banská Bystrica, Slovak Republic

Izabella Sowier-Kasprzyk Faculty of Management, Czestochowa University of Technology, Poland

Anna Staszewska Academy of Physical Education and Sport, Gdansk, Poland

Jolanta Staszewska Faculty of Materials Engineering and Metallurgy, Silesia University of Technology, Gliwice, Poland

Rhodri Thomas UK Centre for Events Management, Leeds Metropolitan University, UK

Nadine Veerapermal Student the International Marketing Master, Ecole Supérieure des Affaires (ESA), University of Lille 2, France

Paul Westhead Centre for Small and Medium-Sized Enterprises, University of Warwick, UK

Preface

Over the past 50 years or so, the European Union has enlarged in a piecemeal manner, sometimes incorporating relatively prosperous countries while at other times encouraging the accession of those that will be, for many years, net recipients of finance. The recent enlargement falls into the latter category. Ten new member states joined the 'community' in 2004, all of whom had significantly lower GDP than existing members and, often, quite different economic and political traditions. This attempt at creating a unified market of 25 member states raises numerous fascinating issues for tourism production and consumption. Some of these — as they relate to tourism SMEs — are examined in this book.

It was never our intention to create a textbook. As a consequence, we do not claim to provide a standardised account of SME policy and practice in each member state. Our experience tells us that such a task would, at the moment, be unrealistic. There are insufficient data available and few academics working in the field, who could contribute robust research in English. Our preference for a rather selective research-based approach is, therefore, primarily pragmatic. Critics may point out — with some justification — that there are gaps in coverage. We make no exaggerated claims about comprehensiveness, though we are confident that this volume represents a solid start of a longer-term research agenda. Our aim in assembling and editing this book has been to draw together work that has been undertaken in the 'new' Europe, to map out a research agenda and stimulate greater research effort. In that, we feel the collective effort of colleagues represents an advance in tourism research, as demanded by this book series.

We are grateful to Stephen Page and others at Elsevier for their support from the outset; it is always satisfying to work with people who share similar visions. As always, we are most grateful to the contributors for their participation. They appreciated the challenges involved in trying to bring some degree of stylistic unity to the project, and responded positively to suggestions accordingly.

Producing a book of this kind, provides a rare opportunity to thank those who consistently give intellectual and emotional succour, notably of late: Glenn Bowdin, Karen Conway, Lauren Conway, Andrew Eaglen, Agata Maccarrone-Eaglen, Liam Hayden, David Hind, Stephanie Jameson, Marianna Kornilaki, Guy Lincoln, Conrad Lashley, Jonathan Long, Paul Lynch, Annemarie Piso, Huw Thomas, Andreas Walmsley, and Emma Wood. Finally, we would like to thank Nia Thomas for her work on the index.

Rhodri Thomas
Marcjanna Augustyn
Editors

Chapter 1

Small Firms in the New Europe: An Overview

Marcjanna Augustyn and Rhodri Thomas

Introduction

If it is meaningful to speak of the European Union (EU) as *an* economy (rather than association of 25 member states),[1] it is the world's largest. Its combined GDP is greater than
that of advanced capitalist countries such as the USA and Japan, and emerging global
economic powers such as China and India still have some way to go before they equal
European economic output (World Bank, 2006). Yet, such an observation conceals critical national differences in the economies of EU member states. Using an index to represent GDP per capita (100 = average GDP of the 15 states that comprised the EU until it
expanded in 2004), Luxembourg's GDP per capita was 229 in 2005 whereas Latvia's
was merely 16; Ireland's was 146 during the same year and Estonia's was 28 (European
Commission, 2005a). Although these examples show the differences at their most
extreme, they demonstrate clearly the variety in levels of output and wealth contained
within the EU.

The scale of tourism activity also varies significantly between the member states. In
2004, for example, France and Spain accounted for 18 per cent and 13 per cent, respectively, of European international arrivals (13 per cent and 14 per cent, respectively, of
international tourism receipts), whereas Norway and Sweden each accounted for 1 per
cent of arrivals, and 1 per cent and 2 per cent, respectively, of international receipts
(WTO, 2005).

The existence of a single currency (the Euro) in twelve member states[2] further complicates
the European economic terrain. Tourists face a more meaningful single market when visiting
certain combinations of countries compared with others. Equally, small and medium-sized

---

[1] The 25 members of the EU are Austria, Belgium, Cyprus, Czech Republic, Denmark, Estonia, Finland, France,
Germany, Greece, Hungary, Ireland, Italy, Latvia, Lithuania, Luxembourg, Malta, Netherlands, Poland, Portugal,
Slovakia, Slovenia, Spain, Sweden and United Kingdom.
[2] The 12 members that have adopted the Euro as their currency are Austria, Belgium, Finland, France, Germany,
Greece, Ireland, Italy, Luxembourg, the Netherlands, Portugal and Spain.

Tourism in the New Europe
Copyright © 2007 by Elsevier Ltd.
All rights of reproduction in any form reserved.
ISBN: 0-08-044706-6

enterprises (SMEs) in some states can more easily trade beyond their borders than their counterparts elsewhere.[3]

Some of the most recent members of the EU have only been fully functioning democracies with market economies since the early 1990s. This throws up significant differences of business culture and political tradition, which, in turn, can reasonably be expected to influence the kind of policies aimed at tourism SMEs in the different countries.

It seems that the EU has not welcomed its last members. There are five candidate countries: Bulgaria, Croatia, Macedonia, Romania and Turkey. Each of these is currently seeking to develop domestic economic and social policies that will enable it to qualify for membership. This complex evolving scene — illustrated by the characteristics described above — represents the 'New Europe' referred to in the title of this book.

Though the economic, social and political contexts vary between countries, they are all dominated numerically by SMEs. Indeed, it is hard to imagine tourists visiting any country in Europe and not coming into contact with SMEs. As a consequence, the European Commission and the governments of each member state have taken an interest in creating conditions that are conducive to SME development (European Commission, 2005b). This book seeks to cast light on some of the most interesting SME policies and business practices that emerge from the different member states. No claims are made about comprehensiveness — with so many members and so many potential interventions, such a claim would be naive — but the book represents a significant advance on earlier efforts (e.g. Thomas, 1996) which, though well received,[4] came to the conclusion that little could be said about the impact of European interventions on tourism and tourism SMEs until significantly more research had been undertaken. This volume suggests that we have started this process in earnest.

The distinctive feature of this volume is the fact that it presents results of primary and secondary studies concerning tourism SMEs that operate in a range of European contexts. There are chapters that discuss research into tourism SMEs in established EU member states (i.e. the 15 countries that joined the EU before 2004), notably Finland, Ireland, Portugal, Spain and the UK, although there is also reference to tourism SMEs operating in Greece, France, Luxembourg and the Netherlands.

There are also chapters concerning SMEs in European countries that are new EU member states (i.e. the ten countries that joined the EU on May 1st 2004). These include Poland, Slovakia and Slovenia, although there are also references to the Czech Republic and Hungary. The candidate EU member states are also considered and the volume contains one chapter on tourism SMEs in Turkey, and reference is also made to Bulgaria and Romania. Finally, other European countries (i.e. the 15 non-EU European countries) are represented in this volume by Norway and Russia but reference is also made to tourism SMEs that operate in Bosnia-Herzegovina. In addition, some chapters discuss issues

---

[3]Most contributors to this volume use the standard European Commission classification of SME: micro enterprises are those employing fewer than 10 people, small enterprises are those employing between 10 and 49 people and medium enterprises are those employing between 50 and 249 people. In the case of Russia, small businesses are defined as those that employ fewer than 50 people or fewer than 100 people in the case of hospitality enterprises. There are no guidelines for determining medium-sized enterprises in Russia.

[4]As one review noted, 'this publication succeeds in bringing together a number of specialists on the topic, and in offering a comprehensive and detailed analysis of the influence of European Union policies on hospitality and tourism in the region' *Annals of Tourism Research* (1997).

concerning European tourism SMEs, indicating the particular features of those that operate within Western Europe and Central and Eastern Europe, the latter frequently being referred to as transition economies.

The remainder of this chapter provides an overview of the various contributions contained in this volume. Key themes and issues that emerge from the studies are identified.

Tourism SMEs in the New Europe: An Overview

Matlay and Westhead's contribution (Chapter 2) considers how small businesses can adopt various entrepreneurial strategies in order to achieve sustainable competitive advantage. Within the context of corporate strategy this would be attainable via Porter's approach by employing one of his generic strategies, i.e. cost leadership, differentiation and focus (Porter, 1985). Matlay and Westhead resist adopting this approach to identifying strategies within the SME context. They recognise that small businesses are different and, therefore, need to be treated differently. Central to their analysis is the concept of Virtual Teams of e-Entrepreneurs, based upon collaborative entrepreneurship, virtual teams and e-Entrepreneurship, the latter being defined as the process of buying and selling products, services and information across a digital network. The authors present case studies of virtual teams of e-Entrepreneurs that involve tourism SMEs from both Western and Central and Eastern Europe. These teams usually operate in niche markets and conduct joint national and Europe-wide marketing campaigns. This approach clearly appears to contribute towards more small business start-ups and better growth prospects once established. The chapter demonstrates that there are significant advantages for small businesses to being part of virtual teams. These include the high quality of information that such teams generate and the pooling of human, financial and technical resources. However, the chapter also alludes to disadvantages associated with virtual teams such as problematic working practices across teams. In spite of these, the authors conclude that virtual teams represent an excellent strategy for SMEs to adopt.

The challenges facing Slovak tourism SMEs are examined by Baláž in Chapter 3. His analysis suggests that Slovakia's recent accession to the EU provides a welcome development that could assist tourism SMEs in overcoming difficulties associated with immature capital markets. The author recognises, however, that some problems besetting the Slovakian tourism industry are so deep-seated that it will be a long process before significant development occurs.

Dale and Robinson's contribution (Chapter 4) deals with the issue of strategic capabilities within SMEs, with particular reference to the newly acceded EU countries. They identify several strategic challenges that face SMEs in these countries, which include the fact that the tourism sector is characterised by fragmentation with typically family-run enterprises that bring with them all of the emotion and potential dysfunctionalism so frequently associated with families. Furthermore, SMEs are very independent in the way they conduct their business. This frequently results in a somewhat relaxed approach towards their business with poor management skills creating a situation where strategic decisions are neither very focused nor analytical. In addition, tourism SMEs operate within a business environment that is highly competitive and fluctuating. Such strategic challenges are intensified in Central and Eastern Europe owing to the kinds of resource constraints recognised in the previous chapter.

The authors identify a number of strategic options that tourism SMEs in Central and Eastern Europe can adopt in order to become more competitive. One of the most important options identified is that of networking and alliance formation. There is clearly a spectrum associated with this approach that ranges from relatively loose networking arrangements at one end to very formal and tight alliance agreements at the other. However, this contributes significantly to adding to the pool of resources that SMEs can draw upon. Intrapreneurship is another element that can galvanise the operations of SMEs. This enables employees or, in the case of family-owned business, family members to become more empowered to contribute towards ideas and to be rewarded accordingly. If such a strategy is effective, it can radically alter the way SMEs are run. The typical image of the autocratic leader could be transformed into an operation that deploys the ideas and skills of a team more completely. With these types of strategies being adopted, the authors argue that tourism SMEs in Central and Eastern Europe may be able to cope more confidently with the ongoing transitional process that they must contend with.

The next chapter, by Mottiar and Ryan, considers the role of tourism SMEs with respect to economic development in the Killarney area of Ireland. They begin by considering different models of tourism development. However, they note that very little is written about one of the key stakeholders in such models — the firms involved. They argue that industrial district theory is likely to provide an approach that will go some way towards dealing with this omission. They identify several characteristics that constitute an industrial district in a contemporary context. Geographical and sectoral clustering provide industrial districts with a clearly defined area, be it a town or a region. Firms located within such areas are usually SMEs. This is significant because it ensures a degree of interdependence and therefore co-operation between small firms. Consequently, strong interfirm relations are normally established. Although firms are competitive particularly in terms of quality and innovation rather than price, in industrial districts firms also co-operate significantly. Such co-operation can take the form of sharing tools and undertaking combined marketing. Another feature is that a strong social embeddedness between the firms operating within an industrial district and the individuals living within it is encountered. The authors feel that this notion of industrial districts is particularly relevant for the tourism industry as it normally defines a particular geographical area. The authors then conduct a detailed analysis of the industrial district model to consider whether it applies within the context of Killarney. They find that it is helpful in explaining the success of this area as a tourism region and how the SMEs within the area are vital in contributing towards this success.

Pheby's contribution (Chapter 6) considers the role of a relatively new form of tourism SME — the social enterprise. Despite the numerous definitions and legal forms of social enterprise, a definition of an organisation that is market oriented, socially led, aiming for community profits and intending to achieve financial sustainability is adopted. Several limitations with social enterprises are identified. For example, Pheby stresses that social enterprises find it very difficult to obtain finance. This is due to the fact that they are organisations that endeavour to deal with situations of market failure in both the public and private sectors. However, this very fact often means that the type of activities that they are associated with are not viable without significant public sector or charitable subsidy.

A more optimistic picture emerges when we consider how social enterprises have contributed significantly towards development within the tourism industry. A notable example is the Eden Project in Cornwall, which is now ranked fourth on the UK visitor attraction list and contributes significantly towards the economic development of that area. Other examples that Pheby draws from the tourism industry indicate that social enterprises may play a significant role in enhancing the competitiveness and sustainability of tourism destinations, thus making tourism SMEs that operate within these areas more viable. The chapter concludes with a number of suggestions as to how this sector can be encouraged through business support and training programmes.

In Chapter 7, Leslie focuses upon SMEs in the tourism sector that contributes towards the sustainability of rural areas within Scotland. He examines the value of rural tourism SMEs in terms of the potential social benefits they may bring to their communities. He relates his discussion to Agenda 21, which was set out at the Earth Summit in 1992. Essentially, it established a framework designed to encourage progress towards sustainable development in the twenty-first century. This study of tourism SMEs and their attitudes towards sustainability indicates that more progress needs to be made to make them more aware of their environmental responsibilities. The author identifies several factors such as lack of time and interest on the part of owner-managers in such issues. Other contributory aspects may be lack of resources, information, supportive infrastructure and the availability of local products. If the EU is serious about seeking to influence the behaviour of tourism SMEs, it needs to recognise the nature of such businesses and devise initiatives accordingly.

Marciszewska and Staszewska also consider tourism SMEs within the context of sustainability in Chapter 8. The Polish tourism sector contains mainly SMEs, but much larger players such as hotels and foreign tour operators are also included. The authors argue that the structural characteristics of the sector will encourage tourism SMEs to behave more competitively. However, they express concern that such improvements in competitiveness should not be at the expense of preserving the unique and scarce resources that they will be forced to interact with. The chapter reports a study that sought to assess the level of knowledge and understanding of sustainable tourism SMEs in the area of Pomerania in Northern Poland. This area was selected due to its richness in both natural and cultural attractions, and being the location of Poland's most popular seaside resorts. The results indicate a widespread ignorance of the concept of sustainable tourism. Furthermore, there appears to be a gap between tourism SMEs' awareness of the notion of sustainability and their attitudes towards sustainable tourism management. The authors suggest the need for improving educational and training courses as a means of rectifying this situation.

The next contribution is Komppula's examination of rural tourism in Finland (Chapter 9). Rural tourism is frequently portrayed as something that contributes significantly towards economic development in such areas. Rural tourism SMEs in Finland are typically family businesses, couples and portfolio entrepreneurs. Consequently, rural tourism enterprises tend not to be growth oriented or particularly innovative and are risk averse. It seems that both the consumers and firms are happy for this state of affairs to continue. However, unless there are significant developments in quality and co-operation in rural tourism SMEs, their contribution to regional development — according to this study — will be limited.

Lebe continues the rural theme in Chapter 10 by considering the role that entrepreneurship can play in the development of rural areas. Following a comprehensive analysis of the recent history and the current significance of the SME sector in contemporary Slovenia, the chapter focuses on rural issues. A legacy from the communist past arises from the historically severe restrictions on the ownership of land. Although such restrictions have now been eased, the problem of primarily small farms remains. Moreover, they are nowadays typically starved of finance in order to acquire more land, and — in the face of other difficulties — many farmers are keen to give up farming altogether. The author argues that the best route for developing rural tourism in Slovenia is through emphasising the culture and heritage of such areas. This appears to have already paid dividends in one region where an interesting visitor centre serves as an important focal point for promoting a myriad of other SMEs such as arts and crafts and small restaurants. However, the emphasis is upon the indigenous population pursuing their traditional way of life that is intended to be of interest to visitors.

Gúčik, Maráková and Šípková undertake an analysis of the Slovak Republic's SME hotels in Chapter 11. They suggest that this is an important sector for helping any of the transitional economies' tourism industry to be appealing to indigenous populations, but particularly to foreign visitors. It transpires that the Slovak hotel industry is dominated by SMEs. Furthermore, these hotels experience low occupancy rates and consequently low profitability. The authors make a case for the necessity of quality improvement and more effective marketing by Slovak hotels. It is argued that there are too many small, independent hotels that are struggling. Thus, they point to the need for greater concentration in the hotel business through a process of business integration and the establishment of national hotel chains. Furthermore, more competitive hotels will need to join multinational hotel chains in order to realistically aspire to international standards. Although the authors foresee the trend towards greater concentration within the Slovak hotel industry, they are optimistic that SMEs can still play a role if they develop appropriate niche strategies and alliances. The authors also emphasise that government support, through training in quality standards, management and finance, is imperative.

The next chapter by Staszewska, Klisinski and Sowier-Kasprzyk considers the effectiveness of promoting package tours by Polish travel agents. The important point to recognise here is the links that exist between tourism organisers that are typically large organisations and travel agents that tend to be SMEs. There is evidence of a symbiotic relationship that requires appropriate strategies for both parties in order to achieve beneficial results. Clearly, the tour operators play a key role in as much as they are responsible for creating the overall package tours. Consequently, the effectiveness of the promotional activities undertaken by individual travel agents will depend crucially upon how well the tour operators market their products. Chapter 12 reports that this process does not work well, and that greater co-operation between both parties needs to be achieved. It was also found that travel agents need to be more concerned with developing repeat custom.

In a contribution from Spain, Verdugo, Oviedo-Garcia and Veerapermal focus on the importance of relationship quality for improving the competitiveness of accommodation SMEs (Chapter 13). They recognise that this sector is highly competitive. One of the important strategies that they advocate is the deployment of relationship marketing. Despite the different notions of this concept, the authors focus upon the quality dimension of the relationship. With this in mind, the authors regard relationship marketing as something that encourages, retains and improves relationships with customers, which are beneficial to all sides with the important emphasis being placed upon the retention of existing customers. Their analysis of hotels in Seville produced some interesting results. They found that smaller hotels scored better than larger hotels in providing a quality service that was designed to build relationships with customers. This could have been owing to a more personal and friendly service in smaller hotels, or simply that customers expectations were modest and that they were pleasantly surprised. However, larger hotels appear to be ignoring an excellent opportunity to gain competitive advantage, as they are seemingly not providing their customers with an appropriate level of relationship quality.

Holmengen's work in Chapter 14 is concerned with explaining the relationship between the motivation for starting a business and the firm's performance. He found in a survey of 95 tourism enterprises that operate in the eastern part of Norway that there were four groups of motives for running tourism enterprises: self-development, lifestyle, control, and profits. However, he stresses that these motives change over time. Holmengen emphasises that it is important to employ meaningful measures of business performance. As the author argues that business performance is influenced by the motivations for running an enterprise, using risk measurements is appropriate. Risk management also has the advantage of possessing relevance for budgeting, marketing and strategic planning.

Aykın and Altıntaş provide an analysis of tourism SMEs in Turkey, a country that is currently aspiring towards EU membership (Chapter 15). Unlike many of the Central and Eastern European countries previously discussed, Turkey is already a well-established tourist destination. Turkish governments in recent years have undertaken a programme of developing poorer regions within the country. However, government spending on tourism is well below the average for countries across the EU. To assist tourism development, Turkish governments have implemented a Tourism Incentive Act. This entails improving the infrastructure, providing credit facilities for construction purposes and allocating public land to investors. An important condition for receipt of such incentives is that tourism enterprises must be regarded as exporters who generate a certain threshold of foreign exchange. Clearly, this type of restriction will impact significantly upon SMEs. However, it is argued that stimulating the development of larger organisations and therefore the tourism infrastructure could ultimately bring benefits to tourism SMEs. The conclusions drawn are that the bureaucracy associated with tourism incentives and other barriers such as high VAT rates are likely to threaten the impressive growth rates that the tourism industry in Turkey has enjoyed in recent years.

The penultimate chapter, from Saprunova, considers the problems and prospects facing tourism SMEs in Russia. An important feature of the Russian tourism market is that affluent Russians who are the main tourist element tend to go outside Russia for their holidays. This is because of the poor quality and service found within the Russian accommodation sector. In addition, the tourism infrastructure in most parts of the country is seriously underdeveloped. All of this is not helped by a raft of restrictions that are imposed upon tourism SMEs that are not conducive to both their establishment and development. However, there are examples of innovative product development by small tourism businesses, particularly in poorer parts of the country where a tourism business is seen as one of the very few options for survival. Saprunova stresses that government intervention is seen

as being the best way forward to encourage tourism SMEs. The recent major simplification of the national accounting rules significantly facilitated development of SMEs.
However, it is argued that a wide range of measures needs to be implemented to significantly improve the situation.

Conclusions

The studies presented in this volume discuss a range of issues concerning European
tourism SMEs that operate in all sectors of the tourism industry, including visitor attractions, hospitality facilities, tour operators, travel agents and ancillary services. The subjects discussed are as diverse as the contributors' research and professional backgrounds
and experiences, and indeed, the countries themselves. Nevertheless, two distinct themes
that run through the chapters can be identified: firstly, the contribution of tourism SMEs
towards regional development, which includes issues of networking, collaboration and
sustainability; secondly, business strategies, behaviour and performance of tourism SMEs.
Underpinning both themes is a concern with the competitiveness of tourism SMEs at the
local, regional, national and European levels. Many argue that public sector support is central to achieving high levels of tourism SME competitiveness. In addition, many chapters
present the characteristics of tourism SMEs in European countries and barriers that they
face in attaining their goals.

The final chapter of this volume compares and contrasts the business environments,
behaviour, strategies and practices of tourism SMEs operating within the 'New Europe'.
The book concludes by considering the implications for policy makers, managers and
researchers.

References

European Commission (2005a). *Statistical annex of European economy*. Luxembourg: DG ECFIN
    Economic and Financial Affairs.
European Commission (2005b). *Commission staff working paper: The activities of the European
    union for small and medium-sized enterprises (SMEs)*. SEC (2005) 170. Brussels: European
    Commission.
Porter, M. E. (1985). *Competitive advantage: Creating and sustaining superior performance*. New
    York: Free Press.
Thomas, R. (Ed.). (1996). *The hospitality industry, tourism and Europe: Perspectives on policies and
    practices*. London: Cassell.
World Bank (2006). *Little data book*. Washington, DC: World Bank Group.
WTO (2005). *Tourism highlights*. Madrid: World Tourism Organisation.

Chapter 2

Competitive Advantage in Virtual Teams of e-Entrepreneurs: Evidence from the European Tourism Industry

Harry Matlay and Paul Westhead

Introduction

It is widely recognised that, in recent years, entrepreneurship has undergone a fundamental transformation from a mostly traditional form of small business to a more collaborative approach to product manufacturing, service provision and knowledge sharing. There are a number of complex reasons underlying this departure from long-established, conventional models of small-scale economic activity (Matlay & Westhead, 2005).

The ongoing transformation of entrepreneurial activities reflects the rapid changes affecting the contemporary global market place (Kreindler, Maislish, & Wang, 2004). Primarily, the emergence of the Internet and related advances in Information and Communication Technologies (ICTs) have opened new markets and radically altered existing ones (Brynjolfsson & Kahin, 2002). Furthermore, a number of traditional local and regional markets have been replaced by global e-Markets, which are driven by innovative new technologies that bring producers as well as corporate and private consumers into close, cost-efficient and mutually beneficial proximity (Chaston, 2001). Importantly, these changes have removed most of the barriers that impeded traditional market performance, including imperfect information relating to the willingness and ability to supply or purchase, at a given price, a vast portfolio of internationally sourced goods and services (Matlay & Addis, 2003). In this context, a variety of adaptive entrepreneurship strategies have emerged to facilitate small businesses in their pursuit of sustainable competitive advantage at local, national and European levels (Lechner & Dowling, 2003).

From a small business perspective, the full economic impact of the Internet and related ICTs upon the European economy is yet to be fully understood (Matlay, 2004). The results of recent Pan-European research studies have highlighted a shift in entrepreneurial equilibrium that affects an increasing proportion of small businesses in this region (Matlay & Westhead, 2005). At macro-economic level, it is increasingly apparent that much of the context in which small business operations are taking place has changed dramatically over the last decade or so. In the contemporary 'Networked Economy', collaborative entrepreneurship has emerged as a strategic catalyst in the quest for a larger share of the economic value that is generated within rapidly evolving e-Markets (Mistri, 2003). Collaborative strategies tend to facilitate the convergence of innovative small business activities into entrepreneurial networks, strategic alliances and clusters that offer a greater degree of sustainable competitive advantage (Anderson, Jack, & Dodd, 2005; Feldman & Francis, 2001; Zeleny, 2001). In this rapidly evolving economic milieu, new and innovative organisational forms have emerged, including 'Virtual Enterprises' (D'Atri & Pauselli, 2004) and a highly competitive brand of 'e-Entrepreneurs' (Matlay, 2003). Arguably, however, one of the most successful, adaptable and sustainable forms of entrepreneurship is embodied in 'Virtual Teams of e-Entrepreneurs', which were found to operate in most, if not all, the industrial sectors of the European economy (Matlay & Westhead, 2005). Unfortunately, due to a notable paucity of empirically rigorous research in this area, little is known about virtual teams of e-Entrepreneurs and the characteristics and competitive strategies of their component small businesses.

This chapter aims to redress the knowledge imbalance in this area of small business competitiveness by focussing on virtual teams of e-Entrepreneurs that operate in the rapidly expanding European tourism industry. It is based upon the results of 15 illustrative case studies, chosen to reflect both common trends and divergent small business competitive strategies across Eastern, Central and Western Europe. We identify and analyse the various stages and processes involved in virtual team operation, from formation to the fulfilment or adjournment of specific tasks and projects. The advantages and disadvantages of virtual teaming are addressed, and their managerial implications and strategic recommendations for improving small business competitiveness are presented.

e-Entrepreneurship in Europe: Conceptual and Contextual Issues

The Internet and related ICT developments have significantly affected the socio-economic and political infrastructure of the European economy (Brynjolfsson & Kahin, 2002). Early estimates predicted that few areas of human activity would remain unaffected by the e-Revolution (Thelwall, 2000). Research has shown that expectations were exceeded by new developments that involve all the major aspects of human activity (Matlay, 2003). Significant changes are taking place in the way that 'online' economic transactions have become routinised within the global e-Market place (Timmers, 2000; Elliot, 2002). In the context of entrepreneurship and small business development, the Internet and related ICTs provide significant new opportunities for 'online' trading (Turban, Lee, King, & Chung, 2000). In the specialist literature, e-Entrepreneurship is defined as the process of buying and selling products, services and information across a digital network (Kalakota & Robinson, 1999). Dutta and Segev (2001) argue that the Internet has created a shared, real-time commercial 'Cyberspace' that can facilitate not only safe online transactions but also co-operation amongst trading partners. In response to rapid developments and changes in the global e-Market, organisations of various sizes, economic activity and geographical location have been adapting their business models to exploit the opportunities afforded by the Internet (Martin & Matlay, 2003).

The competitive 'Marketspace Model' proposed by Dutta and Segev (1999) involves two interrelated entrepreneurial dimensions: (i) *technological capability* and (ii) *strategic business*. In turn, the technological capability of the model comprises two crucial elements: *interactivity* and *connectivity*. Increasingly, e-Entrepreneurs found that the competitive edge of their businesses was greatly enhanced by the real-time, online nature of Internet-based transactions. Furthermore, as the trading links between businesses and their customers become more *interactive*, innovative product designs and customer services are created (Martin & Matlay, 2001). Thus, a radical change in *connectivity*, enabled by the open and global nature of the Internet, is promoting a range of new and innovative communication and co-ordination mechanisms. These can facilitate more effective interactions and links among small businesses, their customers and relevant support agencies (Thelwall, 2000). Furthermore, the dual aspect of Internet-based interactivity and connectivity is increasingly transforming small business competitive strategies and goals (Li & Williams, 2001).

Most successful business strategies rely upon better customer interaction and utilise relevant feedback to improve products and services on a continuous basis. The magnitude of managerial and strategic challenges associated with online trading can be considerable and should not be underestimated (Matlay, 2003). The key management decisions required by small businesses moving into online trading extend beyond choosing the latest technology as a platform to automate existing processes (Matlay & Addis, 2003). Importantly, to achieve and maintain sustainable competitive advantage, a wide range of internal knowledge and competencies is required, involving economic processes and activities across the 'value chain', manufacturing, product development, marketing and procurement as well as transactional logistics (Deise, Nowikow, King, & Wright, 2000). Furthermore, to complement internal resources, external support might be also required, at least during the initial stages of Internet adoption.

In the early stages of e-Entrepreneurship, online businesses were based largely upon the cumulative competencies of the founding team. In search of sustainable competitive advantage, many of these e-Entrepreneurs chose the 'high risk, quick returns' route, which relied largely upon external sources of funding. Human resources, business strategy development and technical support were bought in from outside providers (Boddy, Boonstra, & Kennedy, 2001; Plant, 2000). Typically, e-Entrepreneurs in this type of Internet-based set-up were under considerable pressure from backers to move rapidly from concept to trading and profit. During the same period, an acute shortage of relevant skills and resources was exacerbated by a difficulty in selecting from amongst the portfolio of existing services on offer to e-Entrepreneurs. Entrepreneurial and investor greed, fuelled by one of the longest 'bull markets' in recent history, added further pressure on e-Entrepreneurs for rapid expansion and capitalisation. Interestingly, however, not all e-Entrepreneurs chose the 'high risk, quick returns' business strategy. Some e-Entrepreneurs decided to either gradually adopt online strategies into their existing small businesses or start up new, Internet-based enterprises, on a 'low risk, low return' basis (Martin & Matlay, 2001; Matlay & Addis, 2003).

It is often argued that online trading offers small businesses the opportunity to compete on equal terms with larger and better-resourced organisations (Matlay & Westhead, 2005; Mellor, 1998). In terms of cooperation, the Internet has facilitated better communication and interaction between entrepreneurs, allowing documents, spreadsheets, databases and technical drawings to be exchanged across geographical divides in 'real time' mode. The removal of geographical and time barriers allows the sharing of data and information on a global basis, with the potential to provide a cost-efficient multiple channel for advertising, marketing and direct distribution of a wide range of goods and services. In terms of adoption constraints, Chapman, More, Szczygiel, and Thompson (2000) found that some small businesses were prevented to join online trading by a number of barriers. In their experience, barriers to Internet trading involved: (i) a lack of understanding of the opportunities offered by ICTs; (ii) the perceived price of new technologies and related support; and (iii) a lack of relevant knowledge and skills amongst the workforce. In contrast, Matlay and Addis (2003) found that small business owner-managers understood the potential benefits of Internet trading; they were computer literate and possessed basic ICT techniques. Furthermore, in recent years the price of hardware and software has decreased to a level that was considered low enough to be within the budget of the majority of their respondents.

Nevertheless, an acute lack of intermediate and higher skills amongst owner-managers and their workforce constituted a substantial barrier to online trading amongst small businesses. The extent, quality and effectiveness of external support relevant to the implementation and maintenance of Internet trading varied considerably across regions. When and where available, small business owner-managers preferred to use financial incentives or government support as a subsidised entry point into their chosen e-Markets. The adoption of online trading cannot be viewed as a 'simple' innovation and must be construed as a 'cluster' of interrelated changes (Van Slyke, 1997). Therefore, when considering adoption, e-Entrepreneurs are often able to choose which of these innovations to adopt as the most suitable competitive strategy for their e-Market niche (Daniel, Wilson, & Myers, 2002).

As an entry point, a basic ICT platform can be implemented as part of a competitive strategy and specific innovations developed or adopted as and when appropriate (Matlay, 2003). In the UK, the 'cluster of innovation' approach is evidenced by a growing number of initiatives targeting the small business sector and supported by the Department of Trade and Industry's 'Adoption Ladder' system (DTI, 2000). This model involves a series of stages, ordered in a well-planned, sequential process. It has, however, been criticised for its 'linearity' and also for its failure to encompass key small business competitive factors such as size, sector, gender and ethnicity, human and financial resources, customer base and degree of internationalisation. Furthermore, the lack of relevant owner-manager and workforce skills is likely to negatively affect the outcome of each stage of Internet adoption (Matlay & Addis, 2003).

The Rise of Virtual Teams of e-Entrepreneurs

Beginning with the 1990s, there has been growing interest in entrepreneurial teams and their impact upon small business start-up, growth and success. It appears that the occurrence of entrepreneurial teams amongst small businesses is more common than it was suggested by the specialist literature on entrepreneurship (Vyakarnam, Jacobs, & Handelberg, 1999). Interestingly, the existence and leadership provided by entrepreneurial teams often make a considerable difference to the competitive potential of a small business. Vyakarnam and Jacobs (1993) claim that, as a rule, 'lifestyle' entrepreneurs tend not to add significantly to wealth creation. Timmons (1994) however found that team-led small businesses were more successful than single ownership start-ups, in terms of both longevity and long-term profitability. Similarly, successful small businesses are more often established and managed by entrepreneurial teams than by individual entrepreneurs (Doutriaux, 1992).

Evidence from the US shows that 94% of 'hypergrowth' enterprises were started by teams of two or more entrepreneurs (Brockaw, 1993). Likewise, there is evidence that about two-thirds of the US fastest growing, privately owned small businesses were started by teams of two or more entrepreneurs (Mangelsdorf, 1992). According to Kamm, Shuman, Seeger, and Nurick (1990), other success indicators, such as net income, operating profit and market capitalisation, also favoured small businesses that were established by teams of entrepreneurs rather than individual founders. In term of product, service or process innovation, it appears that small businesses managed by entrepreneurial teams tend to outclass their owner-managed counterparts (Michel & Hambrick, 1992). Regarding team size, larger entrepreneurial star-up teams were considerably more successful than smaller groups of founders. Nevertheless, Birley and Stockley (2000) concede that the impact of entrepreneurial teams upon small business survival and growth is a dynamic and highly contingent concept, and that it is difficult to realistically establish competitive impact due to a lack of generally accepted definitions.

From an opportunity recognition perspective, external data, information and knowledge become crucial to the development of entrepreneurial teams (Kirzner, 1997). Those teams that are able to access a wide range of relevant information are likely to perform better than those that are retrieving a narrower range. Through inherent firm-specific mechanisms or processes, entrepreneurial teams ensure the transformation of data and information into competitive knowledge and strategy as well as economic goods and services. Drawing upon the concept of dispersed knowledge where no two individuals or teams possess the same mix of strategic knowledge, Sarasvathy, Dew, Velamuri, and Venkataraman (2003, p. 145) propose a model of entrepreneurial opportunities based upon three distinct, yet interrelated, perspectives: *recognition*, *discovery* and *creation*. Their proposed model embraces three entrepreneurial opportunity permutations:

1. *Opportunity Recognition* — both sources of supply and demand already exist. Entrepreneurial teams recognise such opportunities and match them, either through an existing small business or a new start-up.
2. *Opportunity Discovery* — only one side (supply or demand) exists and the other needs to be discovered. Entrepreneurial teams focus upon the exploitation of existing or latent niche markets.
3. *Opportunity Creation* — neither supply nor demand exists and both need to be created or discovered. Knowledge, product and process innovations can facilitate entrepreneurial teams in their creation of new niche markets.

Two main factors appear to influence access to new knowledge, its distribution and use by entrepreneurial teams. The first involves advantageous network positions that can facilitate the flow of new information to entrepreneurial teams. Informational flows to and from entrepreneurial teams and their networks are sometimes affected by the 'stickiness' of knowledge and its restricted availability to only those who have direct contact with users (Szulanski, 2003). In addition, to be competitive, new information needs to be matched by complementary internal resources, including relevant knowledge or experience or both (Shane, 2000). Human, financial and knowledge resources tend to enhance the 'absorptive capacity' of entrepreneurial teams and facilitate opportunity recognition, discovery or creation. The second factor to affect the distribution and usage of new information relates to the uncertainty of its sources. From a competitiveness perspective, uncertainty relating to source and accuracy of information can affect an entrepreneurial team's predictions of supply and demand and renders them dependent on individual beliefs and personal opinions (Kirzner, 1997). Both knowledge stickiness and informational uncertainty can be mitigated by the collective interaction and diversity of skills found amongst the members of an entrepreneurial team. According to Timmons (1994), entrepreneurial teams usually have a lead entrepreneur who unites and clarifies the competitive strategy of a small business.

The rise of virtual teams of e-Entrepreneurs has been attributed to a number of interrelated factors associated with the Internet and the globalisation of e-Markets (Matlay, 2003). In order to take advantage of the virtual environment in the e-Marketplace, small businesses need continuous access to a wide range of online information sources (Tetteh & Burn, 2001). However, Feher and Towell (1997) argue that during the 1990s small businesses experienced considerable difficulties in overcoming knowledge gaps and exploiting the opportunities created by the Internet. It appears that some small business owner-managers lacked the skills and competencies needed to strategically engage in online trading. Generally, small businesses that adopted online trading as a competitive strategy relied on poor-quality websites and missed e-Market opportunities for early growth and development (Thelwall, 2000).

There is a paucity of empirically rigorous research to document the initial period (1995–1999) of Internet-based trading by small businesses (Martin & Matlay, 2001). Therefore, the specialist literature tends to rely on most recent research results (Martin & Matlay, 2003). Similarly, most of the research on 'Virtual Teams' tends to focus on collaborative activities within large, geographically dispersed organisation and multinationals corporations (Kelley, 2001). Most aspects of virtual teams of e-Entrepreneurs, their characteristics and competitive strategies remain under-researched. In this chapter we aim to redress the imbalance in this area of small business research by focussing on 15 virtual teams of e-Entrepreneurs that operate in the rapidly expanding Pan-European tourism industry.

Research Sample and Methodology

Tourism represents one of the world's largest industries and the fastest growing sector of economic activity in Europe (Matlay, 2004). Mainstream tour operators dominate roughly the tourism industry in Europe, through the high-volume supply of economically priced package holidays (Matlay, 1998). An independent, niche market-oriented sector of specialist operators complements the package holiday aspect of the industry. The sample of 15 illustrative case studies upon which this chapter is based has been chosen from a large Pan-European research database of small businesses operating in the tourism industry. It currently holds the details of over 60,000 small businesses located in Western, Central and Eastern Europe. Exploratory telephone interviews were carried out during 1993–94, to collect relevant data relating to businesses involved in this sector of economic activity.

The initial research established that 1287 virtual teams of entrepreneurs strategically interacted or collaborated on tourism-related activities. On a yearly basis, from 1995 to 2003, follow-up telephone interviews were carried out with these teams. The longitudinal research study charted the nature, extent and context of collaborative links within virtual teams as well as relevant changes in composition, strategy and profitability. In addition, every three years (i.e. 1997, 2000 and 2003) we undertook in-depth, face-to-face interviews in a sub-sample of 60 virtual teams. The 15 case studies presented in this chapter were chosen as illustrative of the virtual teams that increasingly form the competitive core of successful e-Entrepreneurship in the European tourism industry.

Where appropriate, case studies were grouped together, to facilitate comparisons in terms of membership composition, organisational structure and competitive strategy. For example, virtual teams that were involved in three specialised family holidays (SFH1-3) exhibited similarities in terms of membership composition and target-market orientation. Core membership comprised those entrepreneurs that were significantly and consistently involved in the activities of their virtual team. Core entrepreneurs derived the main proportion of their turnover from the collaborative activities of their respective virtual teams. In contrast, peripheral members were usually involved on a temporary basis, and were called upon as and when necessary. Only a small proportion of the peripheral members' turnover was attributable to transactions generated by their virtual teams. The membership of the three SFH1-3 virtual teams was comparatively large and their core entrepreneurs outnumber peripheral members by at least three-to-one. These virtual teams focussed exclusively on domestic and European markets. In another group with a large membership, the three European postcards, stamps and currency (ECH1-3) virtual teams, core entrepreneurs were twice as numerous as their peripheral counterparts, but their focus involved domestic, European and international markets. At *prima facie* it appears that competitive strategies specific to each virtual team of e-Entrepreneurs determined both the size of the membership and the proportion of core to peripheral entrepreneurs (Table 2.1).

Competitive Strategies and Virtual Team Dynamics

A comparative approach to competitive strategies and e-Market dynamics has highlighted a number of common trends as well as considerable differences in the formation and development of these virtual teams of e-Entrepreneurs. The main finding is outlined below:

Competitive Strategies and Virtual Team Formation

In Western Europe, small businesses play an important and stabilising role, and since the 1980s, governments promoted a more enterprising society. After the 1989 collapse of communism in Central and Eastern Europe, most countries have undergone a transition period from a centrally planned system to a liberalised, Western European style market economy. In forming virtual teams, the entrepreneurs in our research sample sought to enhance the competitive strategies of their small businesses in terms of flexibility, responsiveness and cost efficiency as well as to lower operational costs and improve resource utilisation. The virtual teams in the sample were formed between 1990 and 1993, soon after the

Table 2.1: Research sample by economic activity, membership and target market (2003).

Descriptor code	Main economic activity description	Membership		Target market		
		Core	Peripheral	Domestic	Europe	Other
SFH1	Specialised family breaks	28	8	Yes	Yes	No
SFH2	Specialised family holidays	25	7	Yes	Yes	No
SFH3	Multi-generation family holidays	22	5	Yes	Yes	No
HCM1	Roman forts and medieval castles	7	3	Yes	Yes	No
HCH2	Churches and monasteries	18	8	Yes	Yes	Yes
ECH1	European postcards	21	9	Yes	Yes	Yes
ECH2	European stamps	26	11	Yes	Yes	Yes
ECH3	European coins and banknotes	25	12	Yes	Yes	Yes
CWT1	Culinary and wine testing clubs	5	2	Yes	Yes	No
CWT2	Whiskey and brandy clubs	6	2	Yes	Yes	No
WSM1	Winter sports and mountaineering	26	7	Yes	Yes	No
FSH1	River, lakes and reservoir fishing	29	16	Yes	Yes	Yes
FSH2	Pleasure, game and sea fishing	23	12	Yes	Yes	Yes
FSH3	Small and large game hunting	8	4	Yes	Yes	No
BWH1	Birds watching	6	3	Yes	Yes	No
	Total	**275**	**109**			

widespread economic reforms in Central and Eastern Europe. Their inception appears to have been triggered by rapid changes in the socio-economic and political infrastructure of Europe and a substantial increase in demand for both specific and general tourist destinations (Table 2.2). Initial membership consisted of a mixture of newly formed, young and well-established small businesses located in Western, Central and Eastern Europe. It comprised a total of 88 small businesses, representing an average of six economic units per team. Their location was distributed between 45 businesses in Western Europe and 43 in Central and Eastern Europe. The virtual team formation appears to closely conform

Table 2.2: Virtual team formation and membership location.

Descriptor code	Main economic activity description	Year of formation	Number of businesses	Business location in Europe	
				Western	Central/ Eastern
SFH1	Specialised family breaks	1990	6	2	4
SFH2	Specialised family holidays	1990	8	4	4
SFH3	Multi-generation family holidays	1992	5	3	2
HCM1	Roman forts and medieval castles	1993	3	1	2
HCH2	Churches and monasteries	1992	7	4	3
ECH1	European postcards	1991	6	3	3
ECH2	European stamps	1990	8	4	4
ECH3	European coins and banknotes	1990	7	4	3
CWT1	Culinary and wine testing clubs	1992	4	2	2
CWT2	Whiskey and brandy clubs	1993	3	2	1
WSM1	Winter sports and mountaineering	1991	7	3	4
FSH1	River, lakes and reservoir fishing	1991	6	4	2
FSH2	Pleasure, game and sea fishing	1992	8	4	4
FSH3	Small and large game hunting	1992	6	3	3
BWH1	Birds watching	1991	4	2	2
	Total		**88**	**45**	**43**

to the opportunity recognition, discovery and creation model proposed by Sarasvathy et al. (2003).

The initial membership consisted exclusively of 88 core entrepreneurs (Table 2.3). Numerically, portfolio entrepreneurs (41) dominated the overall membership, followed by serial (29) and novice (18) owner-managers. Most of the portfolio and serial entrepreneurs claimed to be experienced in setting up and managing small businesses. The novice entrepreneurs had already set up their businesses and were operating profitably in their chosen niche market before joining the respective virtual teams. In terms of formative dynamics, during inception, the virtual teams comprised a small number of entrepreneurs who considered themselves as 'drivers' of the team.

Table 2.3: Core and peripheral membership characteristics at inception date.

Descriptor code	Main economic activity description	Number of entrepreneurs	Type of core entrepreneur		
			Novice	Serial	Portfolio
SFH1	Specialised family breaks	6	1	1	4
SFH2	Specialised family holidays	8	1	2	5
SFH3	Multi-generation family holidays	5	1	1	3
HCM1	Roman forts and medieval castles	3	1	2	0
HCH2	Churches and monasteries	7	2	5	0
ECH1	European postcards	6	0	3	3
ECH2	European stamps	8	0	2	6
ECH3	European coins and banknotes	7	0	2	5
CWT1	Culinary and wine-testing clubs	4	4	0	0
CWT2	Whiskey and brandy clubs	3	3	0	0
WSM1	Winter sports and mountaineering	7	0	7	0
FSH1	River, lakes and reservoir fishing	6	2	2	2
FSH2	Pleasure, game and sea fishing	8	1	1	6
FSH3	Small and large game hunting	6	2	1	3
BWH1	Birds watching	4	0	0	4
	Total	**88**	**18**	**29**	**41**

These core entrepreneurs either knew each other or have had successful business dealings prior to inception. In the case of the SFH1-3, the drivers were members of extended family groups. There were some family links amongst the drivers of other virtual teams, notably the European ECH1-3 and the Fishing (FSH1-3) groups. By drawing upon proven family, personal or business contacts operating in the same economic sub-sector, these entrepreneurs were able to complete the membership of their virtual teams within a relatively short span of time, averaging six weeks. Interestingly, although the 'driver' group of entrepreneurs perceived themselves as firmly committed to the competitive strategies of their virtual teams, other members were often considered 'on probation' until they proved themselves worthy of 'full membership'. In other aspects, however, including access to local market information and team-based benefits and obligations, there were no significant differences noted amongst core entrepreneurs.

Virtual Team Growth and Development

The longitudinal development of virtual teams in the research sample seems to have been influenced by two important competitive factors:

(i) An ability to recognise, discover or create entrepreneurial opportunities in terms of demand for niche market products and services.

(ii) A capacity to match demand with a supply of discriminant or quality products and services from within virtual teams.

Although some of the competitive strategies and growth orientation in these virtual teams differed, all proved successful in providing their members with profitable domestic and Pan-European niche markets. Furthermore, their chosen competitive strategies ensured both the longevity and sustainability of these small businesses. A number of similarities and differences emerged from the analysis of the development and maturisation process of these virtual teams. For instance, two-thirds (10) of the virtual teams in the research sample were growth-oriented from inception and these entrepreneurs increased demand for their products and services. Their chosen competitive strategies were aimed at expanding their share of the market. In the case of the SFH1-3, ECH1-3, winter sports (WSM1) and fishing (FSH1-2) virtual teams, core entrepreneurs initially opted to carry out national and Europe-wide marketing campaigns in specialist magazines, periodicals and selected newspapers.

Interestingly, the expense of national advertisements was born by respective core entrepreneurs, while the cost of Europe wide advertisements was pooled and divided equally between all the small businesses in a team. The initial marketing drive produced better than expected results in terms of increased demand, but also highlighted considerable gaps within the initial core membership in relation to national market representation. These gaps were bridged by peripheral entrepreneurs who, on joining the team, were expected to mop-up the excess demand in marginal locations. The longitudinal growth in overall membership can also be attributed to strategic campaigns that brought requests for inclusion from a large and widely dispersed geographical area (Table 2.4).

Rapid expansion also brought considerable membership difficulties to growth-oriented virtual teams. This was reflected in the size of the overall membership as well as the high turnover of both core and peripheral entrepreneurs. Over the span of the research study, the core membership has increased from 88 entrepreneurs at inception to 187 by the end of 2003. In addition, a total of 109 peripheral entrepreneurs gained membership status. Core and peripheral membership turbulence varied considerably between fast growth and the less competitive virtual teams. One-third (5) of virtual teams in the sample, such as the Roman Forts and Medieval Castles (HCM1), Culinary and Wine Testing (CWT1), Vintage Whiskey and Brandy (CWT2), Small and Large Game Hunting (FSH3) and Birds Watching (BWH1), chose a competitive strategy aimed at the high-quality, exclusive end of their niche market. Core entrepreneurs in these virtual teams appear not to have been pressurised by market conditions to expand their overall membership (Table 2.5).

Thus, in terms of turbulence, membership changes were comparatively small: in total 14 core entrepreneurs had joined these virtual teams and only 2 left. In terms of peripheral membership, 15 entrepreneurs had joined and 1 exited the team. To a large extent, the

Table 2.4: Virtual team membership turbulence (1990–2003).

Descriptor code	Main economic activity description	Core membership turbulence			Peripheral membership turbulence		
		Joined	Exited	Total	Joined	Exited	Total
SFH1	Specialised family breaks	31	9	22	11	3	8
SFH2	Specialised family holidays	25	8	17	10	3	7
SFH3	Multi-generation family holidays	23	6	17	7	2	5
HCM1	Roman forts and medieval castles	6	2	4	4	1	3
HCH2	Churches and monasteries	14	3	11	11	3	8
ECH1	European postcards	22	7	15	13	4	9
ECH2	European stamps	26	8	18	17	6	11
ECH3	European coins and banknotes	25	7	18	20	8	12
CWT1	Culinary and wine-testing clubs	1	0	1	2	0	2
CWT2	Whiskey and brandy clubs	3	0	3	2	0	2
WSM1	Winter sports and mountaineering	28	9	19	10	3	7
FSH1	River, lakes and reservoir fishing	31	8	23	18	2	16
FSH2	Pleasure, game and sea fishing	18	3	15	14	2	12
FSH3	Small and large game hunting	2	0	2	4	0	4
BWH1	Birds watching	2	0	2	3	0	3
	Total	**257**	**70**	**187**	**146**	**37**	**109**

relatively slow development of these teams was perceived to be a function of the nature of the chosen niche markets as well as the slower competitive pace preferred by the drivers (Table 2.6).

e-Entrepreneurship and Virtual Team Interaction

An in-depth, longitudinal analysis of Internet trading adoption amongst the 15 virtual teams in the research sample highlighted that core entrepreneurs in both the growth-oriented and

Table 2.5: Fast growth virtual team membership turbulence (1990–2003).

Descriptor code	Main economic activity description	Core membership turbulence			Peripheral membership turbulence		
		Joined	Exited	Total	Joined	Exited	Total
SFH1	Specialised family breaks	31	9	22	11	3	8
SFH2	Specialised family holidays	25	8	17	10	3	7
SFH3	Multi-generation family holidays	23	6	17	7	2	5
	Total (SFH1-3)	**79**	**23**	**56**	**28**	**8**	**20**
ECH1	European postcards	22	7	15	13	4	9
ECH2	European stamps	26	8	18	17	6	11
ECH3	European coins and banknotes	25	7	18	20	8	12
	Total (ECH1-3)	**73**	**22**	**51**	**50**	**18**	**32**
FSH1	River, lakes and reservoir Fishing	31	8	23	18	2	16
FSH2	Pleasure, game and sea fishing	18	3	15	14	2	12
	Total (FSH1-2)	**49**	**11**	**38**	**32**	**4**	**28**
HCH2	Cathedrals, churches and monasteries	14	3	11	11	3	8
WSM1	Winter sports and mountaineering	28	9	19	10	3	7
	Total	**243**	**68**	**175**	**131**	**36**	**95**

the high-quality virtual teams recognised the importance of these market developments in terms of future competitive strategies. Compared with other, similar-sized small businesses, these virtual teams seem to have achieved an early and relatively faster route to ICT and Internet adoption (Matlay, 2003). Three main factors appear to have facilitated the speedy adoption of advanced technologies by these entrepreneurs:

i. The realisation of the chosen competitive strategies in these virtual teams often depended upon regular and concerted coverage of large geographical areas by a relatively small number of entrepreneurs. As an e-Marketing platform, the Internet could facilitate a focused, fast and efficient coverage of individual as well as team territories.

ii. A large proportion of business activities in tourism is 'interactive' and often involves large volumes of communications between suppliers, intermediaries and buyers. Within a virtual team, a considerable proportion of communications traffic relies upon and involves core and peripheral entrepreneurs.

Table 2.6: High-quality and exclusivity virtual team membership turbulence (1990–2003).

Descriptor code	Main economic activity description	Core membership turbulence			Peripheral membership turbulence		
		Joined	Exited	Total	Joined	Exited	Total
HCM1	Roman forts and medieval castles	6	2	4	4	1	3
CWT1	Culinary and wine testing clubs	1	0	1	2	0	2
CWT2	Vintage whiskey and brandy clubs	3	0	3	2	0	2
FSH3	Small and large game hunting	2	0	2	4	0	4
BWH1	Birds watching	2	0	2	3	0	3
	Total	**14**	**2**	**12**	**15**	**1**	**14**

iii. At inception, the individual and cumulative knowledge base of core entrepreneurs was considerable, and involved not only tourism information and experience but also a considerable ICT element. The availability of financial resources needed to accomplish an early and rapid Internet adoption across the team complemented the skills and knowledge base of core entrepreneurs.

On average, fast growth-oriented virtual teams completed Internet adoption in 4 months, inclusive of functionality and compatibility tests. The smaller, quality-oriented virtual teams claim to have completed adoption in about 3 months. All agreed that team-based knowledge as well as human, financial and support resources available to members helped considerably in choosing, implementing and testing the relevant systems. Interestingly, local hardware and software suppliers as well as installers seem to have understood and supported team decisions and choices. Only minor technical difficulties or price variations were reported, all of which were resolved locally. Importantly, rapid adoption appears to have succeeded in polarising the competitive strategies of these e-Entrepreneurs and ensured a common e-Trading platform. This also provided virtual team members with opportunities to increase their volume of transactions as well as achieve higher than average profit margins. The cumulative effect of lower costs and higher volumes brought not only competitive advantages to virtual team members but also the pressures and problems associated with growths. On balance, however, Internet adoption appears to have had a beneficial impact upon the competitiveness and profitability of both core and peripheral members.

Competitive Advantages in Virtual Teams

Respondents attributed a number of important advantages as well as some disadvantages to their membership of virtual teams. It appears that the larger the virtual team membership (both core and peripheral) the more extensive are the perceived benefits that could accrue to e-Entrepreneurs. Similarly, e-Entrepreneurs in larger groups tended to perceive proportionally more disadvantages related to virtual team membership. The most important advantage relates to the data and knowledge on tourism-related supply and demand that is made available to virtual team members. To achieve and maintain 'knowledge advantage', both core and peripheral e-Entrepreneurs are given access to verified knowledge on actual and potential e-Market opportunities. Importantly, the quantity, quality and reliability of information brokered within virtual teams are significantly higher than what is usually available to other small tour operators. In addition, the expense of gathering, testing and validating data and information relating to the tourism industry can be considerably lower than average. Similarly, the cost of analysing, updating and exploiting related entrepreneurial opportunities could be spread across the wider core and peripheral membership. Furthermore, the provision of high-quality, accurate and lucrative knowledge invariably adds to the 'internal prestige' of members as well as to the overall 'virtual successes' of a team.

Another important virtual team benefit involves the inherent pool of readily accessible human, financial and technical resources. These are typically available in virtual teams as 'task-related support'. This type of internal support tends to ensure the longevity of a virtual team in general, and that of individual members in particular. The main task for which such support is available to members focuses upon overall profitability, both at small business and virtual team levels. Usually, a member can access a range of team-wide resources by requesting it directly from other e-Entrepreneurs or through the virtual team. Training and human resource advice and support is widely available from within a team, offering considerable advantages in terms of cost and sector-specific skill development. The knowledge resources available from within a virtual team can be considerable and inform most, if not all, the decision making of individual e-Entrepreneurs. In some instances, experienced core members were 'seconded' to less successful e-Entrepreneurs in order to support and coach them or restructure their loss-making small businesses. Occasionally, some small businesses experienced fraud-related losses and were supported and rescued from failure by team members who purchased interest-free virtual shares that financed recovery and growth.

Considerable niche market benefits were also derived by e-Entrepreneurs in terms of individual operational territories and access to a more lucrative, Pan-European customer base. Individual territories delineated areas of tourism destinations to be serviced exclusively by e-Entrepreneurs from within the virtual team. The customer base, however, was widened significantly by advertising links on the websites of all the other members. The sustainability of a Pan-European presence was ensured not only by territorial marketing but also by fully functioning Internet trading facilities, such as ordering, remittance and documentation delivery to and from the purchaser's location. A wider, professionally presented and maintained e-Marketing base tended to enhance both the presence and the credibility of virtual team members and ensure sustainable competitive advantage beyond its domestic reach. Other, minor niche market benefits included technical and linguistic support, website maintenance, cash flow security and legal advice. Interestingly, most of these e-Entrepreneurs professed a strong sense of integration within a 'virtual community' that incorporated their chosen sector of economic activity. They also claimed to share in a 'virtual trust', which covered not only their own small business activities but also the commercial interests of their fellow team members.

There were some disadvantages attributed by some e-Entrepreneurs to their membership of virtual teams. One of the most important of these related to perceived changes to their status and working practices. Although they were the owner-managers of their small businesses, membership of a virtual team imposed certain obligations and limitations upon them. They were no longer free to operate as they liked or saw fit and felt obliged to consider their decisions in relation to other core and peripheral members. Their own business strategy and market orientation invariably reflected that of their team, and this also restricted their freedom of action. A related disadvantage involved the added complexity and stress of cross-team communication and collaboration. Some members complained about the restrictive structure of their virtual teams. The fast growth-oriented teams tended to exhibit an informal hierarchy, which stratified the status of core and peripheral members. It was sometimes felt that drivers and core entrepreneurs had privileged positions and access to better and more lucrative markets. Some e-Entrepreneurs were accused of belonging to 'cliques' within virtual teams, which restricted the benefits accruable to peripheral members. Similarly, most peripheral entrepreneurs felt that, due to their less prestigious status, the real decision-making process largely bypassed them. This appears to explain the higher turnover experienced in the peripheral membership category.

The alleged rigidity of virtual teams in terms of membership and niche market territory had a demotivating effect on some members who felt oppressed and stressed by 'unwritten rules' and 'covert conventions'. Similarly, some members resented the rigidity of the profit-oriented strategy of their virtual teams. They felt that this caused conflict amongst members, who felt disadvantaged by the overall lack of flexibility or stressed by long hours and extensive work schedules. It appears that individual circumstances and local conditions were neglected for the alleged benefit of the virtual team as a whole. Conflict resolution mechanisms were in place only in a minority of the smaller teams in the sample. The majority of these e-Entrepreneurs relied upon the terms and condition contained in virtual team agreements. On balance, however, most of the e-Entrepreneurs interviewed admitted that membership of their virtual teams had a very positive and profitable effect upon their small businesses.

Concluding Remarks

Entrepreneurship is currently undergoing a fundamental change from a mostly traditional form to a more collaborative approach to online trading. This reflects the rapid changes that are impacting upon the global e-Market, including the emergence of the Internet and innovative advances in related ICTs. In this chapter, we focused upon 15 case studies of virtual teams of e-Entrepreneurs that operate in the rapidly expanding tourism industry of Europe. A number of important finding have emerged from the in-depth analyses of these virtual teams.

The virtual teams in the research sample were formed between 1990 and 1993, in order to enhance the competitive strategies of the constituent small businesses. The membership strategically sought to improve flexibility, responsiveness and cost efficiency as well as to lower operational costs and enhance resource utilisation. Initial membership consisted of a mix of newly formed and well-established small businesses, in conformity with the opportunity recognition, discovery and creation model proposed by Sarasvathy et al. (2003). In terms of formative dynamics, during inception the teams comprised a small number of core entrepreneurs who considered themselves 'drivers' within team. Furthermore, the initial membership involved mainly core entrepreneurs who either knew each other from previous transactions or were connected through family links.

Even though the competitive strategies and growth orientation of these virtual teams differed, they all provided their members with profitable domestic and Pan-European niche markets. Nevertheless, fast growth-oriented virtual teams exhibited larger memberships as well as increased turnover of both core and peripheral entrepreneurs. Core entrepreneurs in both growth-oriented and high-quality virtual teams claimed to have recognised the importance of the Internet and related ICT development, and decided to incorporate them into their competitive strategies. Compared with other similar-sized small businesses operating in this important sector of the European economy, these virtual teams achieved an early and considerably faster route to new technology adoption. This has greatly facilitated entrepreneurial interaction within virtual teams as well as growth in market share and profitability.

A number of important advantages were attributed by respondents to their membership of virtual teams. One of the most important advantages related to the high quality of data, information and knowledge on supply and demand that was available to all virtual team members. The quantity, quality and reliability of information brokered within virtual teams were significantly higher than what was usually available to the competition. Furthermore, the cost of gathering, testing and validating relevant data was considerably lower. In addition, the cost of analysing, updating and exploiting related entrepreneurial opportunities was spread across the wider core and peripheral membership. Another important virtual team benefit involved 'task-related support' and access to an internal pool of human, financial and technical resources. Considerable niche market benefits were also accrued to these e-Entrepreneurs in terms of individual territories and access to wider customer bases. In particular, professionally presented and maintained e-Marketing websites tended to enhance both the presence and the credibility of virtual team members and ensured sustainable competitive advantage beyond domestic reach.

There were some disadvantages attributed by e-Entrepreneurs to their membership of virtual teams, including changes and restrictions to their status and working practices. In addition, the complexity and stress of team-wide communication and collaboration tended to pressurise some e-Entrepreneurs beyond their acknowledged comfort zones. Some virtual team members complained about restrictive structures, stratified hierarchies and favouritism in the distribution of individual trading territories. Conflict resolution mechanisms were in place only in a small number of virtual teams and this caused problems in relation to actual or perceived grievances. Nevertheless, the vast majority of e-Entrepreneurs in the research sample felt that, on balance, membership of their virtual teams had a very positive and profitable effect upon the competitive strategy of their small businesses.

References

Anderson, A., Jack, S., & Dodd, S. (2005). The role of family members in entrepreneurial networks: Beyond the boundaries of the family firm. *Family Business Review, 18*(2), 135–154.

Birley, S., & Stockley, S. (2000). Entrepreneurial teams and venture growth. In D. Sexton & H. Landstrom (Eds.), *Handbook of entrepreneurship*. Oxford: Blackwell Publishers Ltd.

Boddy, D., Boonstra, A., & Kennedy, G. (2001). *Managing the information revolution.* Harlow: Pearson Education.

Brockaw, L. (1993). The Truth About Start-Ups. *Inc., 15*(3), 56–64.

Brynjolfsson, E., & Kahin, B. (Eds.) (2002). *Understanding the digital economy: Data, tools and research.* Cambridge, MA: MIT Press.

Chapman, P., More, J., Szczygiel, M., & Thompson, D. (2000). Building internet capabilities in SMEs. *Logistic Information Management, 13*(6), 353–360.

Chaston, I. (2001). e-*Marketing strategy.* Maidenhead: McGraw-Hill Publishing Company.

Daniel, E., Wilson, H., & Myers, A. (2002). Adoption of e-commerce by SMEs in the UK. *International Small Business Journal, 20*(3), 253–270.

D'Atri, A., & Pauselli, E. (2004). *Virtual enterprises to develop learning environments in an* e-*marketplace,* Paper presented at the IASTED International Conference on WEB-Based Education, Innsbruck, Austria, February.

Deise, M., Nowikow, C., King, P., & Wright, A. (2000). *Executive's guide to e-business: From tactics to strategy.* New York: John Wiley & Sons.

Doutriaux, J. (1992). High-tech start-ups, better off with government contracts than with subsidies: New evidence in Canada. *IEEE Transactions on Engineering Management, 38*(3), 127–135.

DTI (2000). *International Benchmarking Survey for ICT Use,* London: Department for Trade and Industry, www.ukonline.gov.uk (Accessed 6th January 2001).

Dutta, S., & Segev, A. (1999). Business transformation on the Internet. *European Management Journal, 17*(5), 466–476.

Dutta, S., & Segev, A. (2001). Business transformation on the Internet. In S. Barnes& B. Hunt (Eds.), e-*Commerce and v-business: Business models for global success.* Oxford: Butterworth-Heinemann.

Elliot, S. (Ed.) (2002). *Electronic commerce, B2C strategies and models.* Chichester: John Wiley & Sons Ltd.

Feher, A., & Towell, E. (1997). Business use of the Internet. *Internet Research: Electronic Networking Application and Policy, 7*(3), 195–200.

Feldman, M., & Francis, J. (2001). *Entrepreneurs and the formation of industrial clusters.* Paper Presented at the Complexity and Industrial Clusters Conference, Milan, Italy, June.

Kalakota, R., & Robinson, M. (1999). e-*Business: Roadmap for success.* Boston, MA: Addison Wesley.

Kamm, J., Shuman, J., Seeger, J., & Nurick, A. (1990). Entrepreneurial teams in a new venture creation: A research agenda. *Entrepreneurship Theory and Practice, 14*(4), 7–17.

Kelley, E. (2001). Keys to effective virtual global teams. *The Academy of Management Executive, 15*(2), 132–143.

Kirzner, I. (1997). Entrepreneurial discovery and the competitive market process: An Austrian approach. *Journal of Economic Literature, 35*(1), 60–85.

Kreindler, M., Maislish, R., & Wang, S. (2004). An empirical test of the impact of electronic commerce on organizations. *Human Systems Management, 23*(1), 59–68.

Lechner, C., & Dowling, M.(2003). Firm networks: external relationships as sources for the growth and competitiveness of entrepreneurial firms. *Entrepreneurship & Regional Development, 15*(1), 1–26.

Li, F., & Williams, H. (2001). Inter-organisational systems to support strategic collaboration between firms. In S. Barnes & B. Hunt (Eds.), e-*Commerce and v-business: Business models for global success.* Oxford: Butterworth-Heinemann.

Mangelsdorf, M. (1992). The Ink. 500: America's fastest growing private companies. *INC., 14*(10), 71–80.

Martin, L., & Matlay, H. (2001). Blanket approaches to promoting ICT in small firms: Some lessons from the DTI ladder adoption model in the UK. *Internet Research, 11*(5), 399–410.

Martin, L., & Matlay, H. (2003). Innovative use of the Internet in established small firms: The impact of knowledge management and organisational learning in accessing new opportunities. *Qualitative Market Research, 6*(1), 18–26.

Matlay, H. (1998). *Small tourism firms in Eastern, Central and Western Europe: An empirical overview.* Paper presented at the International Tourism Conference, Llandudno, Wales, May.

Matlay, H. (2003). Managerial work in smaller firms: Past, present and future. *Journal of Management Research, 26*(9), 39–48.

Matlay, H. (2004). Small tourism firms in e-Europe: Definitional, conceptual and contextual considerations. In R. Thomas (Ed.), *Small firms in tourism: International perspective* (pp. 297–312). Amsterdam: Elsevier.

Matlay, H., & Addis, M. (2003). Adoption of ICT and e-Commerce in small businesses: An HEI-based consultancy perspective. *Journal of Small Business and Enterprise Development, 10*(3), 321–335.

Matlay, H., & Westhead, P. (2005). Virtual teams and the rise of e-entrepreneurship in Europe. *International Small Business Journal, 23*(3), 279–300.

Mellor, N. (1998). e-*Commerce and the way forward.* e-Business Seminar, University of Wolverhampton, April.

Michel, J., & Hambrick, D. (1992) Diversification posture and the characteristics of the top management team. *Academy of Management Journal, 35*, 9–37.

Mistri, M. (2003). The emergence of cooperation and the case of the "Italian industrial district" as a socio-economic habitat. *Human Systems Management, 22*(4), 147–156.

Plant, R. (2000). *e-Commerce: Formulation of strategy.* Upper Saddle River, New Jersey: Prentice Hall.

Sarasvathy, S., Dew, N., Velamuri, S., & Venkataraman, S. (2003). Three views of entrepreneurial opportunity. In Z. Acs & D. Audretsch (Eds.), *Handbook of entrepreneurship research — An interdisciplinary survey and introduction.* Dordrecht: Kluwer Academic Publishers.

Shane, S. (2000). Prior knowledge and the discovery of entrepreneurial opportunities. *Organisational Science, 11*(4), 448–469.

Szulanski, G. (2003). *Sticky knowledge — barriers to knowing in the firm.* London: SAGE Publications.

Tetteh, E., & Burn, J. (2001). Global strategies for SME-business: Applying small framework. *Logistics Information Management, 14*(1/2), 171–180.

Thelwall, M. (2000). Effective websites for small and medium-sized enterprises. *Journal of Small Business and Enterprise Development, 7*(2), 149–159.

Timmers, P. (2000). *Electronic commerce: Strategies and models for business-to-business trading.* Chichester: John Wiley & Sons Ltd.

Timmons, J. (1994). *New venture creation: Entrepreneurship for the 21st century.* Homewood, IL: Irwin.

Turban, E., Lee, J., King, D., & Chung, H. (2000). *Electronic commerce: A managerial perspective.* New Jersey: Prentice Hall.

Van Slyke, C. (1997). *The diffusion of technology cluster innovation: The case of the Internet.* Paper presented at the American Conference on Information Systems, Indianapolis, August.

Vyakarnam, S., & Jacobs, R. (1993). *Teamstart — Overcoming blockages to growth.* Paper presented at the 16th National Small Firms Research and Policy Conference, Nottingham Trent University, November.

Vyakarnam, S., Jacobs, R., & Handelberg, J. (1999). Exploring the formation of entrepreneurial teams: The key to rapid growth business?' *Journal of Small Business and Enterprise Development, 6*(2), 153–165.

Zeleny, M. (2001). Autopoiesis (self-production) in SME networks. *Human Systems Management, 20*(3), 201–207.

Chapter 3

The Economic Performance of the Slovak Tourism Businesses

Vladimír Baláž

Introduction: Tourism in The National Economy

After 1989, international tourism was seen as an important source of growth, employment and income in the transition economies. The growing volumes of international tourism receipts were reflected in their increasing share of GDP, exports and the National Bank's currency reserves, as can be seen in Slovakia. International tourism was of considerable importance for the Slovak economy, especially in the earlier years of the economic transition.

In 1990, international tourist receipts generated mere 0.5 per cent of the Slovak GDP, while international tourist expenditure was 1.3 per cent, so the total balance was negative. In next 6 years Slovakia, like other countries in Central Eastern Europe (CEE), experienced a boom in international tourist exchange. In 1996, when the international travel peaked in Slovakia, the share of international tourist receipts in GDP was 3.5 per cent and some 6.1 per cent of the goods and services exports. Net positive international tourism receipts made significant contributions to current accounts, partly offsetting deficits generated in the trade of goods and other services, and helping to build up international currency reserves (Baláž, 1996). For example, international currency derived from tourism considerably helped Slovakia to stabilise its new national currency after 1993. Increases in tourist receipts would be hard to achieve without a proper supply of tourist services. Early 1990s saw a great rise in numbers of tourist facilities. Thousands of new hotels, inns and pubs were established within a short period of 1990–1993.

In the second half of the transition, the relative economic importance of international tourism decreased. By 2003, international tourist receipts generated some 2.7 per cent of the GDP (Figure 3.1) and 3.4 per cent of exports. It does not, however, mean that development of tourism industry stopped. This change should be seen in context of overall transformation of Slovakia's economy. In the period 1998–2004, Slovak government undertook a number of thorough social and economic reforms. The reform agenda was highly acclaimed by foreign investors, and helped to attract a great volume of foreign investment. Stocks of direct foreign investment, for example, increased from 22.9 per cent of GDP in 2000 to 37.2 per cent in 2003 (NBS, 2004). By early 2000s, Slovakia definitely integrated into world production networks. Foreign direct investment (FDI) helped to restructure Slovak economy towards more sophisticated manufacturing industries and services, which accounted for growing GDP shares after 2000. Business services, manufacturing and car assembly, in particular, grew by higher rates than tourism industry and became major production and export activities in Slovakia.

Growth in manufacturing and service sector had positive impact on development of domestic tourism. It helped to improve employment levels and income situation of the Slovak households. This development was reflected in rapidly growing numbers of nights spent by domestic tourists in Slovak accommodation facilities, which increased from 4.8 million in 1992 to 7.1 million in 2003. Rise in domestic tourism demand was another impetus for growth in tourism supply.

In the longer term, this suggests that the economic contribution of tourism in Slovakia (and other CEE countries), within the EU, may become more akin to the modest role it occupies in countries such as Denmark or Belgium than the more significant role it plays in, say, Greece or Portugal (Williams & Baláž, 2002).

The Hotel and Restaurant Sector: Business Performance

The rapidly growing numbers of tourism businesses in early transition period may have suggested an unproblematic growth trajectory. In fact, development of tourism businesses was far from being easy, for small and medium enterprises (SMEs) in particular.

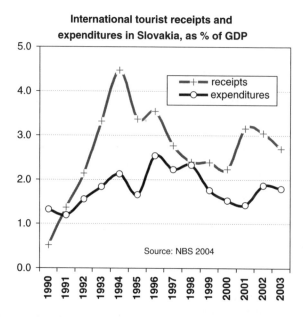

Figure 3.1: International tourist receipts and expenditures in Slovakia, as % of GDP.

Tourism businesses in the transition economies had to overcome several major shocks in a relatively short time: a switch from a planned to a market economy, privatisation, the loss of traditional markets, changes in the structure of demand, and numerous re-organisations and changes in corporate governance. Most of these changes occurred in the period 1991–1993. Because of these shocks, a very differently structured tourism sector emerged after a few years of transformation. By 2004 very few of the original business units operated within the same organisational structure as before 1989, since almost all the original businesses had been privatised. Not surprisingly, these 'wild times' affected the old hotel and restaurant businesses negatively. The new owners had to face the same difficulties as other small businesses in the transition economies: lack of capital, high interest rates, incomplete and unclear regulation, mounting bureaucratic obstacles, corruption and increasing crime. Many privatised businesses accumulated debts and were bankrupted in relatively short time periods. There were rapid ownership changes in such companies, which had further negative results. In contrast, hundreds of new tourism companies and thousands of successful personal businesses emerged in this period.

The importance of tourism depended on the legal form of the businesses, for its share decreased inversely with increasing capital adequacy (the minimum amounts of capital and the capital structure required to establish a company) and was greatest in the personal business sector. Personal businesses (mostly family businesses) were the most widespread ownership form in Slovak tourism, as in most market economies. By 2002 there were some 16 thousand hotel and restaurants businesses, of which 14.2 thousand were personal. These businesses were mostly in the restaurant sub-sector (pubs, inns, cafes etc.), and their numbers increased rapidly 1990–1993 (Figure 3.2). Many were established under the *Small Privatisation* programme (Williams & Baláž, 2000, p. 104), in which tourism had played

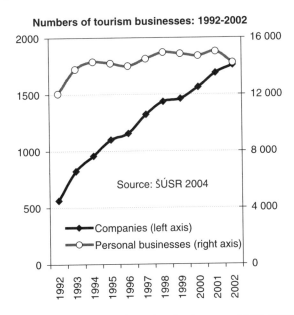

Numbers of tourism businesses: 1992-2002

Source: ŠÚSR 2004

Companies (left axis)
Personal businesses (right axis)

Figure 3.2: Number of tourism businesses: 1992–2002.

a major role. Later, these businesses faced market saturation because of the large numbers of new (or revamped) entrants into the sector. After 1993 the total number of personal businesses changed very little. Share of hotel and restaurant personal businesses in total personal businesses was 3.0 per cent and this share remained stable after 1993.

With tourism companies, situation was rather different. Hotels and restaurants companies (Plc and Ltd-type) accounted for some 4.5 per cent of the total companies in Slovakia in 2002. Privatisation produced a very fragmented tourism industry. The former state socialist enterprises had been large firms, often comprising 20 or more units, incorporating hotels, restaurants, cable cars and other tourism activities. In the course of the transition, these units were first reconstituted as separate firms, and later were either sold to various kinds of investors or transferred to municipal ownership. In Slovakia, transfers to municipalities mostly occurred in 1993. After 1993, the importance of juridical (i.e. non-personal and partnership) ownership increased. Large hotels were privatised in the form of Ltd or Plc (joint-stock) companies. In the period 1996–1998, most of the spas and several large hotels in the High Tatras were privatised in this way in Slovakia, with ownership usually being acquired by domestic private firms.

Privatisation usually was accompanied by fragmentation of the former state-owned hotel chains, as most investors acquired one or two facilities. Privatised hotel and spa enterprises usually had size of 10–49 employees, which explains above-average share of this company size in tourism sector (Figure 3.3). Most of privatisation in tourism sector happened during the period of the undemocratic Mečiar's government (1992–1998), and many of the new owners were allowed to privatise tourism facilities because they were 'government friendly'. Few of the new owners however proved to be good managers. Large numbers of privatised facilities was mismanaged and passed to hands of either financial institutions or foreign and domestic investors. This explains drop in numbers of tourism enterprises in mid 1990s (Figure 3.4).

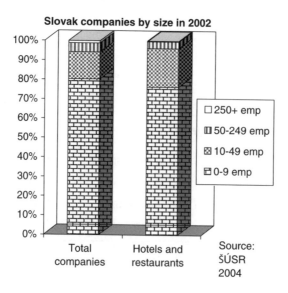

Figure 3.3: Slovak companies by size in 2002.

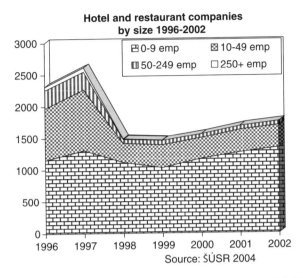

Figure 3.4: Hotel and restaurant companies by size 1996–2002.

Process of privatisation and re-privatisation contributed to polarisation of the tourism industry. By 2002 there was a large number (1341) of very small companies (with 0–9 employees) and limited number (411) of small- and medium-sized ones (with 10–249 employees). In contrast, there were just five companies with 250+ employees. A look at the structure of the companies by their size reveals that numbers of small-sized companies increased, while numbers of medium and large-sized ones decreased in the period 1996–2002 (Figure 3.4).

What assessment can be made of the economic performances of Slovak tourism enterprises during the transformation? This depends, of course, on the indicators selected, but some consistent variations can be identified.

Capital Shortages and Debt-Servicing Costs

There has been a generalised capital shortage in the transition economies, so that most enterprises have relied on their own financial sources. In Slovakia, the share of own funds was significantly higher than the OECD average and was close to the maximum OECD value (56.5% in the UK). Tourism, however, was different. Their share of own funds was much lower than the Slovak average and, furthermore, it decreased during the transformation. Most tourism businesses were either privatised or newly established after 1989. The new owners had to borrow capital, initially for the privatisation purchase and later to restructure their businesses. Non-tourism establishments were mostly privatised via coupon privatisation or direct sales at very low prices, so that their owners had relatively smaller borrowing requirements.

The above-average proportions of borrowed capital in the total funds of tourism businesses contributed to their above-average debt-servicing costs. Funds for privatisation were

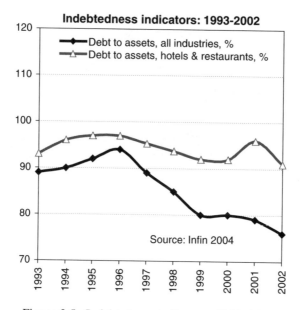

Figure 3.5: Indebtedness indicators: 1993–2002.

borrowed over short time periods, and debts had to be repaid relatively quickly. The short-term nature of loans (and a falling inflation rate) meant that the amount of debt and interest somewhat decreased over time; there was also an upturn in the share of debt in total assets. Decrease in indebtedness levels in HORECA sector (hotels, restaurants, cafes, bars, pubs and camping), however, was much less pronounced than in the rest of economy (Figure 3.5).

Profitability

A further insight into firm performance is provided by the Banking and Clearing Centre of Slovakia, which, since 1993, has been computing the median values of the financial indica-tors of Slovak businesses (Infin, 2004). This information, originally designed for investment banking, provides a unique insight into the performances of Slovak tourism businesses. The statistics summarise information from all types and sizes of enterprises. Selected indicators for tourism businesses are shown in Table 3.1. It is important to stress Table 3.1 that summarises data on all types of enterprises (Ltd, Plc, co-operatives), except personal businesses.

An overwhelming majority of enterprises — 896 out of a total of 936 — in HORECA sector in Slovakia had less than Sk 50 million (Euro 1.2 million) in assets in 2002. Most had basic capital of only Sk 200,000 (Euro 5000), which is the lowest capital requirement for the Ltd-type company in Slovakia. The low capital requirement explains the very low share of own funds in the total capital of most Slovak tourism businesses. In contrast, large enterprises, with assets over Euro 3.5 million (12 units) and turnover over Euro 2.3 million (8 units), mostly relied on their own capital. However, the rapidly growing numbers of small companies explain the decreasing average share of own funds in the period 1993–2002 and high level of indebtedness in the HORECA sector. This contrasted with decreasing levels of indebtedness in the rest of Slovak economy (Figure 3.5).

Table 3.1: Selected financial indicators for Slovak tourism business, 1999–2002.

1999	2000	2001	2002	Indicator	2002: assets, (€) mill.			2002: turnover, (€) mill.		
					Up to 1.2	1.2–3.5	Over 3.5	Up to 0.6	0.6–2.3	Over 2.3
All enterprises				**Total HORECA sector**						
927	1076	1198	936	No. of companies	896	28	12	881	47	8
−7.69	−8.58	−8.03	−5.26	Net profits/ own funds (%)	−5.77	0.03	−0.35	−5.77	2.31	−6.12
−1.62	−1.73	−1.29	−0.23	Operating profits/ sales (%)	−0.37	3.42	1.50	−0.88	1.95	4.62
21.78	22.45	22.83	24.35	Value-added/ sales (%)	23.18	47.48	53.47	23.61	38.26	46.93
0.79	0.29	0.74	1.60	EBITDA/sales (%)	1.36	10.78	14.56	1.36	6.60	11.21
				Hotels						
217	261	261	180	No. of companies	155	17	8	155	20	5
−8.40	−5.26	−3.66	−3.54	Net profits/ own funds (%)	−3.89	−1.03	−0.35	−4.32	5.59	−0.70
−3.62	−1.66	−0.34	0.51	Operating profits/ sales (%)	0.42	5.59	1.50	0.04	5.32	6.44
36.00	37.24	37.15	36.81	Value-added/ sales (%)	33.92	49.97	53.47	34.36	47.46	53.58
1.25	1.34	3.01	5.39	EBITDA/ sales. (%)	3.18	12.38	14.56	3.18	10.90	19.77
				Restaurants						
493	546	630	489	No. of companies	480	6	3	471	16	2

(Continued)

Table 3.1: (Continued)

1999	2000	2001	2002	Indicator	2002: assets, (€) mill.			2002: turnover, (€) mill.		
					Up to 1.2	1.2–3.5	Over 3.5	Up to 0.6	0.6–2.3	Over 2.3
All enterprises										
-7.64	-9.76	-12.06	-9.65	Net profits/own funds (%)	-9.96	1.53	1.97	-9.65	-4.19	idp
-1.19	-1.77	-2.13	-1.81	Operating profits/sales (%)	-2.07	2.55	6.60	-2.27	1.75	idp
18.34	18.66	19.35	20.81	Value-added/sales (%)	20.62	35.03	62.45	20.81	20.51	idp
0.39	-0.10	0.01	0.57	EBITDA/sales. %	0.53	5.26	41.68	0.45	2.16	idp
				All Slovak industries						
39 162	43 415	47 004	34 200	No. of companies	31 404	1 656	1 140	28 774	3 640	1 786
-2.16	-1.94	-0.48	0.00	Net profits/own funds (%)	-0.12	1.83	1.37	-0.52	10.97	13.54
0.32	0.41	0.98	1.35	Operating profits/sales (%)	1.19	3.15	3.24	0.95	2.33	2.96
14.77	14.99	15.29	16.19	Value-added/sales (%)	15.45	24.17	23.30	16.67	14.95	14.99
1.86	1.95	2.52	2.91	EBITDA/sales. (%)	2.56	7.47	8.15	2.49	3.88	4.86

Source: Infin (2004).
Notes: The data refer only to Ltd and Plc companies and exclude personal businesses. idp = data suppressed due to individual data protection (2 or less units).

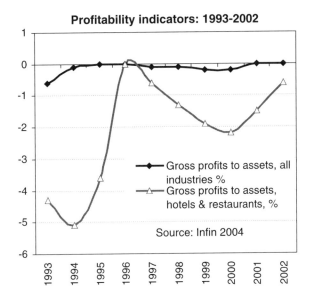

Figure 3.6: Profitability indicators: 1993–2002.

High levels of indebtedness generated high shares of debt costs in total costs. Additionally, interest rates stood as high as 15–20 per cent in 1990s and 8–10 per cent in early 2000s. As pointed above, most HORECA sector enterprises were small and had short business history, and banks charged their credits with above-average interest rates. High costs of debt heavily impacted profitability of tourism industries. Enterprises in HORECA sector accounted for much worse gross profit/asset ratios than other Slovak companies in the period 1993–2002 (Figure 3.6).

Size Does Matter

In general, there is a positive relationship between the size of assets or turnover and the profitability of the enterprise. The industry, in aggregate, made a net loss, mostly because of the performances of smaller enterprises. This has to be seen against the growth in the number of enterprises (Figure 3.2) and the fact that newly established firms tend to record losses initially. By 2002, however, the average (median) loss (virtually zero) had declined significantly compared to the equivalent figure for 1993. Additionally, small enterprises had to maintain relatively high levels of financial assets, in relation to their capital require-ments (only Euro 5 thousands) for small enterprises, whereas many have turnover of Euro 25–250 thousands because of the increasing demands of suppliers for cash transac-tions and the large share of trade credits in their total capital. The average (median) share of financial assets, however, was very low.

Table 3.1 also provides an insight into the structure of the tourism industry. Most medium- and large-scale enterprises were in the hotel sub-sector. In contrast, only two restaurant chains had a turnover of more than Euro 2.3 million in 2002. Profitability also differed in the hotel and restaurant sub-sectors. In the hotel sub-sector, medium-sized and large enterprises were more profitable (ratios of net profits/own funds and operating profits/sales) than small firms. However, overall profitability improved in the hotel sub-sector in particular, during the observed period, after the initial costs of privatisation had been absorbed, interest rates decreased and tax collection became more efficient.

Low profitability of enterprises in the HORECA sector contrasted with the above-average levels of value-added and income generations (ratios of value-added/sales and EBITDA/sales, EBITDA = Earnings Before Interest, Taxes, Depreciation and Amortization). Service sector industries use to have lower material costs and higher levels of wages costs, which explains relatively higher levels of the value-added generation. Medium and large Slovak hotel enterprises, in particular, had high EBITDA levels. Significant part of the income, however, was spent for debt servicing. Profitability of the own funds was thus low.

Tourism Versus Non-Tourism Enterprises

Finally, it was clear that Slovak tourist enterprises were, generally, less efficient than the remainder of the economy. This is mostly due to the establishment of large numbers of new, small tourism businesses after 1989. These had lower shares of own funds and financial assets in their total assets, and many were burdened with privatisation debts. In contrast, tourism businesses shared in the more generalised trend for the economic performance of Slovak firms to improve during the transition.

While the published data provide insights into the transition process, especially into changes over time, their reliability has to be seen in context of the operational realities, in period of economic transition in particular. Most market institutions had to be created in transition economies, including the tax and statistical systems. There has been a thriving shadow economy, and tax evasion is known to be widespread. The tourism industry in a transformation economy is usually characterised by large shares of cash payments and a failure to issue receipts for payments made by foreigner visitors. These conditions favoured the non-reporting of income, particularly amongst small businesses. This was underlined the difference between the US$ 672.8 million of international currency receipts reported by the National Bank of Slovakia (computed according to recommended IMF methods) and the receipts of at least US$ 1808 million indicated by a market survey in 1998. This means that the actual profitability of Slovak tourism businesses was probably far stronger than was reported in their financial statements. During 1992–2002 the numbers of tourism-related companies multiplied by 3.1 times in Slovakia, and this is only likely to have occurred if the profits outlook was favourable.

Travel Agents

While three state and co-operative travel agencies (plus the federal *Čedok*) accounted for the entire turnover of this sector in Slovakia in 1989, some 1000 licences were issued subsequently in the period 1989–2004. Most of these licences, however, were never or sparsely used and, in fact, there were some 160 active travel agents by 2004. Some 150 members of the Slovak Association of the Tour-Operators and Travel Agents (SATOTA) covered about 95 per cent of the total turnover in this industry.

The year 1989 was therefore a watershed in the travel agency sector as in most segments of the tourism industry. Most of the new firms in the sector originated as family businesses, and the founder usually had some previous experience of working in a state-owned travel agency. Except for *Satur Plc.* (the Slovak part of the former *Čedok*) and *Tatratour*, almost all the domestically owned agencies suffered from a lack of capital, technical equipment and professional staff. The new firms began operating by creating simple products for the domestic market. The very first products were short bus trips to Vienna and Venice — the buses being hired from local bus networks and the offices being established in the entrepreneurs' own homes. A typical product in the 1990–1995 period was a bus trip to an Italian or Spanish resort for US$ 200 per capita per week. The 'mortality rate' amongst such firms was very high. Only a small number of the 150 members of the SATOTA in 2004 could date their origins back to 1990. There was no large firm (with 250+ employees) in the travel agents sector in Slovakia. Very few agents had more than ten employees. An overwhelming majority of travel agents in Slovakia were small companies and personal businesses.

There is, however, evidence that the travel agency sub-sector was becoming more sophisticated, for there was increasing involvement in outbound tourism, particularly for 'sunshine, sea and sand' holidays. This was linked to improved living standards after 1994 as well as to more sophisticated product development and marketing. Many agents established working contacts with partners in the destination countries or with major European tour companies, such as Neckerman and TUI. The total number of clients and the volume of days sold increased three-fold in the period 1989–2003 (Figure 3.7), with the most significant increases being in 1996 and 1997. Also, there was change in the average length

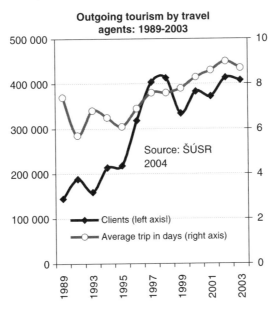

Figure 3.7: Outgoing tourism by travel agents: 1989–2003.

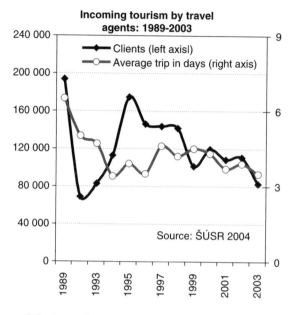

Figure 3.8: Incoming tourism by travel agents: 1989–2003.

of stay. It first decreased from 6.5 days in 1989 to 3.4 days in 1994 (perhaps because of declining incomes) but increased to 4.6 days in 1997 and 3.5 days in 2003. There were more significant changes in quality. The market share of cheap bus trips has fallen and standard travel packages, inclusive of flights and accommodation, have become more important, such as air inclusive package trips. As their potential customer base has become more solvent and selective, the product supply of Slovak travel agencies has converged towards Western European models (Williams & Baláž, 2001).

While outgoing tourism boomed, incoming tourism stagnated (Figure 3.8). In 2003, incoming tourists accounted for only 20.3 per cent of total travel agency clients. The average length of inbound trip has fallen from 6.5 days in 1989 to 5.0 days in 1992, and to 3.4 days in 1994. This is probably due to the diminishing level of organised travel amongst the post-socialist countries, and to the decreasing quality of travel agency services in this early transition period. After 1995 the 'core' Slovakian travel agencies improved the quality of their services and developed closer collaboration with major EU tour operators, but the length of stay by incoming tourists did not change much and was 3.5 days in 2003.

In many ways, the travel agents were the most 'enlightened' entrepreneurs in the Slovakian tourism industry. The SATOTA was the most effective self-regulation tourism body in the country and had designed, for example, its own code of conduct of business rules, was a member of Universal Federation of the Travel Agents Association (UFTAA), successfully lobbied for a reduction in VAT on incoming tourism from 25 per cent to zero and had prepared a system of customer protection based on the EU's 314/90/EEC Travel Package Directive. There was strong geographical concentration in the sector, with the headquarters of 75 of the 150 SATOTA members being in Bratislava in 2004.

There were a number of spectacular failures amongst the Slovakian travel agents in the course of 1996 and 2004. After a successful 1995 season, some agents tried to act as tour operators and booked charter flights. Supply considerably exceeded demand, and the agents resorted to selling the packages at what were effectively 'dumping' prices, but many flights remained half-empty. When these agents were unable to pay their foreign creditors, several hundreds of Slovak citizens were stranded without return tickets at Greek airports. Fortunately, these crashes were relatively small scale. The major Slovakian tour companies had sufficient finance and experience to avoid such an ignominious fate. The crashes however highlighted need for some kind of insurance in case of bankruptcy by the travel agent. Slovak Ministry of Economy, responsible for regulation of the tourism sector, reviewed the Travel Package Directive No. 90/314 of the European Communities and tried to incorporate it into the Slovak laws. The Act No. 281/2001 defined tour operators and travel agents and required 'all tour operators to have a valid contract with an insurance company, or a bank guarantee, or to be a member of a guarantee fund in case of bankruptcy by the tour operator'. Most tour operators wanted to follow the law and tried to have contracts with insurance companies. This, however, was far from being easy:

- Slovak financial market was small, and insurance companies had little experience with risks encountered by tour-operators. Most tour operators had short business history and did not pass risk tests by insurance companies. Insurance companies did not consider bankruptcy insurance products for tour-operators attractive and refused many applicants.
- Some banks agreed to provide bank guarantees, but had excessive requirements on collaterals to be pledged by tour operators. There was very small number of bank guarantees provided for Slovak tour operators.
- There was no guarantee fund for tour operators.

As a result, many tour operators had no bankruptcy insurance and developed their business on the verge of law. Ministry of Economy (MoE) tried to establish the Tourism Guarantee Fund, with a compulsory membership by all tour operators. The ministry prepared a special act on the fund in 2003. The fund should have a basic capital of 2.5 million euro (provided by the Ministry of Finance). By 2006, the funds has not been established and travel agents had to hedge their trips via the bankruptcy insurance.

Business Environment

Like in other European countries, SMEs played an important role in economic development in Slovakia. By 2002, Slovak SMEs generated 62 per cent of total employment, 45 per cent of total value-added and 26.7 per cent of total exports. Economic activities of SMEs, however, were hampered by a number of barriers:

- Slovak SMEs were quite small by European standards. Some 26 per cent of SMEs had turnover less than €25,000 and some 28 per cent between €25,000–€125,000. Some 4 per cent of SMEs only had turnover higher than Euro 2.5 million. Less than one quarter of SMEs was able to export their products (NADSME, 2003). Because of their size and short business history, most of the SMEs had problems to get bank credits.

- Regular surveys done by the Business Alliance of Slovakia (BAS, 2004), for example, revealed that SMEs quoted enforcement of law, great number of changes in regulations applied to business environment, corruption and bureaucracy as major problems of their developments. This view was supported by international agencies engaged in scoring economic freedom and corruption. By 2004 Slovakia occupied 59th place (out of 133 countries in the world) in the Corruption Perception Index (TIS, 2004) and 51st place (out of 123 countries) in the Economic Freedom Index (HF, 2004).

These difficulties generated by poor business environment were common for all SMEs. It explains why they were considered more important than the problems encountered by particular sectors of economy, including tourism. Business environment reform was for SMEs active in tourism, far more important than specific government initiatives aimed at tourism.

Business Environment Reform

Administrative simplification has been one of the key points of the reform agenda by the Slovak government since 2002. Old administrative environment was a significant hindrance for dynamic development of Slovak enterprises in general and small- and medium-sized enterprises in particular. A thorough reform of the business environment was a major event in the life of SMEs in Slovakia during 2003–2004. While not specifically aimed at tourism SMEs, these reforms were a great step towards the creation of a stable, flexible and transparent business framework in the country. The main objective of the business environment reform was simplifying conditions for entry of and activities undertaken by enterprises. The reform included the following major themes:

- *Tax Reform*: It was a major event in Slovak economy in 2004. The basic goal of the tax reform was to create light, non-distorting, simple and transparent tax system. The reform radically decreased economic distortions created by the old tax system. There were five rates for personal income tax, one rate for corporate income tax and two rates of VAT in 2003. Since 2004 these eight rates have been replaced by one flat tax of 19 per cent. The new tax system also erased a great number of exceptions, exemptions and special regimes.
- *Regulation of entry*: New Business Code (Law No 530/2003) provided for simplifying requirements for entry and shortening numbers of administrative procedures for new business when entering the market. While it took, on average, some 40 days to start a business in the EU-15 area, it took some 98 days in Slovakia. The new regulations enabled business to be registered in 5–15 days.
- *Labour market regulations*: New Labour Code (Law No 311/2001 as amended via Laws No 165/2002, 408/2002, 413/2002 and 210/2003) provided for re-codification of the employee–employer relations, towards greater flexibility of business when hiring/firing employees, negotiating wages, holidays, trade-union participation on the corporate governance etc.
- *Credit market regulation*: Credit register was established by three leading Slovak banks. It was aimed to protect banks from lending to dubious business and enabled an easier access to credit by efficient enterprises. The register obtained approval by the National

Bank of Slovakia and started in September 2004; The Amendment of the Act No. 526/2002 of the Civil Code was another important step towards an easier access to credit by small- and medium-sized enterprises. The act widened the range of assets eligible for credit collaterals (cars, equipment or intellectual property rights).

- *Bankruptcy regulation amendments*: An amendment of the Bankruptcy Law No 566/2001 was prepared by the Slovak Government in May 2004. It aimed to strengthen protection of creditors, speed up the bankruptcy process and increase income by creditors from the bankruptcy proceedings.

Tourism-Specific Initiatives

There were two major government initiatives aimed at promoting tourism SMEs: (i) the 1998 Pilot Tourism Development Grant Scheme (PTDGS) and (ii) the 2002 Tourism Development Grant Scheme (TDGS). Both schemes heavily relied on the finance provided by the EU-Phare Programme.

Prior to the PTDGS, government financial incentives were available through the Nation Agency for Development of Small and Medium Enterprises (NADSME) and the Slovak Guarantee and Development Bank's Tourism Development Programme in Slovakia No. I–VI. Both were too limited in their scale and not well structured for tourism sector SMEs, and offered no preparatory benefits for SMEs to gain the 'know-how' to access future large-scale financing under EU Structural Funding.

The MoE issued the 'Call for Proposals' for the 1998 PTDGS in March 2001. The scheme had three components: (i) investment component aimed at development of tourism infrastructure by SMEs, (ii) training and (iii) network and private–public partnership development. During the following 6 months over 2000 expressions of interest were submitted of which over 650 were reported through the project's website. Actual applications received numbered 504 of which 153 were successful and awarded grants. The breakdown of grant awards by each of the three TDGS measures was as follows: enterprise 37, people-based development 5 and partnerships and the regions 111. The value of the grants awarded accounted for more than 90 per cent of the totally available grant of Euro 2.0 million.

Significantly, the 'pilot' scheme issued grants to only 30 per cent of applicants. This was mainly due to applicant's lack of capacity to satisfactorily formulate and present projects. Investment-based applications formed 30 per cent of grants awarded (max. 35% grant support) and non-investment 70 per cent (max. 75% grant support). This skew in favour of non-investment applications was likely due to investment projects that require access to higher levels of matching finance and the more demanding requirements of the grant scheme (business plans and independent financial assessment). Regardless of this imbalance, it is estimated that the Euro 1.8 million awarded in grants levered a further Euro 2.0 million investment from applicants (1.11 leverage ratio). Success of the PTDGS was a clear indication that appropriately designed financial incentive instruments stimulated a popular response from the sector and signalled the potential to act as a major catalyst of regional development.

It is evident that the latent absorption capacity exits in the sector. With increased technical assistance in project preparation and improvements in the general business environment, the proportion of successful applicants would increase and a better balance between investment and non-investment grant awards would be achieved. This can be anticipated over the duration of the Phare 2002 programme and would significantly raise the leverage effects of the grant scheme. The 2002 TDGS call was published in September 2003, and first grants were awarded in July 2004. This scheme was managed by the NADSME. Total funds of 5.7 million Euro were envisaged for the scheme, of which 3.5 million Euro was contributed by the Phare Programme. At a 1.20 average leverage ratio, and a similar level of support under Phare 2002 and future programmes, the scheme would potentially yield Euro 7.2 million investment by applicants. This improved performance should be indicated by achievement of the following results:

- A better balance between investment and non-investment projects supported by the grant scheme should be achieved. Approximately 40–50 investment and around 60–70 non-investment projects were set as a target.
- Best practice examples of product development should feature strongly in the 'output' results of the grant scheme and demonstrate both qualitative and quantitative improvements in the standard of tourism facilities.
- MoE's support to more optimal conditions within which SME tourism sector entrepreneurial activities can prosper should be indicated by a significant increase in complimentary activities by local and regional tourism associations created.

The investment component TDGS was aimed solely at the SMEs and met by great interest by Slovak entrepreneurs. The NADSME received over 800 applications, but only small numbers of projects were envisaged to be awarded. When the total number of tourism business in Slovakia (over 16 thousand) was compared with the expected total 100–120 grants under the TDGS, it was evident that tourism-specific initiatives were not able to have a significant impact on development of tourism sector in Slovakia.

Conclusions: Interpreting Economic Performance

The tourism boom after 1989 was reflected in different ways at the macroeconomic and microeconomic levels in Slovakia. The boom had been generated by external changes in the general economic and political environment (especially re-internationalisation and establishment of a market economy), which helped to increase the volumes of tourist inflows and international tourism receipts. These receipts increased 12 times (in current US $ prices) in Slovakia in the period 1990–2003. The development stimulus provided by the boom, however, was less powerful than might be expected from these ratios. The shares of value-added and investment in the tourism industry decreased, mostly due to more rapid growth in other sectors of national economy. Most investment activities in Slovakia in this period were carried out by multi-national firms, especially in the service and manufacturing sectors. The access to finance by small businesses (including tourism establishments) was restricted via capital shortages and high costs of debt. Development of the tourism sector was partly financed from personal sources accumulated by entrepreneurs via various activities (including those in the shadow economy).

In 1989–1993, several thousand personal tourism businesses were established in Slovakia. Later, they faced saturated markets and increasingly competitive conditions, even if the tourism sector in aggregate continued to expand. In contrast, larger companies, mostly established in the Ltd form, had access to wider pools of capital and expertise, and emerged as the main players in the tourism market.

The overall profitability of Slovak businesses increased over the period under review. There were some differences between the hotel and restaurant sub-sectors. Generally, tourism businesses seem to be less profitable than the rest of the Slovakian economy, but the real situation may be different if unreported income is included.

Perhaps the most important conclusion that can be drawn in this chapter is that any attempt to assess the relative economic performance of firms needs to take into account the nature of privatisation and creation of business environment. Failure of many of the original owners of small- and medium-sized businesses meant that these were effectively taken over by the financial institutions that had provided loans for their initial purchases. There was, therefore, no simple linear process of converting public into private property rights but, instead, there was 'an intersection of old and new pathways' (Smith & Pickles, 1998; p. 15).

With these comments in mind, some brief reflections can be made about changing structure of the tourism industry mediated by Slovakia's EU-membership. It is realistic to suppose that there would be no great or rapid changes, assuming there are no fundamental shifts in other economic and political parameters (such as relationships with the Commonwealth of Independent States or in the price of oil). Most of the fundamental changes already happened in 1990s and were related to process of economic and social transition and political integration to the EU and NATO structures. Borders to the West have been opened, and EU membership has no major implications for tourism in this respect. The processes of privatisation of property rights are virtually complete in the tourism sector, and limited EU regulation in this area, such as the package holiday directive, have already been incorporated into the legislation of the new member states in anticipation of accession.

There will of course be some changes in the economic performance of the tourism businesses.

- Rising income levels, convergence on EU GDP per capita levels (at exchange rates) and foreign investment may facilitate increased outlays on domestic and outbound tourism oriented towards business and leisure purposes. Rising demand (matched by improved supply) is likely to increase profitability ratios of the Slovak SMEs in tourism sector.
- After all the Slovak banks were privatised by renowned foreign financial institutions during 1998–2002, access to credit by SMEs improved. Debt-servicing costs decreased and approached those in the Eurozone. This may provide another impetus for improving economic performance by the tourism businesses.
- Some inbound tourism may be facilitated by perceived reduced risks of trading with Slovak companies by the EU firms. Structural aid that flows into transport infrastructure, farm tourism and environmental and urban assistance programmes may provide for another impetus for development of tourism supply in Slovakia. There is no doubt that many tourism businesses will rely on financial assistance from the structural funds in Slovakia in the future.
- Major incentives for tourism sector development may be provided by the far-reaching reform of the business environment. Reform agenda of the Slovak government

addressed issues important for all kind of businesses. SMEs, in particular, were likely to profit from amelioration of administrative barriers and creation of a stable, flexible and transparent business framework in the country.

However, any such changes and growth in tourism sector are likely to be relatively modest in comparison with the shifts that occurred in the 1990s, and given global rather than European competition. Hence, there is more scope for path dependence than path creation as a consequence of EU membership per se. The scale and structure of the tourism sector have already been reshaped substantially in anticipation of EU membership.

References

Baláž, V. (1996). *International tourism in the economies of central European countries.* Tourism Research Group, Discussion Paper No.9, University of Exeter: Exeter.

BAS, Business Alliance of Slovakia (2004). *The state of the business environment in Slovakia — business environment index (BEI),* http://www.alianciapas.sk/pas/.

HF, Hayek Foundation (2004). *Economic freedom index,* www.hayek.sk.

Infin (2004). *Medium values of financial indicators for economic activities in Slovakia,* Infin Bratislava, www.infin.sk.

NADSME, National Agency for Development of Small and Medium Enterprises (2003). *State of small and medium enterprises in the Slovak Republic,* NADSME, Bratislava, December 2003.

NBS, National Bank of Slovakia (2004). *Balance of payments statistics.* NBS Bratislava, July 2004.

Smith, A., & Pickles, J. (1998). Introduction: theorising transition and the political economy of transformation. In J. Pickles & A. Smith (Eds.), *Theorising transition: The political economy of post-communist transformations* (pp. 1–24). London: Routledge.

ŠÚSR, Štatistický úrad Slovenskej republiky (1993–2004). *Štatistická ročenka Slovenskej republiky,* {Slovak Statistical Office: *Statistical yearbook of the Slovak Republic*}, Bratislava, 1993–2004.

TIS, Transparency International Slovakia (2004). *Corruption perception index.* http://www.transparency.sk.

Williams, A. M., & Baláž, V. (2000). *Tourism in transition.* London and New York: I.B.Tauris & Co. Ltd, p. 256.

Williams, A. M., & Baláž, V. (2001). *From collective provision to commodification of tourism? Annals of Tourism Research, 28*(1/2001), 27–49.

Williams A. M., & Baláž, V. (2002). The Czech and Slovak Republics: Conceptual issues in the economic analysis of tourism in transition. *Tourism Management, 23*(1), 37–45.

Chapter 4

Strategic Imperatives for Tourism SMEs in Europe

Crispin Dale and Neil Robinson

Introduction

The most recent accession of new member states to the European Union (EU) has generated a wealth of opportunities for tourism SMEs to exploit the potential demand from international tourism. At the same time, however, it has increased the level of competition amongst European tourism SMEs, which need to employ appropriate strategies to achieve their business objectives in such a competitive market. While the literature on strategic management is growing, it is still at an embryonic stage in relation to the SME sector. The strategic management theories developed within the context of large enterprises are frequently inappropriate for application within the sector of SMEs (Jones, 2003). Indeed, small firms are not scaled-down versions of large corporations (Bridge, O'Neil, & Cromie, 1998) and differ greatly both in *employee* collectivization (numbers and training), *organizational* configuration (make up and structure) and operational manner. The unique characteristics of the tourism sector within the New Europe also call for developing strategies that can address the new challenges that are present in this new competitive landscape. In particular, tourism SMEs based in the new member states — which mostly represent transition economies — possess less experience in competing in the European market. Consequently, they need to accelerate their learning curve if they are to match the strategic capabilities of tourism SMEs operating in the established EU states and to effectively compete in the European and global markets. Central to this learning process is gaining an understanding of the dynamic external tourism environment, the new and emerging stakeholder priorities and the development of capabilities and competences that would enable those SMEs to compete on an equal footing with the established European tourism SMEs.

With a particular focus on the new EU member states, this chapter discusses the fundamental strategic issues and imperatives that tourism SMEs need to consider if they are to compete effectively in the New Europe. The enhancement of SME competitiveness is

Tourism in the New Europe
Copyright © 2007 by Elsevier Ltd.
All rights of reproduction in any form reserved.
ISBN: 0-08-044706-6

important, as according to Szamosi, Duxbury, and Higgins (2004), it is the strong SME infrastructure that is critical to a nation's economic growth.

The European SME Economy

At the European level, the limited diffusion of knowledge of strategic management practices in SMEs has the potential to destabilize a section of commerce, which is key to the economic well being of the global economy. National economies are often highly dependent upon SME development and play a key role in creating employment and contributing towards gross national product (GNP) (Yap & Thong, 1997). Buhalis and Peters (2006) raise the importance of SME contribution and detail how European economies are predominately SME orientated. For instance, small businesses represented 98.8% of all enterprises employing 140 million people in Western Europe in 2003 (European Commission, 2003). In the same year, there were nearly 6 million small businesses in the "accession" states (represented by many of the Central and Eastern European countries) and the "candidate" states (Bulgaria, Croatia, Romania and Turkey) employing 30 million people (European Commission, 2003). In fact, employment growth in SMEs within the accession states far exceeds that in larger enterprises, which is in a state of decline (European Commission, 2003). The above statistics indicate that the input, which SMEs make to local and national economies, is pivotal to establishing a fully functioning economy. Whilst many governments attempt to devise support mechanisms via policy designed to facilitate SME development, it could be argued that much of this support is little more than tokenism. Furthermore, owing to the limited understanding of SMEs on the part of these support agencies, such policies can be ineffective with regulatory pressures acting as a major barrier to small business success (Atkinson & Hurstfield, 2003).

Small and medium-sized enterprises are exposed to a multitude of negative macro-environmental factors, which are in many cases exclusive to the small business sector and which are not shared by larger organizations. Problems faced by SMEs that inhibit their ability to gain competitive advantage include ineffective/limited labour supply, inept management skills, a poor resource base and low levels of education and training (Jones & Tilley, 2003). As trade barriers become increasingly liberalized and deregulated across Europe, a wealth of opportunities exist for tourism entrepreneurs and SME start-ups. However, the process of globalization increasingly generates entry opportunities for multi-nationals to gain a foothold in the growing economies of the new member states and acts as a direct threat to SMEs (Robinson, 2005). This is particularly true for large multi-national corporations such as Hilton, Holiday Inn and InterContinental that can dominate the market through brand recognition and greater capital resources. This itself can cause many problems in fledgling, developing economies where much of the business revenue created by an international enterprise is exported back to the country of origin. This benefits few in the local communities resulting in negative host–visitor relations and economic leakage (Mason, 2003). Given the challenges in the business environment, it is essential that both the EU and individual member states, particularly the new member states, create an environment conducive to enhancing competitiveness of tourism SMEs.

Tourism Development in Europe

Europe as a whole has the greatest number of international tourist arrivals that account for 57% of the total market (WTO, 2003). While the market is maturing in Western Europe, the growth in visitor arrivals is forecast to occur primarily within the Central and Eastern European states. This is being driven by a number of factors including low-cost airlines entering Central and Eastern European nations (Coles & Hall, 2005), the trend towards Internet bookings, the growth in the demand for short-break holidays and the desire of travellers to experience alternative forms of tourism (WTO, 2003). From a supply side, a number of competitive factors also enable this growth to occur. Firstly, owing to the low barriers to entry compared to manufacturing firms, tourism SMEs can start up fairly quickly (Wood, 2002). Secondly, the environmental diversity of EU member states facilitates and enables visitors to experience a multitude of climatic regions, cultures and scenery. Thirdly, the superstructure of neighbouring EU states enables access to all but a few in the newly emerging member countries. As the accession states begin to capitalize on the benefits of joining the European Union, entrepreneurial activity in the tourism industry will become increasingly prevalent. Indeed, the growing entrepreneurial culture associated with SME development within the accession states, offers opportunities for those SMEs astute enough to match provision with customer expectations. It should be noted that visitors from other EU states will have a high level of expectations in terms of delivery and continuity of provision. If such expectations are not met, those tourism SMEs not delivering an appropriate product will potentially lose out to competitors and countries where provision is perceived as being superior. Therefore, it is crucial that tourism SMEs throughout Europe are aware of the strategic challenges that they might face in gaining and maintaining their competitiveness.

Strategic Challenges

Small and medium-sized enterprises are often family run with emphasis upon individuality and product differentiation and are crucial to the national economies of Europe, which offer employment opportunities and support to local businesses that supply goods and services (Buhalis & Main, 1998). However, the tourism industry is characterized by fragmentation, high staff turnover, seasonality and labour-intensive production/work patterns (Evans, Campbell, & Stonehouse, 2003). Furthermore, the independent and often autonomous nature of SMEs has created a culture of inertia and poor strategic focus, resulting in outdated management and development practices (Buick, 2003; Main, 1995; Mutch, 1995). Small businesses are subject to a number of economic and environmental factors including fluctuation of demand, elasticity, capacity constraints and changing customer preferences, resulting in an uncertain and unstable business environment. In addition, tourism SMEs are often affected by limited IT investment, seasonal infrastructure pressures, limited long-term quality job creation and poor levels of innovation amongst existing companies, all compounding the pressures on service sector SMEs (SCC, 2004).

These strategic challenges are further compounded in Central and Eastern Europe where SME development and entrepreneurship has been a difficult process but has acted as a catalyst to the transition states orientating themselves towards a market economy (Bateman & Lloyd-Reason, 2000). It is important to note the historical context in which the growth of SMEs has occurred within Central and Eastern Europe. During the communist era, the centralization of the political process made it almost impossible for any kind of self-managed entrepreneurial activity to take place. Entrepreneurial activity was restrained due to SMEs over complicating the planning process, with the authorities having to manage a myriad of further small businesses in addition to the larger enterprises. There was also a fear that SME development would create a culture of capitalist activity and thus generate an uprising. SMEs were also unable to gain economies of scale due to their relative size which was fundamental to the communist production mentality (Bateman & Lloyd-Reason, 2000).

Owing to highly limited international tourism activity to the communist states, tourism SME development was limited. However, in states such as the former Yugoslavia a level of market socialism was allowed to develop during the 1960s and tourism SMEs were encouraged. However, even this development was heavily regulated with restrictions on the number of people that could be employed outside of family members.

Since the fall of communism, the European Union has actively encouraged SME development in the form of its "Phare" and "Tacis" initiatives and the creation of the European Bank for Reconstruction and Development (ERBD). In addition, during the 1990s Business Support Centres (BSC) were created to assist SME development in Central and Eastern Europe offering information, training and capital, though many of these are now under threat due to a lack of continuing finance (Bateman & Lloyd-Reason, 2000). This has major strategic implications for SMEs in the transition states, which need such knowledge-based resources for their long-term viability.

Although tourism SME development has been prominent in some transition states including Poland, Hungary and the Czech Republic (Bateman & Lloyd-Reason, 2000), this is not the case for all Central and Eastern European countries. Indeed, some transition states have found it difficult to develop an economic system conducive to SME development and as a consequence a lack of entrepreneurialism has occurred (Ateljevic, O'Rouke, & Todorvic, 2004). Quoting an Organisation for Economic Cooperation & Development (OECD) report, Ateljevic et al. (2004, p. 241) argue that "most governments in transition economies have failed to create conditions (e.g. tax system, bodies of law, efficient administration, education) favourable for small and medium-sized enterprises". Analyzing the growth of SMEs in Bosnia and Herzegovina, Ateljevic et al. (2004) identify a number of barriers to SME development. This includes, taxation, lack of access to capital, high rates of interest and bureaucratic governmental structures both nationally and regionally. Ateljevic et al. (2004) also note a number of other specific issues pertinent to Bosnia and Herzegovina including the high entry and cost barriers for small businesses, labour immobility due to inter-ethnic tensions, a poor education and training system and negative media towards entrepreneurialism focusing on small business failures. Studying Russia, Barkhatova (2000) acknowledges the level of bureaucracy involved in starting a small business in comparison to the likes of the UK where policies are conducive to starting a business. The development of a small business also depends upon relations with local authorities which can be based upon corruption and being on the "inside" of the power networks at play. Further barriers also include negative opinions and different social values regarding entrepreneurialism and profit making in Central and Eastern Europe, and the difficulty in obtaining a small loan from banks which can be a time-consuming process and orientated towards the financing of larger organizations (Barkhatova, 2000). These barriers consequently lead to a black market economy of SME activity with governments unable to obtain taxes from small businesses.

As opposed to the rapid transition policies of many Central and Eastern European states, Hungary has taken a gradualist approach to economic and political change (Szivas, 2005). Part of this process was the development of empowering policies for the growth of SMEs in the region. Nevertheless, Berko and Gueullette (2003) note how small businesses in Hungary are still lacking competitiveness in comparison to larger enterprises and to the rest of Europe in general. Ultimately, those countries that are perceived to be reticent to reform are affected by corporate reluctance to invest (Matlay, 2004) therefore leading to a lack of economic growth in Central and Eastern Europe.

The aforementioned strategic challenges illustrate a situation where SMEs, particularly in Central and Eastern Europe, need to gain competitiveness if they are to compete effectively with their Western European counterparts.

Gaining Competitiveness

The trading conditions for tourism SMEs within Europe has become increasingly difficult over the past few years with a maturing market and increased competition. The need to sustain competitiveness has therefore become crucial for tourism SMEs. According to Fielden et al. (cited from Jones & Tilley, 2003, p. 4) the competitiveness of any SME is based upon a range of situational and contextual factors. Small businesses need to be aware of the range of macro- and micro-environmental factors that can influence their businesses so as to obtain an advantage over competitors. It should be noted, however, that the pursuit of competitive advantage is not necessarily the primary concern of all SMEs, with ongoing viability, return on investment and lifestyle options being the main focus for many of them (Getz, Carlsen, & Morrison, 2004). However, the enlargement of the EU has created a number of threats that bring the issue of competitive advantage to the fore for tourism SMEs. Thus, the pursuit of competitive advantage may be the only way in which an SME can ensure its long-term viability.

Beaver et al. (cited from Morrison & Teixeira, 2004, p. 167) argue that ". . . competitive advantage in small businesses is an elusive concept. It is fashioned by the actions and abilities of the principal role players, and owes much to their personal perception of satisfactory performance and business direction". The fact that a tourism SME is in itself family orientated can bring about a number of competitive advantages. These include effective stakeholder relationships, niche market advantages, market and labour flexibility and market credibility (Peters & Buhalis, 2004). Furthermore, for tourism SMEs the need to retain "smallness" is the key to sustaining competitive advantage, and enterprise development could actually negate this process (Morrison & Teixeira, 2004). Indeed, the flexibility of the small firm in being able to respond to market changes and opportunities enables the firm to obtain an advantage over larger competitors (O'Gorman, 2000). Furthermore, such flexibility of tourism SMEs is essential in enhancing not only the performance of individual enterprises but also the competitiveness of the destination as a whole (Brent-Ritchie & Crouch, 2003). The decline of many English seaside resorts, for example, was partly due to the lack of continuous improvement of SMEs in these destinations (Shaw & Williams, 1997). Although flexibility and continuous improvement is an important source of gaining competitive advantage, it is not the only one. Getz et al. (2004) note, for example, that a static tourism SME can also retain its competitive advantage if it meets one or more of the following criteria: the business is unique, it has a better location, it offers superior service quality, it has cost advantages or it has a better perceived value for money. Getz et al. (2004) also acknowledge that access to a combination of tangible (i.e., financial capital) and intangible (i.e., brand assets) resources is a pre-condition for SME growth.

According to Tomer (cited from Szamosi et al., 2004, p. 445) for transition of the new EU states to be successful there needs to be an alignment between both intangible (socio factors) and tangible (economic factors) capital. However, this alignment will not be immediate and SMEs in the transition states will pursue a rapid experience curve as their business and market structures become more closely paralleled with the established European states. This kind of scenario has been played out in former Eastern Bloc countries such as Romania, where financial infrastructure has been opened up to free market forces, resulting in an uncomfortable period of time for many businesses, including SMEs. In addition, many of the service industries have found it increasingly hard to match Westernized service expectations with their own human resource provision, which has itself often been criticized for being off par with the requirements of the International tourist. As a consequence, service sector SMEs can suffer from human and financial "resource poverty" (Morrison & Teixeira, 2004) and this may affect the overall performance of the small business. Though it should be noted that resource scarcity does not necessarily inhibit continuous growth amongst tourism SMEs (Augustyn, 2004).

With these factors in mind a range of strategic imperatives (Figure 4.1) can be identified which SMEs, particularly in Central and Eastern Europe, need to embrace if they are to compete effectively. However, these factors are not exclusive to SMEs operating within these countries and can just as easily be applied to all European tourism SMEs.

Strategic Imperatives

Strategic Planning and Options

The first stage of any strategic development is for SMEs to formulate strategic plans. According to Peters and Buhalis (2004) those SMEs that engage in strategic planning are more successful and growth oriented. The benefits of a formal strategic planning process for small firms include gaining external financial support, which offers a goal/results orientation to the business and provides a control and benchmarking device (O'Gorman, 2000). However, owing to a lack of time, experience and the fear of failure, strategic plans often fail to materialize within SMEs (O'Gorman, 2000). Furthermore, it could be argued that the actual benchmarking process for understanding competitive advantage for SMEs is difficult. To know and understand who has a competitive advantage and what this advantage actually is, are somewhat challenging where there are many competing SMEs.

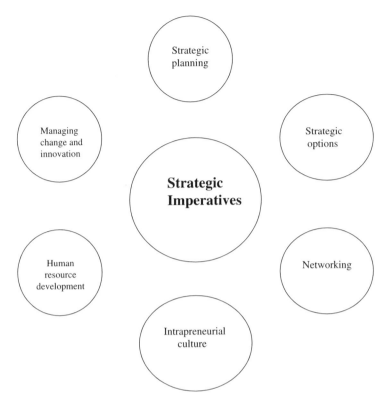

Figure 4.1: The wheel of strategic imperatives for SMEs in the New Europe.

Nevertheless, systematic scanning of the macro- and micro-environment is crucial for tourism SMEs to identify threats and opportunities which may arise.

Tourism SMEs then need to consider the strategic options that are available to them. O'Gorman (2000) notes how SMEs tend to adopt a "me too" strategy, simply imitating existing provision of competing SME providers. Referring to Porter's (1985) generic strategies, the ability of a small business to gain cost leadership can be very difficult due to increased overheads, difficulties in obtaining cheap labour and the inability to gain economies of scale. In addition, though a low price may attract customers, the perceived quality maybe lower leading to a lack of expected sales (O'Gorman, 2000). Therefore, competitive advantage for SMEs is not so much locationally specific but more a case of the extent to which the firm differentiates itself from its competitors (Bennett & Smith, 2002; Jones & Tilley, 2003). The fact that tourism products offered by Western and Eastern Europe are arguably similar in nature can lead to a lack of differentiation and a cannibal-ization of the European total tourism product. Examples of this include the similar resources of the Baltic and Spanish coastal lines, the heritage and cultural monuments of Prague and Paris and the mountainous landscapes of The Tatras in Poland and the Lake District in North-West England (Coles & Hall, 2005; Dale & Robinson, 2005). This con-sequently generates a highly competitive environment amongst the different European states, placing demands on tourism SMEs and their need to differentiate themselves from their rivals. Differentiation can therefore be achieved by offering better quality or faster service, a better location or a superior perceived brand in the mind of the consumer (Wickham, 2004). Owing to resource limitations, Porter (1985) also argues that a focus strategy is the most viable for SMEs. However, dangers of pursuing this strategy include targeting a niche market that fails to materialize or focusing on too small a market (O'Gorman, 2000). The development of agri-based environmental tourism in Poland is an example of the way in which SME farm providers have diversified their businesses to target tourists via a focus-differentiation strategy (Hegarty & Przezborska, 2005). While Hegarty and Przezborska (2005) note that this is largely an unconscious strategy, it is a good example of the way in which tourism SMEs can differentiate themselves whilst concurrently diversifying their core business in pursuit of income generation.

Getz et al. (2004) discuss a range of strategic options that SMEs can pursue for their businesses. Firstly, the sustainability option where SMEs do their up most to remain small, controllable and viable. For this to happen SMEs need to ensure they re-invest in their businesses to remain modern, up-to-date abut also receptive to changes in the market place. This may be difficult for tourism SMEs in the transition states that are lagging behind the service and product standards of the more established European states (Robinson, 2005). Secondly, the value-adding option where businesses seek to add value through, for example, the use of technology, efficiency gains, adding new services or products and the continuous improvement of service quality. Thirdly, the diversification option where SMEs could enter new market or product areas or even vertically integrate the business to achieve additional revenue sources from the same market. Fourthly, the physical expansion option where the SME may decide to increase the volume of the business via its physical space in terms of increasing rooming or restaurant cover size, or extending the times of opening, for example. Fifthly, the plan to sell option where the business is simply sold to retrieve its asset value. Finally, the professionalisation option, where the SME owners decide to hand over the functioning of the business to professional managers. According to Getz et al. (2004) most family oriented businesses pursue a "value-adding" strategy to enable their ongoing survival and viability. The aforementioned strategic options which can be pursued by businesses looking to develop market share and profitability can be best described using business examples from the growing development of adventure tourism in Central and Eastern Europe. A number of small adventure tourism enterprises such as Sport-S in Czech Republic, Inteco Travel in Bulgaria and Adventure Transylvania in Romania have employed strategies which have seen them adding value in terms of the utilization of technology to aid distribution, diversification into new markets, business expansion and employment of management specialists to further develop their businesses (Mintel, 2005).

Networking and Alliance Formation

In a Council of Europe (1997) report, one of the resolutions for Central and Eastern Europe stated the need "to stimulate the creation of lasting partnerships between the public and the private sectors, to encourage the development of small and medium-sized enterprises in the travel and tourism fields as a means of creating employment opportunities, and to ensure that such enterprises are not overburdened by excessive regulations". This process can be facilitated via the process of effective networking and alliance formation with SME stakeholders. Carson et al. (cited from Donnell, 2004) define networking in a small business context as "an activity in which the entrepreneurially oriented SME owners build and manage personal relationships with particular individuals in their surroundings". Indeed, Donnell (2004) notes the use of networking by SMEs as a means to successfully market the business. In his research study exploring the extent of networking activities amongst small businesses, Donnell (2004) finds that businesses that rely on one-off transactions will not expend considerable effort in forging networks. However, for tourism businesses where relationships are crucial for the long-term viability of the business and for developing innovation, networking is essential (Getz et al., 2004). In their research into the strategic planning of family hotel businesses, Peters and Buhalis (2004) note the lack of understanding of how small business competitiveness could be enhanced through cooperation and networking with partners. Bennet and Smith (2002) also argue that SMEs can gain competitive advantage from trading relationships with other regions or countries beyond their own locality. For tourism SMEs the process of networking with partners across the European states will be crucial in effectively marketing and distributing their goods and services which could otherwise be a strategic problem for many SMEs (O'Gorman, 2000). Even more so for SMEs in Central and Eastern Europe which may have limited access to the physical, knowledge-based and financial resources to market their goods and services effectively.

Jarratt (1998) explores the use of alliance formation by SMEs as a means of cross-selling and building upon innovative capability and technological competences. This is particularly the case within the tourism industry where the dissemination and distribution of the tourism product is driven predominately by technology. Particularly via the use of, for example, destination management systems (DMS) which generate awareness of the goods and services available and enable sales to be driven via technological channels. However, for tourism SMEs in the accession states the challenges of poor network infrastructure and resources will act as an increasing barrier to gaining an advantage over their Western European SME counterparts. SMEs should therefore endeavour to collaborate and build regional clusters so as to enhance their resource capabilities that will enable them to compete effectively against larger tourism organizations. Networking via trade associations and professional bodies still needs to be established and developed in some Central and Eastern European states (Wood, 2002).

Intrapreneurial Culture

Developing a culture of intrapreneurship, where employees feel valued and empowered to contribute to the development of the small business is also another crucial factor. However, in family oriented businesses where a dominant and centrally controlled power culture (Handy, 1993) may exist, employees outside of the "family nucleus" may find it difficult to have their ideas embraced by the firm. Indeed, the centrality of such a work culture where the strategic leadership is driven by the owner manager at the expense of employees, may actually inhibit the growth of the firm. This issue may be further compounded in transition states within Europe where human resources are often underdeveloped and there may also be some resistance to change (Szamosi et al., 2004). Therefore, the education and training of employees in developing arguments that convince the other family members is crucial in embedding intrapreneurial spirit within the firm (Peters & Buhalis, 2004). By allowing the executive family members to concentrate more on the strategic direction and development of the business, a clearer management structure emerges which utilizes demarcation mechanisms to ensure that all employees are familiar with their role and responsibilities. It is often the case that in micro-SMEs the owner manager is responsible for the multitude of day-to-day activities which include debtor control, personnel-related issues, sales and marketing and operational management. This approach whilst unavoid-able due to financial constraints might see the owner manager spreading themselves too thinly within the organization. By empowering less senior staff members to make deci-sions which impact on the day-to-day business activities, owner managers are able to focus on the strategic development of the firm (Peters & Buhalis, 2004). The embedding of a reward-based culture that stimulates creativity can facilitate this process of idea generation and intrapreneurialism.

Human Resource Development

One of the threats that many Central and Eastern European tourism SMEs face is the move-ment of labour across the frontiers of the EU member states, which generates a labour drain and loss of human capital and expertise (Coles & Hall, 2005). The need to invest in human resources is thus imperative. This is compounded further by the under-resourced training and development infrastructure in some of the accession states that consequently may pro-hibit the competitiveness of SMEs. In their research of the SME sector in Hungary, Berko and Gueullette (2003) found that small businesses were not greatly interested in the train-ing programmes that were available. In addition, owing to low labour costs, SMEs in the transition states maybe reliant on outsourced business that, according to Smallbone, Piasecki, Venesaar, Todorov, and Labrianidis (1998), can be volatile and unstable. Though, it has been acknowledged that formal training does not necessarily impact directly on a small firm's performance (Jameson, 2000; Wood, 2002) it is still important that tourism SMEs invest in the development of their employees so as to instil a sense of commitment to the goals of the business and to develop a culture of intrapreneurialism. Formalized edu-cation within the transition states also needs to focus on entrepreneurial development. Ateljevic et al. (2004) note the use of courses based around enterprise development and the impact this has on entrepreneurialism in European communities. However, some transition states have been slow to react to course development focusing on entrepreneurialism, in part due to an older teaching resource base that has been reticent to change, but also to a lack of funding in the education system (Ateljevic et al., 2004).

Managing Change

At the heart of developing an intrapreneurial culture is the process of change management. For the transition states, this process needs to occur both organizationally and internationally. However, according to Ateljevic et al. (2004, p. 251) the ". . . change from the welfare state and an egalitarian society to deregulated, liberal economic order has caught many unprepared for the transformation". In sustaining competitiveness therefore, Jones (2003) recognizes the need for innovation and change within SMEs and proposes a conceptual framework of competitive advantage in small firms with change at the heart of the process. Firstly, SME owner–managers need to understand the strategic framework within which the organization is operating. This includes a full understanding of the firm's existing strengths, weaknesses, opportunities and threats. This process should involve the consultation of all staff so as to gain commitment to change and innovation. The second stage involves identifying the change agent. This should be delegated to a junior member of staff within the firm so as to act as a champion or intrapreneur to change within the organization. The change agent needs to network both internally and externally if the change process is to be successful. This involves a process of boundary spanning with external providers and the successful dissemination of information across all levels of the organizational structure. The organization needs to be receptive to factors that occur within the external environment. Therefore, the organization and its employees need to be flexible to change. This will imbue a sense of innovation within the SME and its ability to be creative in its approach to developing new products and services and also reacting to the exchange of information received by the organizations stakeholders. Such a process should ultimately lead to the firm developing an enhanced competitive position. From a value and supply chain perspective those SMEs which are reluctant to innovate will find it hard to trade with larger organizations which often outsource business. In addition, the change process, particularly for tourism SMEs in Central and Eastern Europe, may involve a cultural shift away from centralized management cultures to an overall more participative approach. Case study 1 illustrates a typical situation where an SME is finding it difficult to change in the face of strategic challenges.

Conclusion

This chapter has outlined the strategic context within which tourism SMEs in the New Europe operate and has identified the strategic imperatives for such enterprises. It is firstly essential for a tourism SME to adopt a strategic plan that pursues a selected strategic option. Secondly, the tourism SME needs to engage in the process of networking and alliance formation so as to build collaborative resources and facilitate enhanced distribution of goods and services to target markets. Thirdly, the tourism SME needs to build a culture of intrapreneurial spirit where idea generation is fostered. Fourthly, if this intrapreneurial culture is to be successfully developed, human resources need to be educated and trained so as to meet the service standards that customers expect in today's tourism industry. Finally, at the heart of this process is the need to respond to the changes in the environment and to manage such change. By embracing these strategic imperatives tourism SMEs will be in a position to enhance their overall competitiveness. While the chapter has focused on strategic issues that impact predominately upon the new member states in Central and Eastern Europe, the discussed issues are not exclusive to these states and impact upon all tourism SMEs throughout Europe.

   The EU policy needs to be directed towards developing measures that enable SMEs to effectively embrace these strategic imperatives. Examples of this may include offering financial incentives to SME start-ups to encourage entrepreneurial activity to take place. This maybe in the form of grants, low-interest loans or tax breaks. It is also important for the EU to ensure that excessive administrative processes do not hinder SMEs. This philosophy needs to be driven down to local level to ensure that authorities develop an environment that is conducive to SMEs to develop. The EU also needs to encourage knowledge transfer, across and between, Western and Central and Eastern European states. Partnerships between Western academic institutions and SMEs in Central and Eastern Europe could be developed to contribute significant expertise to the development of the business. This would enable SMEs in Central and Eastern Europe to develop competences, skills and knowledge resources to be able to compete effectively with their Western counterparts. To some extent the aforementioned suggestions are being addressed and benchmarked within the context of the DG Enterprise initiatives on the European Charter for Small Businesses and the Action Plan for Entrepreneurship. Hopefully these will go someway to ensuring the continued competitiveness of SMEs in the new Europe.

Case Study 1 — Rossini's, Bratislava

Rossini's[1] is an Italian-themed restaurant, in Bratislava, the capital city of Slovakia, and has been in operation since 1998. The business is jointly owned and managed by the father and his two sons who are responsible for running the operational and managerial activities of the business. Whilst the father holds a general managerial/administrative role, the eldest son has responsibility for food production, whilst the younger son has operational responsibilities in the front of house. A team of waiting staff and kitchen personnel supports the three family members. Rossini's also has an associated factory shop specializing in the production of gateau's and cakes which they often produce, on demand, for the multi-national hotels that are located in Bratislava. This acts as an additional revenue stream for the business enabling its continued viability. However, the restaurant has been faced with a number of key challenges. Service standards are not at par with expectations required by the increasing flow of Western visitors to the restaurant. This includes below standard food service delivery times, a lack of Italian authenticity and poor toilet facilities. Owing to seasonality factors, the restaurant has to lay off staff during periods of low demand. The business therefore finds it difficult to retain competent staff that it may need when demand rises. There is also reticence to change within the firm with some family members wishing to concentrate more on the restaurant side of the business as opposed to the food production side of the enterprise.

Opportunities exist for developing the production side, due to a growing demand from corporate clientele and the embassies in the capital. However, the firm, at present, is not equipped sufficiently for a growth in the mass production of its food-related products. Owing to capacity constraints, the business is also unable to expand the size of the restaurant. The business has also found it difficult to get loans from banks because of an inability

---

[1] The name of the firm has been changed for the purposes of anonymity. Information for this case study was based upon interviews conducted with the owner manager during April 2004 and was part of a Leonardo funded visit.

to guarantee consistent demand. Whilst the long-term development of the business is crucial, the owners appear reluctant to commit themselves to developing a strategy and instead continue on a day-to-day basis with little or no strategic management thinking. With the overstretching of its resources and having no clear focus or direction the firm, therefore, faces a number of strategic challenges.[2]

References

Ateljevic, J., O'Rouke, T., & Todorvic, Z. (2004) Entrepreneurship and SMEs in Bosnia and Herzegovina. *Entrepreneurship and Innovation, 5*(4), 241–253.

Atkinson, J., & Hurstfield, J. (2003). *Annual small business survey 2003.* Small Business Service, Department of Trade and Industry, Kingsgate, London.

Augustyn, M. (2004). Coping with resource scarcity: The experience of UK Tourism SMEs. In R. Thomas (Ed.), *Small firms in tourism: International perspectives* (pp. 257–275). Oxford: Elsevier.

Barkhatova, N. (2000). Russian small business, authorities and the state. *Europe-Asia Studies, 52*(4), 657–676.

Bateman, M., & Lloyd-Reason, L. (2000). Entrepreneurship in transitional economies. In S. Carter & D. Jones-Evans (Eds.), *Enterprise and small business: Principles, practice and policy.* Harlow: FT-Prentice Hall.

Bennett, R. J., & Smith, C. (2002). Competitive conditions, competitive advantage and the location of SMEs. *Journal of Small Business and Enterprise Development, 9*(1), 73–86.

Berko, L., & Gueullette, A. (2003). Policy for support of small and medium-size enterprises in hungary: The case of the central region. *Post-communist economies, 15*(2), 243–257.

Brent-Ritchie, J. R., & Crouch, G. (2003). *The competitive destination: A sustainable tourism perspective.* Wallingford, UK: CABI.

Bridge, S., O'Neil, K., & Cromie, S. (1998). Understanding enterprise, entrepreneurship and small business. London, UK: Macmillan Business.

Buhalis, D., & Main, H. (1998). Information technology in small and medium hospitality enterprises: Strategic analysis and critical factors. *International Journal of Contemporary Hospitality Management, 10*(5), 198–202.

Buhalis, D., & Peters, M. (2006). SMEs in tourism. In D. Buhalis & C. Costa (Eds.), *Tourism management dynamics* (pp. 116–129). Oxford, UK: Elsevier.

Buick, I. (2003). Information technology in small scottish hotels: Is it working? *International Journal of Contemporary Hospitality Management, 15*(4), 243–247.

Coles, T., & Hall, D. (2005). Tourism and the European union enlargement: Plus ca change? *International Journal of Tourism Research, 7*(2), 51–61.

Council of Europe (1997). Need to accelerate the development of tourism in central and Eastern Europe. Report by the *Committee on Economic Affairs and Development.* Strasbourg: Council of Europe, http://assembly.coe.int/Documents/WorkingDocs/doc97/edoc7976.htm, (accessed 30 March 2006).

Dale, C., & Robinson, N. (2005). Tourism attractions and entertainment. In L. Ineson (Ed.), *Current issues in international tourism development* (pp. 101–115). Sunderland, UK: Business Education Publishers.

Donnell, A. (2004). The nature of networking in small firms. *Qualitative market research: An international journal, 7*(3), 206–217.

European Commission (2003). *Observatory of SMEs in Europe 2003,* Enterprise Publications, Luxemburg: European Commission.

European Commission (2004). *Action plan: The European agenda for entrepreneurship*. Brussels: European Commission.

Evans, N., Campbell, D., & Stonehouse, G. (2003). *Strategic management for travel and tourism*. Oxford, UK: Butterworth-Heinemann.

Getz, D., Carlsen, J., & Morrison, A. (2004). *The family business in tourism and hospitality*. Wallingford, UK: CABI.

Handy, C. (1993). *Understanding organizations* (4th ed.). Oxford, UK: Blackwell.

Hegarty, C., & Przezborska, L. (2005). Rural and agri-tourism as a tool for reorganising rural areas in old and new member states — a comparison study of Ireland and Poland. *International Journal of Tourism Research, 7*(2), 63–77.

Jameson, S. M. (2000). Recruitment and training in small firms. *Journal of European Industrial Training, 24*(1), 43–49.

Jansen-Verbeke, M. (1998). *Leisure, recreation and tourism policy*. Mansell: London.

Jarratt, D. (1998). A strategic classification of business alliances. *Qualitative Market Research: An International Journal, 1*(1), 39–49.

Jones, O. (2003). Competitive advantage in SMEs: Towards a conceptual framework. In O. Jones, & F. Tilley(Eds.), *Competitive advantage in SMEs: Organising for innovation and change*. Chichester, UK: Wiley.

Jones, O., & Tilley, F. (2003). Conclusion. In O. Jones & F. Tilley(Eds.), *Competitive advantage in SMEs: Organising for innovation and change*. Chichester, UK: Wiley.

Main, H. (1995). Information technology and the independent hotels — failing to make the connection? *International Journal of Contemporary Hospitality Management, 7*(6), 30–32.

Mason, P. (2003). *Tourism impacts, planning and management*. Oxford, UK: Butterworth-Heinemann.

Matlay, H. (2004). Small tourism firms in eEurope: Definitional, conceptual and contextual considerations. In: R. Thomas(Ed.), *Small firms in tourism: International perspectives* (pp. 297–312). Oxford, UK: Elsevier.

Mintel (2005). *Adventure Travel — Central and Eastern Europe*, May, Mintel.

Morrison and Teixeira (2004). Small business performance: A tourism sector focus. *Journal of Small Business and Enterprise Development, 11*(2), 166–173.

Mutch, A. (1995). IT and small tourism enterprises a case study of cottage-letting agencies. *Tourism Management, 16*(7), 533–538.

O'Gorman, C. (2000). Strategy and the small firm. In S. Carter, & D. Jones-Evans (Eds.), *Enterprise and small business: Principles, practice and policy*. Harlow, UK: FT-Prentice Hall, pp. 283–299.

Peters, M., & Buhalis, D. (2004). Family hotels businesses: Strategic planning and the need for education and training. *Education and training, 46*(8/9), 406–415.

Porter, M. E. (1985). *Competitive advantage: Creating and sustaining superior performance*. New York: Free Press.

Robinson, N. (2005). Accommodation development: Focusing on a case study of Eastern Europe. In L. Ineson (Ed.), *Current issues in international tourism development* (pp. 43–60). Sunderland, UK: Business Education Publishers.

SCC (2004). *Economic Development, Employment and Business*, Shropshire County Council.

Shaw, G., & Williams, A. (Ed.), (1997). *Rise and fall of British coastal resorts: Cultural and economic perspectives*. London: Pinter.

Smallbone, D., Piasecki, B., Venesaar, U., Todorov, K., & Labrianidis, L. (1998). Internationalisation and SME development in transition economies: an international comparison. *Journal of Small Business and Enterprise Development, 5*(4), pp. 363–375.

Szamosi, L.T., Duxbury, L., & Higgins, C. (2004). Toward an understanding of people management issues in SMEs: a South-Eastern European perspective. *Education and Training, 46*(8/9), 444–453.

Szivas, E. (2005). European union accession: Passport to development for the hungarian tourism industry? *International Journal of Tourism Research, 7*(2), 95–107.

Wickham, P. A. (2004). *Strategic entrepreneurship* (3rd ed.). Harlow, UK: FT-Prentice Hall.

Wood, E. H. (2002). Predictors of business performance in small tourism and hospitality firms. *Entrepreneurship and Innovation, 3*(3), 201–210.

WTO (2003). *Tourism market trends 2003.* World Tourism Organization.

Yap, C. S., & Thong, J. (1997). Programme evaluation of a government information technology programme for small business. *Journal of Information Technology, 12*(2), 107–120.

Chapter 5

The Role of SMEs in Tourism Development: An Industrial District Approach Applied to Killarney, Ireland

Ziene Mottiar and Theresa Ryan

Introduction

A primary concern for many policy makers and academics alike has been the development of tourism areas. Butler's (1980) article is concerned with this very issue and he constructs a model that charts the development of a typical tourism area. There are many lessons to be learnt from this view of a path of development, but what is most interesting are the dynamics of this development. What is it that makes a tourism area move through the six stages? What is it that makes some resorts rejuvenate and others decline? Butler outlines these triggers as, 'innovations in areas such as transportation, and in marketing as well as initiatives at the local and subsequently regional, national and international levels by developers' (Butler, 2000, p. 290). This chapter briefly reviews some of the attempts that have been made at modelling tourism development and explaining its development, and concludes that an important stakeholder has been omitted from these models. It then goes on to use the industrial district approach to incorporate the vital role of small firms in the development of tourism areas.

Butler is not the only one to have developed tourism development models. Many other less well-known theories have been developed and each has concentrated on the importance of a particular factor for the successful development of tourism areas. For example, Gormsen (1981) highlights the importance of local participation and local control, Miossec (1976) emphasises the importance of transport hierarchies, speciality and co-operation and Lundgren (1982) concentrates on the physical attributes of the area. More recent work by Ritchie and Crouch (2003) takes a much broader perspective and develops a model of tourism destination competitiveness. They concentrate on five broad areas including supporting factors and resources, core resources and attractors, destination

Tourism in the New Europe
Copyright © 2007 by Elsevier Ltd.
All rights of reproduction in any form reserved.
ISBN: 0-08-044706-6

management, destination policy, planning and development, and qualifying and amplifying determinants.

This brief overview of the literature that develops the models of tourism development shows a glaring omission. What the existing models have in common is the focus on the tourist and resources and, to a lesser extent, the importance of local community involvement. A vital stakeholder in the tourism area and product has been ignored, and that is the firms. That said, it must be noted that in Ritchie and Crouch's (2003) grounded approach they have relied extensively on the views of industry in developing their model, yet the firms do not appear as an important element in the model. Lewis's (1998) work does accredit individual business owners and entrepreneurs for a great deal of the tourism development in the community and also notes the important role of community leaders, but while this is identified as an issue, in-depth analysis of this contribution is not undertaken.

It is in this vein of research that this chapter is concerned. Industrial district theory, developed in the economic geography literature, explains the economic success of an area by factors such as the geographical and sectoral concentration of predominantly small firms, strong inter-firm relations and the existence of a social or professional milieu and high levels of innovation. The focus is on the firms, but importantly rather than the individual firm it is the community of firms and the relationships between them that is of primary concern. This chapter investigates whether this type of approach is useful in explaining successful tourism development. Section one will outline industrial district theory, section two will discuss the relevance of industrial district theory to tourism and section three will present a case study of a successful tourism area in Ireland to evaluate whether its success can be explained using industrial district theory. Comment will then be made on the usefulness of introducing this approach to the tourism development literature.

What Is an Industrial District?

Industrial district theory began in the late nineteenth century with the work of Marshall (1898) who was trying to explain the localisation (geographical concentration) of English industries such as pottery, cutlery and basket making. He outlined three main causes of localisation of industries: physical conditions, the patronage of court (i.e. a ready-made market) and the deliberate invitation of rulers. The advantages of this localisation were then hereditary skills as 'the mysteries of the trade become no mysteries; but are as it were in the air, and children learn many of them unconsciously' (Marshall, 1898, p. 350), the growth of subsidiary trades and the use of highly specialised machinery. The principles and ideas developed by Marshall remain the basis of the literature on this topic almost a century later.

In the late 1970s the theory of industrial districts was applied to an area in Italy that became known as the 'third Italy' (Pyke, Becattini, & Sengenberger, 1992). These regions seemed to be growing faster than the rest of the country and surviving recessions more successfully (Brusco, 1982). In 1984, work by Piore and Sabel brought this concept back to English-speaking audiences and, subsequently, there have been case studies of industrial districts conducted throughout the world, for example in Spain (Benton, 1990), Germany (Schmitz, 1990), the US (Saxenian, 1985, 1994), Brazil (Schmitz, 1993),

Kenya and Zimbabwe (Sverisson, 1992), Korea (Cho, 1994) and India (Knorriga, 1994; Cawthorne, 1995). With the existence of industrial districts having been established, more recent literature has focussed on aspects of an industrial district and how it functions (e.g. Pilotti, 2000; Gottardi, 2000; Bertini, 2000).

The case studies of industrial districts have resulted in a list of common characteristics that constitute an industrial district. These characteristics not only facilitate identification of an industrial district, but are also the features that explain the successful development of that region. The characteristics are discussed below.

Geographical and Sectoral Concentration of Firms

Industrial districts usually comprise a clearly defined area — a town, a valley or a region. There is sectoral concentration and this can be identified in two ways: firstly, in terms of firms producing the same good — for example there are more than 400 shoe firms in the Sinos Valley in Brazil (Schmitz, 1993) — but also in terms of the components of the final product being concentrated in the area. In Sinos Valley,

> within a 50 km radius of Novo Hamburgo, the centre of the Valley, most inputs are produced: uppers, soles, heels, insoles, insocks, shanks, glues, nails, eyelets, dyes etc (Schmitz, 1993, p. 5).

The geographical and sectoral concentration of firms in an industrial district has implications for product development, innovation and inter-firm relations, which will be discussed later.

Firms Are Usually Small

Most case studies of industrial districts portray regions with small firms; in fact, in many cases the firms are micro-enterprises — employing up to nine people. For example, in Valles Oriental in Catalonia (Spain) two-thirds of the firms employ between one and nine people (Benton, 1990, p. 67), and in Emilia-Romagna in Italy, 75 per cent of the firms employ fewer than ten workers (Amin, 1989). The size of the firm is important, as it is this that makes the firms interdependent on each other and thus impacts on inter-firm relations.

Strong Inter-Firm Relations

The relations between firms in an industrial district are not simply competitive in nature, although competition is still intense. They also incorporate co-operative and social and familial elements. Firms often engage in horizontal competition with firms producing the same product, and co-operate vertically with suppliers and customers. However, horizontal co-operation also occurs. This creates a web of inter-firm relations, which is much more complex than just merely competition.

In an industrial district, competition is primarily in terms of quality and innovation rather than cost. As discussed above these firms are interdependent, no one firm could survive on their own, and it is this that provides the impetus for co-operation. Few, if any, firms are involved in every stage of production and so they are reliant on others to be able to produce their final good. Thus, co-operation is evident throughout the district and can be both formal and informal. Formal co-operation in Ikast, Denmark, occurs as the co-operative body, Danikast, employers have 'organised buses to bring women to work from the surrounding areas, have built a dormitory for young women, and have collectively purchased raw materials' (Kristensen, 1990). The geographical concentration of these firms and their willingness to co-operate have resulted in their overcoming some of the difficulties that small firms often experience.

Informal co-operation takes the form of, for example, sharing tools and machinery, joint marketing and joint research. One of the interesting findings in industrial district research is that co-operation is often not defined as that by the firms involved. Kristensen (1990, p. 151) describes how one entrepreneur he interviewed was

> vehemently opposed to any formalised co-operation, yet later during the interview, an upholsterer looked in to tell him that 'their new sofa' had appeared on the front cover of a furniture magazine. Together they had not only produced the sofa, but had worked together several nights a week for six months to develop it.

And yet he did not classify this as co-operation. Schmitz (1990, p. 98) points out that there is probably a great deal of co-operation, which is not strategically pursued but 'just happens in the course of transactions between firms and in the course of contacts between their staff in and outside the place of work'.

An important element in inter-firm relations is social and familial ties. Family members and former employees often establish firms in the same business or a spin-off business locally, and this adds another dimension to business relationships within the district. Kristensen (1990) studies the Durup furniture industry in Denmark and presents a

> story of fathers, brothers and sons, masters and apprentices, and involves the development of a genealogical tree where craft and family relations have become interwoven into 70 years of business history (1990, p. 149).

Similarly in the furniture industry in Co. Monaghan in Ireland, one owner reported that 14 of the 16 people whom he had worked with in his previous employment now had their own firms in the area. Eighty per cent of the owners of wooden furniture firms in this area could be linked directly or indirectly to one of the oldest furniture firms in the area (Mottiar, 1998). This creates a network of owners.

Focussing on inter-firm relations rather than individual firms is an important part of the industrial district approach: 'the single elements of the system flourish as a result of their interdependence; not because any one of them however competent, is capable of playing on the stage alone' (Amin, 1989, pp. 119–120). Their success is embedded in the group of firms within the area and how they relate to each other.

So, it is clear that inter-firm relations are an important element in the success of these districts, and that they represent a complex web of competition, co-operative and social and familial relations. Fundamental to this is the existence of a social or professional milieu that creates the trust required to encourage co-operation.

Social or Professional Milieu

This is perhaps one of the most unique elements of an industrial district. A social milieu and the embeddedness of firms mean that there is a close link between society and firms: the relationships between the actors in the economy are not purely economic (Schmitz, 1993) — the relationship constitutes more than the exchange of labour for wages. What this comprises in summary is a strong community of individuals, families and firms, which is bound together by a 'socio-cultural identity and trust' (Schmitz, 1993, p. 26). The common values that the milieu creates serve both to bind the community together and to set unwritten rules by which firms operate. The operation of an industrial district also creates the possibility of punishing those who behave incorrectly, 'chiefly by withdrawing the willingness to conclude future transactions with them and social disapproval' (Dei Ottati, 1994, p. 531).

What it is that binds the communities together has been identified often as a common background of belief? In Emilia Romagana, Italy, for example, it was the fact that a high proportion of voters were communist and in Sinos Valley in Brazil 'a strong community spirit developed in the region based on the common German heritage' (Schmitz, 1993, pp. 27–28). The social milieu strengthens the links between firms, and as such increases the flow of information and thus levels of innovation. It also encourages trust and, as a consequence, encourages inter-firm co-operation.

In some industrial districts there was no evidence of a social milieu, but what was apparent was a professional milieu whereby being part of a professional community created a group identity similar to that resulting from belonging to the same ethnic group or having the same religious or political beliefs. In the professional milieu, which was identified in the Monaghan furniture industry, having worked together in another firm in the area created a network of professionals who knew each other and 'contact between owners of furniture firms . . . occurs at church, socially, during occasional visits to one another's firms and at exhibitions and fairs' (Mottiar, 1998, p. 206).

Trust is an important by-product of the social or professional milieux. It is important to note that this trust is

> not the type of trust based on idealism or naiveté, but a trust based on the realisation by specialists that they need each other, in such a way that they will also have to trust each other to some extent (Knorringa, 1994, p. 76).

According to Boschma and Lambooy (2002, p. 291),

> trust means easier access to knowledge, primarily from similar firms. Short distances not only facilitate the co-ordination of individual actors, they also play a role in institutionalization of behavioural rules and transfer of knowledge and learning.

This has obvious implications for the continual development of the district.

A social or professional milieu creates a trust between firms and also results in a set of unwritten rules that govern not only social behaviour within the community but also business decisions. Again, industrial district theory challenges us to look at the whole, the group of firms rather than individuals. The relations between these firms and their embed-dedness in the area create a social and professional milieu that influences the way they operate and contribute to the overall economic success of the region.

Innovation

Strong inter-firm relations and the existence of a social or professional milieu encourage the flow of information and this leads to high levels of innovation in an industrial district. Marshall notes that

> inventions and improvements in machinery, in processes and the general organisation of the businesses have their merits promptly discussed: if one man starts a new idea, it is taken up by others and combined with sugges-tions of their own; and thus it becomes the source of further new ideas (1898, p. 350).

In Prato, Italy, information on production techniques diffuses widely and rapidly, 'because owner-operators talk to one another, because families live in the same social context, and because apprentices move easily from one workshop to another' (Harrison, 1994, p. 102). These are examples of incremental innovations that are encouraged by frequent face-to-face contact, close proximity, which allows information to flow quickly, and as a result of the trusting relationships that exist between firms.

Each firm gains from the new idea of others and in turn their ideas benefit others in the district. Pilotti (2000, p. 122) states that places should be considered as 'a context in which learning processes and institutional variables are bound together with economic and social factors'. Using Nonaka's (1998) concept of 'ba', which is like shared space, Pilotti says that knowledge is embedded within the district. Thus, the development of knowledge, through the exchange of ideas encouraged by the social milieu, interdependence, co-operation and trust, is then 'not owned by any particular firm but by the district as a whole, it is one of its tangible productive assets' (Gottardi, 2000, p. 54). This then contributes to the area's success.

The successful development of these many areas identified as industrial districts has been attributed to the dominance of small firms, which are geographically and sectorally concentrated, and their strong inter-firm relations that encompass co-operation and trust and often a social or professional milieu. The group of firms are creators of the regions' success. How is this then relevant for tourism?

Relevance of Industrial District Theory to Tourism

Undeniably, industrial district theory has been primarily concerned with explaining man-ufacturing success and has featured in a very limited way in the tourism literature. Hjalager (1999) concludes that there is no reason why a tourism area could not be an industrial district. Furthermore, Mackum (1998) shows that some of the factors identified in the manufacturing sector in the third Italy are also relevant for the discussion on the development of tourism. This current research, however, the first known attempt to identify an industrial district in a tourism area.

Industrial district theory is relevant for the study of tourism for a number of different reasons. Firstly, because our unit of study in tourism is most often a defined geographical area, concepts that take this type of regional approach are likely to be useful. Secondly, relations between tourism firms are often quite complex (this is exemplified in Mottiar, 2004) and so the industrial district approach, which looks at a variety of different elements in this relationship, is potentially beneficial. In particular, from a rural or resort tourism perspective the idea of a social or professional milieu is fascinating as a way of analysing the complex relations that exist in these tourism areas. Most importantly, using this theory reasserts the importance of firms in the development of a region and hence contributes significantly to a debate that has omitted this vital contribution.

Having outlined the industrial district concept and identified its relevance for tourism, Section four will now apply this concept to a successful tourism area in Ireland to identify if it can be classified as an industrial district. Furthermore, it will determine if this approach is useful in ascertaining which factors have led to the successful development of this area.

Methodology

This section reports the findings of a case study undertaken into tourism development in Killarney, County Kerry, Ireland, in 2004. Information was collected using a process of triangulation employing a number of methods of data collection. Key informant interviews were conducted with representatives of: the Board of Fáilte Ireland (the Irish Tourism Board), the Kerry Branch of the Irish Hotel Federation, Killarney Chamber of Tourism and Commerce, Killarney Urban District Council, Cork/Kerry Regional Tourism as well as a local historian and public relations officer.

The research also involved a survey of local tourism suppliers representing a variety of firms in the local industry. The research tool was a questionnaire that was administered by the researcher with the owner or manager of the firm. It took approximately 20 min to 1 h to complete the questionnaire. Eighty-one firms were surveyed. These firms represent approximately one-third of all tourism businesses in Killarney. They were selected on a random basis, although it was ensured that the sample was representative of the different sub-sectors that operate in Killarney. Snowballing was also used to identify potential interviewees.

In addition, a detailed analysis of archived sources of information on tourism development in the area was carried out. The findings also include data gathered through field notes and observations made during the research period in Killarney.

Does Industrial District Theory Explain Success in Killarney Tourism?

Killarney town is situated in the county of Kerry, in the southwest corner of Ireland. Although traditionally a market town, Killarney owes its growth primarily to the successful development of tourism. It is the oldest tourism centre in Ireland and its tourism dates back to the 1750s when Thomas Browne, 4th Viscount of Kenmare, funded the building of an inn and a hotel to cater to the first intrepid travellers. Killarney is renowned both nationally and internationally as a significant tourism area in Ireland, and tourism is now Killarney's staple industry (Killarney Development Plan, 2003). After the main cities of Dublin, Galway and Cork it is the next most popular tourism destination in Ireland and this is despite the fact that it is relatively inaccessible, is just a small town and relies primarily on natural attractions. While Killarney is famed for its beauty and for the magnificence of its scenery, and its environment has an intrinsic value as an important tourism asset, there are many other factors that have had an important role in the successful development of its tourism industry.

Industrial district theory provides a theoretical and conceptual base and a general framework for examining the dynamics of tourism in Killarney. This section reviews this approach in an effort to explain why Killarney has succeeded in developing a thriving tourism industry.

Geographical and Sectoral Concentration

Killarney is far removed from centres of high population density. The nearest major city, Cork, is 86 km in distance while Dublin, the capital of Ireland, is 345 km. The town itself is quite small, with a population of 11,300 (Kerry County Council, 2003). The south and west of the town are surrounded by an expanse of rugged mountainous country, and at the foot of these mountains nestles the world famous Lakes of Killarney and Killarney National Park.

After Dublin, Killarney has more hotel rooms than any other tourism centre in Ireland (Kenny, 2004). There are 35 hotels in the town plus a thriving bed and breakfast sector (*ibid*). The physical geography of this area with a mountain range and lake, combined with historical development of the town, means that Killarney is a clearly defined area. This area is dominated by tourism firms, and there is a keen awareness in the town of the importance of tourism for the region's continued growth and success. Moreover, within this small area there are not only accommodation suppliers but also restaurants, pubs, jaunting cars (providing horse and buggy tours in Killarney), craft and gift shops, equestrian centres, boat and walking tours as well as a local transport museum. This shows not only sectoral concentration in terms of the number of tourism firms but also diversity in terms of the components of the overall tourist experience that is provided by different firms in the area.

Size of Firms

Tourism in Killarney is characterised by the existence of many small businesses, each providing essential components of the overall tourism product. The majority of tourism firms are small in size employing fewer than twenty people. Figure 5.1 highlights how 49 per cent of those surveyed can be classified as micro-companies, employing fewer than ten people and 78 per cent employing fewer than 40 people.

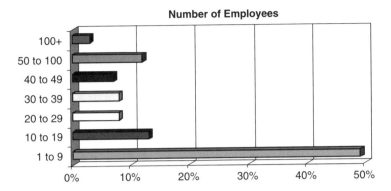

Figure 5.1: Number of employees.

This structure has created an interdependence amongst these firms. For example, most accommodation firms are reliant on the entertainment-providing firms to create an attraction to encourage tourists to come, and, equally, firms supplying entertainment are dependent on accommodation suppliers having beds available so that tourists will come and access their products. Due to this interdependence firms can remain small and survive and the local tourist area can thrive.

It must be noted though that there are a few large-family hotel firms in the area. In 2002, four local families owned 48 per cent of three-, four-, and five-star hotel rooms in the area (Kenny, 2004). This creates a picture quite different from that of an area dominated by micro-enterprises. These four families have played a significant role in the development of Killarney as a tourism destination. What is interesting to note though is that in the main the families have expanded their core business (be it accommodation or entertainment) by establishing new premises or products rather than encroaching on the business of others by providing a new service. It is this that has allowed, and even facilitated, the parallel development of small firms in the area. Many small firms in the area have been able to develop and thrive as a result of the success of the larger, family-run businesses. The larger hotels have the resources to market the area and attract tourists while still relying on the small firms to supply a 'seamless' product to their customers through the provision of rented bicycles, walking tours, boat rides, horse riding and jaunting car rides as well as providing a broad range of places to eat and shop in the town. Through the vertical development of a core product (accommodation and entertainment), these families have encouraged the development of the area in general and, in particular, the development of a range of complimentary products provided by the smaller firms. The interdependence of the firms as well as the focus on core business by the larger firms has been an important element in the region's development.

Strong Inter-firm Relations — Competition and Co-operation

Competition and rivalry is intense between local tourism businesses in Killarney. Seventy per cent of respondents claimed that their main competitors are located in Killarney while only 2 per cent see themselves competing with businesses at a national or an international level.

Despite this intense rivalry, there is strong evidence of co-operation between local businesses. When asked directly if firms in Killarney co-operate with each other, the majority of respondents were adamant that no co-operation took place. However, on closer inspection it is apparent that co-operation between firms takes place on a regular basis. The reason for this contradiction is that much of the co-operation takes place on an informal basis, between people who know each other well, and as a result it is not regarded as co-operation by respondents. This corresponds with the findings discussed earlier in the chapter in relation to other industrial districts. Confirmation of the existence of co-operation existed in a number of ways; there is evidence of vertical co-operation where businesses offering different products recommend each other to tourists. Co-operation with local tour operators and bike rental firms allows hotels to offer extensive and seamless services to tourists within their hotel facility. In addition, there is evidence of horizontal co-operation where tourism operators, such as hotels, refer guests to other hotels when they themselves have full occupancy. In general there is a lot of, what some respondents termed as, 'good neighbourliness' whereby businesses lend equipment to each other and help out in emergencies.

Many businesses in Killarney are involved in co-operative marketing through local marketing groups such as Killarney 250 (a local initiative that was set up to celebrate 250 years of tourism in Killarney and also to re-brand the area as a tourism destination). In 1994, a number of larger businesses in the area came together to form Killarney of the Welcomes, a local marketing group. The initiative for this came from the concern of local businesses regarding the marketing of Killarney being undertaken by the national tourism authority. More recently, local hoteliers have formed Killarney Incentive and Conferencing, (KIC) a marketing group set up to market Killarney as a destination for incentive and conferencing business. One business owner commented, 'there is good networking between hotels in Killarney and this comes about through the realisation that everyone benefits from a co-ordinated approach'.

These types of intitiatives have played an important role in creating and sustaining Killarney's success. The natural beauty of Killarney has become a tourist attraction because initiatives by local firms working together to establish marketing groups have established a national and international brand and reputation for the area.

It is clear that much of the co-operation between businesses in Killarney happens on an informal basis. Many business owners are from Killarney and have grown up together while others have known each other for many years, in some cases as neighbours and in others through the broader national hotel network. Figure 5.2 shows how interaction between businesses comes about in Killarney. Family ties, neighbours, friends or work colleagues are highlighted as key sources of interaction indicating the extent of informal networking in the area.

Killarney's tourism industry is characterised by the existence of a number of family-run businesses. The strength and influence of these local families have played a key role in developing tourism in the area. As early as the 1700s, local landowning families, such as the Earl of Kenmare and Herberts of Muckross, were influential in the development of Killarney's tourism industry. It was these very landlords in fact that encouraged an entrepreneurial pervasiveness throughout Killarney. The Earl of Kenmare not only actively

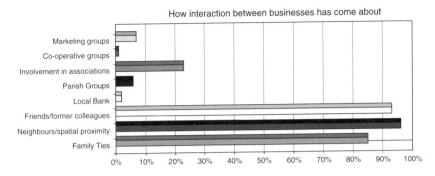

Figure 5.2: Source of interaction between businesses.

developed the area himself through the development of roads and other infrastructure but also encouraged tenants to develop their own holdings. MacLysaght (1970) explains that the Earl of Kenmare's entrepreneurial spirit and goal to encourage visitors to the area were clear in his plans for the development of an inn in the town and in the extended leases and favourable terms offered to tenants who participated in developing Killarney for the benefit of visitors.

Many of the tourism businesses can be linked back through generations of local families. The majority of tourism firms in the area are Irish owned and 61 per cent of the businesses that took part in the survey were owned by people from Killarney specifically. This family ownership can be seen across a range of businesses. Jaunting car drivers, known locally as Jarvey's, spoke of grandfathers and fathers starting the business and passing it down to family members through the generations. Tour companies and hotel owners spoke of tracing their businesses back to the 1800s. Business owners spoke of how being involved in the local tourism industry, either through family connections or through working for other local businesses, had led them to develop their own tourism business in the area.

This involvement in tourism through generations creates a network (although not in a formal sense) of people who have a history together, whose parents and grandparents knew each other and who in many cases have grown up together. This creates closer links between firms and owners and a clear involvement in Killarney, as to them it is something much more than just a place they happen to have a business in.

This connection to the place is evidently important for business owners, with 54 per cent of respondents saying that being from Killarney was important or very important in developing business relations with other firms (see Figure 5.3). Respondents claimed that Killarney is 'very parochial and that you need to fit in or know people'. Another explained that to be accepted in Killarney you 'had to bring something of value to the town'. Being related to other entrepreneurs was also considered very/important by 66 per cent of respondents: 'who you know or who you are related to is very important'. Belonging to a family involved in the industry was considered very/important by 67 per cent of respondents. This was considered 'a sure way of being successful' as 'family businesses support each other'. Respondents spoke of how influential local family businesses are, and one respondent declared that 'it is important to belong to the Killarney mafia'.

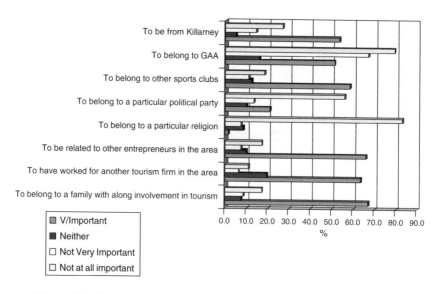

Figure 5.3: Social factors that influence business relations in Killarney.

Social and Professional Milieu

As the literature shows, a social or professional milieu often transgresses business and social life in the area. The fact that tourism has existed in this area since the 1750s and that many of the firms have been passed down through generations creates a social milieu in the area.

An important source of contacts and social networks of business owners was identified as sporting clubs. Belonging to the Gaelic Athletic Association (GAA) was considered very/important by 51 per cent of respondents, while being involved in other sports clubs was considered very/important by 59 per cent of respondents. The level of importance, respondents explained, depended on the business that you were involved in, for example, in the pub industry involvement in sports and GAA would be very important. Membership of golf clubs was also considered an important factor by respondents as this allowed for networking and making contacts.

There is also evidence of a professional milieu in Killarney. Many of the managers of the larger hotels have known each other through involvement in the Irish Hotel Federation (IHF) and have managed the same hotels, throughout Ireland, at different times over the years. For example, one prominent business man in Killarney spoke of how both he and the general manager of a large hotel in Killarney had managed a number of the same hotels over the years; in addition, they had both held the position of President of the Killarney Chamber of Tourism and Commerce besides being active members of both the Kerry branch of the IHF as well as the National branch. This is an example of the type of strong networking and interaction between many of the hotels, and infuences the entire community of businesses in Killarney. A number of hotel managers are involved in the local IHF, the Killarney Chamber of Tourism and Commerce as well as at a national level in Fáilte

Ireland (The Irish Tourism Board) and the national IHF and national tourism steering com-mittes. In this way many of these owners and mangers are active on the national stage and form a strong national lobbying group.

Innovation

For much of its development, Killarney has relied on the natural beauty of the area and the friendliness of the people rather than on any particularly innovative approach to develop-ment. There have been, however, a number of notable innovations by local businesses that have influenced development of tourism in Killarney.

In seeking to maintain market share in the short-break domestic market, hotels have sought to extend the tourist season through the development of bespoke packages in order to allevi-ate the problem of seasonal peaks and troughs. Tourism in Killarney is characterised by hotels offering packages such as golfing breaks and family breaks for one or more nights. This is in reaction to a perceived market need and succeeded in extending the tourism season.

Muckross House and National Park are important attractions in the area. The house was acquired by the Irish state in 1932 but remained closed to the public for three decades dur-ing which time no consensus was reached as to how the house might best be used. Through the initiative of local business people, the house opened to the public in 1964 and is today managed by a Board of Trustees that comprises over 200 members, who share an interest in the preservation of the folklore and history of Killarney (http://www.muckross-house.ie/trustees.htm). Although not necessarily falling into the category of innovative actions, this shows foresight and with reflection this was a vital move in terms of tourism development in the area.

An important element and communicator of innovation in industrial districts has been the flow of information within the industry and area. This is evident in Killarney via groups such as the Killarney 250 and bodies such as the local branch of the IHF and the Chamber of Commerce whereby owners and managers interact with each other regularly. More informally, information about what firms are doing flows through the personal net-works of friends, colleagues and family members as they discuss new occurrences in the industry and in their workplaces.

The tourism sector in Killarney cannot be classified as highly innovative, although there are some indications of small levels of innovation and foresight amongst firms. It is notable that this is not unusual as a number of industrial districts identified in the litera-ture do not appear to exhibit strong levels of innovation (fe.g. Limmasol, (Murray, 1990); Santiago, Mexico (Wilson, 1992)).

Conclusion

It has been established that Killarney is a successful tourism area in Ireland and this research has shown that it has the characteristics of an industrial district. Furthermore, the analysis using an industrial district conceptual framework shows the importance of the local firms in this successful development. While the natural resources that Killarney is endowed with are a significant asset, there are other areas too with similar advantages. Therefore, the explanation has to involve more than natural resources. At each point in the development of Killarney, entrepreneurs and small firms have played a vital role. In the early period of development in the 1750s, Thomas Browne played a leading role in instigating tourism as a business in the area and encouraging others to develop products to sustain this industry. In the 1960s, business owners showed incredible foresight in their campaign to ensure that Muckross House would remain a public asset, which attracts tourists, rather than being sold to private interests. This heritage house and garden remains a major tourist attraction in the area. More recently, firms have worked together to market Killarney independently of the national marketing campaigns undertaken by Fáilte Ireland. At each point in the development of this area, small firms and their owners have played fundamental roles to ensure the continued existence and successful development of this tourism destination.

In addition to these identifiable points in the historical development of the area tourism firms have also contributed to the successful development of this area by the way they operate on a daily basis. The interdependence of firms is critical. Tourism in Killarney is built around the provision of a number of traditional tourism products such as jaunting car rides, boat rides and guided tours, all provided by the smaller firms in the area. Thus, the larger hotels are reliant on the survival of these firms and need their co-operation in order to, for example, attempt to extend the season. These types of relationships create a common vision and goal. Rather than just concentrating on what is good for their own particular firm, owners and managers by necessity have to think about the implications for others and how they may react to their actions, and thus the implications for the area as a whole.

This chapter has clearly shown that the industrial district approach is valuable for the tourist literature. It challenges us to look at the firms in a destination as a group and to pay heed to their embeddedness in the local area and how they inter-relate. Furthermore, it shows clearly that firms must be considered as a vital factor when analyzing and explaining successful tourism development. As such, this chapter is a useful addition to the tourism development model's literature. It also shows other clear avenues of research in terms of identifying tourism industrial districts, investigating inter-firm relations using the industrial district framework and further studying the idea of professional and social milieux in the context of tourist destinations.

References

Amin, A. (1989). A model of the small firm in Italy. In E. Goodman, J. Bamford & P. Saynor (Eds.), *Small firms and industrial districts in Italy* (pp. 111–123). London: Routledge.

Benton, L. (1990). The emergence of industrial districts in Spain: Industrial restructuring and diverging regional responses. In F. Pyke & W. Sengenberger (Eds.), *Industrial districts and local economic regeneration* (pp. 48–86). Geneva: International Institute for Labour Studies.

Bertini, S. (2000). Endogenous development of local systems of SMEs: lessons from practical experience. In F. Belussi & G. Gottardi (Eds.), *Evolutionary patterns of local industrial systems* (pp. 91–113). Aldershot: Ashgate.

Boschma, R., & Lambooy, J. G. (2000). Knowledge, market structure, and economic coordination: Dynamics of industrial districts. *Growth and Change, 33*, 291–311

Brusco, S. (1982). The Emilian model: Productive decentralisation and social integration. *Cambridge Journal of Economics, 6*, 167–184.

Butler, R. W. (1980). The concept of a tourist area cycle of evolution: Implications for management of resources. *Canadian Geographer, xxiv*(1), 5–m12.

Butler, R. W. (2000). The resort cycle two decades on. In B. Faulkner, G. Moscardo & E. Laws (Eds.), *Tourism in the 21st century. Lessons from experience.* London: Continuum.

Cawthorne, P. M. (1995). Of networks and markets: The rise and rise of a South Indian town, the example of Tiruppur's cotton knitwear industry. *World Development, 23*(1), 43–56.

Cho, M. R. (1994). Weaving flexibility: Large-small firm relations, flexibility and regional clusters in South Korea. In: P. D. Pedersen, A. Sverrisson & M. P. van Dijk (Eds.), *Flexible Specialisation: The dynamism of small scale industries in the South* (pp. 111–127). London: Intermediate Technology Publications.

Dei Ottati, G. (1994). Trust, interlinking transactions and credit in the industrial district. *Cambridge Journal of Economics, 18*, 529–546.

Gormsen, E. (1981). The spatio-temporal development of international tourism: Attempt at a centre-periphery model. In *La Consommation d'Espace par le Tourisme et sa preservation* (pp. 150–170). Aix-en-Provence: CHET.

Gottardi, G. (2000). Innovation and the creation of knowledge in Italian industrial districts: A system model. In F. Belussi & G. Gottardi (Eds.), *Evolutionary patterns of local industrial systems* (pp. 49–70). Aldershot: Ashgate.

Hjalager, A. (1999). Tourism destinations and the concept of industrial districts ERSA Conference, Dublin August.

Kenny, T. (2004). Interview with Tony Kenny, Assistant Tourism Officer, Cork/Kerry Regional Tourism.

Kerry County Council (2003). *Submission to the Tourism Policy Review Group, Department of Arts, Sport & Tourism.* Kerry County Council. Tralee.

Killarney Urban District Council (1995). Development plan for the town of Killarney 1995.

Knorringa, P. (1994). Lack of interaction between trader and producers in the Agra footwear industry. In P. D. Pedersen, A. Sverrisson & M. P. van Dijk *Flexible specialisation: The dynamism of small scale industries in the South* (pp. 71–83). London: Intermediate Technology Publications.

Kristensen, P. H. (1990). Industrial districts in West Jutland, Denmark. In F. Pyke & W. Sengenberger (Eds.), *Industrial districts and local economic regeneration* (pp. 122–175). Geneva: International Institute for Labour Studies.

Lee, C. J. (1995). The Industrial Networks of Taiwan's small and medium-sized enterprises. *Journal of industry studies, 2*(2), 75–87.

Lewis, J. B. (1998). A rural tourism development model. *Tourism Analysis, 2*, 91–105.

Lundgren, J. O. J. (1982). The tourist frontier of Nouveau Quebec: Functions and regional linkages. *Tourist Review, 37*(2), 10–16.

MacLysaght, E. (Ed.) (1970, first published 1942). *The Kenmare Manuscripts.* Shannon: Irish University Press for the Irish Manuscripts Commission.

Marshall, A. (1898). *Principles of economics.* New York: McMillan & Co.

Miossec, J. M. (1976). Elèments pour une Thèorie de l'Espace Touristique, Les Cahiers du Tourisme. Aix-en-Provence: CHET. Cited in: Pearce, D. (1995), *Tourism Today, A Geographical Analysis* (2nd ed.). U.K.: Longman Group Limited.

Mottiar, Z. (1998). Unpublished thesis Industrial districts and industrial clusters compared: Applications to Ireland. Dublin City University.

Mottiar, Z. (2004). Islands of power: Small firms in Courtown, Co. Wexford Ireland. ATLAS conference Networking and partnerships in destination development and management Naples, Italy April 3–6.

Murray, R. (1990). Flexible specialisation in small island economies: The case of Cyprus In F. Pyke & W. Sengenberger (Eds.), *Industrial districts and local economic regeneration* (pp. 255–277). Geneva: International Institute for Labour Studies

Pilotti, L. (2000). Networking, strategic positioning and creative knowledge in industrial districts. *Human Systems Management, 19*(2), 121–134.

Piore, M., & Sabel, C. (1984). *The second industrial divide: Possibilities for prosperity.* New York: Basic Books

Pyke, F., Becattini, G., & Sengenberger, W. (1992). *Industrial districts and inter-firm co-operation in Italy.* Geneva: International Institute for Labour Studies.

Ritchie, J. R. B., & Crouch, G. I. (2003). *The competitive destination, a sustainable tourism perspective.* U.K: CABI Publishing.

Saxenian, A. (1985). The genesis of silicon valley. In P. Hall & A. Markusen (Eds.), *Silicon landscapes* (pp. 20–34). Boston: Allen & Unwin

Saxenian, A. (1994). *Regional advantage: Culture and competition in silicon valley and route 128.* Cambridge: Harvard University Press.

Schmitz, H. (1990). Industrial districts: Model and reality in Baden-Württemberg, Germany. In F. Pyke & W. Sengenberger (Eds.), *Industrial Districts and Local Economic Regeneration* (pp. 87–122). Geneva: International Institute for Labour Studies.

Schmitz, H. (1993). Small shoemakers and fordist giants: Tale of a supercluster. *Ids Discussion Paper* 331.

Wilson, F. (1992). Modern workshop industry in Mexico: On its way to collective efficiency? *Ids Bulletin, 23*(3), 57–63.

Chapter 6

Social Enterprise in the UK Tourism Industry

John Pheby

Introduction

In a volume that is dedicated to the role and significance of SMEs within the European tourism industry, it is intriguing to consider an alternative form of SME that is gaining currency as a force to be reckoned with, that is social enterprise. Although social enterprises have been in existence a long time, it is fair to argue that it is only comparatively recently that they have begun to play the significant role in certain European economies that they now possess. It appears that no work has been undertaken to assess whether this unique form of SME can provide a useful contribution towards economic development within the tourism industry in the UK and Europe.

In what follows, we shall consider the nature and particular issues that surround social enterprises. Then we will evaluate whether they could become a significant force within the tourism industry. Finally, we will make some recommendations and draw some conclusions.

Defining Social Enterprise

There are several definitions of social enterprises that we need to consider. For example, the OECD (1999) describes social enterprises as ". . . any private activity conducted in the public interest organised with an entrepreneurial strategy but whose main purpose is not the maximisation of profit but the attainment of certain economic and social goals, and which has a capacity of bringing innovative solutions to the problem of social exclusion and unemployment".

The EU (2005) defines social enterprise in the following terms "Their primary purpose is not to obtain a return on capital. They are, by nature part of a stakeholder economy, where enterprises are created by and for those with common needs and accountable to those they are meant to serve".

Tourism in the New Europe
Copyright © 2007 by Elsevier Ltd.
All rights of reproduction in any form reserved.
ISBN: 0-08-044706-6

The above-mentioned two definitions provide us with a distinctly continental European interpretation of the notion of social enterprise. In the UK, it is interesting to note a slight change in emphasis.

The Social Investment Task Force describes social enterprise as "A business that trades in the market in order to fulfil social aims. Social and community enterprises bring people and communities together for economic development and social gain . . . The Task Force takes the view that not all social and community enterprises need to have social owner-ship. Some are structured as traditional enterprises while still serving a social purpose and placing a great emphasis on their accountability to the communities they serve" (SITF, 2000, p. 31).

The Department of Trade and Industry describes social enterprise in the following terms; "A social enterprise is a business with primarily social objectives whose surpluses are principally reinvested for that purpose in the business or in the community, rather than being driven by the need to maximise profit for shareholders" (DTI, 2002).

Needless to say, social enterprises are found in many different sizes and legal forms. In the UK, there are examples of very large social enterprises such as the Big Issue magazine and the Eden Project. The legal forms of social enterprises include co-operatives, credit unions, LETS (Local Exchange and Trading Schemes), the trading arms of charities, friendly societies, community businesses, and mutual societies.

One of the difficulties with the definitions cited above is that the term social and com-munity enterprise are used inter-changeably. This is unfortunate because there are impor-tant distinctions that are not made as a result. For example, a community enterprise is inevitably focused upon a particular geographical area. This is typically a deprived urban area in need of regeneration. This type of enterprise is unlikely to be of much relevance for the tourism industry. In view of this, we will be focusing our attention on a particular category of social enterprise. Following Watkins-Young, Jackson-Read, and Niel (2004), they have produced a typology that is particularly useful for our purposes (Figure 6.1).

This is a helpful characterisation as it serves to illustrate clearly the diversity of organ-isations that constitute the social enterprise sector. The focus of social enterprise — as something which is socially led, with a market orientation that is designed to achieve a sur-plus for sustainability but is rooted within the community — characterises the type of social enterprise that is most likely to be relevant for the tourism sector.

Commercial			Not For Profit
Commercial Enterprise	**Social Enterprise**	**Community Enterprise**	**Voluntary Community Organisation**
Commercially led	Socially led	Community led	Socially led
Profit driven	Market oriented	Focus on community	Not for profit
	For community profit	impact	Aims to meet
	Intent on financial	Not purely intent on	community need
	sustainability	financial sustainability	

Figure 6.1: Types of enterprise.

This definition is pertinent for our purposes as it focuses upon organisations that are designed to be enterprising within a social and community context. This is important because of the wide range of organisations that fall under the umbrella of social enterprise; a significant proportion of them are not really designed to act entrepreneurially in ways that respond to market forces. Given that the tourism industry is one of the largest global industries, social enterprises operating within this sphere have ample opportunity to develop their entrepreneurial instincts in a way that can serve their social aims and communities.

There is another sense in which our definition proves particularly valuable within the context of the tourism industry. Frequently there are tensions between tourists and indigenous populations. The tourists bring crowds, noise and traffic congestion. In addition, in many situations much of this perceived aggravation does not bring with it strong economic benefits. Considerable amounts of visitor expenditure can benefit larger companies who do not reside within the visited area. Locally based social enterprises can ensure that the visitor/indigenous population tension can be mitigated. Such enterprises will ensure that much of the economic benefits in terms of increased employment and income are retained within their immediate area of operation. Furthermore, the fact that visitors are more clearly perceived as contributing towards the local economy and community is likely to result in their being more welcomed.

It is important to recognise that the notion of social enterprise does not exist outside the context of the social economy. The EU (2005) characterises the social economy as organisations that provide alternative forms of entrepreneurship and employment, are largely founded upon membership-based activities and enhance solidarity and cohesion. Essentially, therefore the social economy can be viewed as providing a network or a support framework for organisations that do not reside either within the public or private sectors. An important point in this connection is made by Smallbone, Evans, Ekanem, and Butters (2001). They argue that evidence exists which indicates that social enterprises are often found in clusters. Such clustering often occurs around support agencies and the links between different social enterprises that they create. Such clustering is often associated with informal networks that help to create a significant element of social capital that social enterprises can draw upon.

The social economy is a means for addressing situations of market failure. Market failure occurs when the needs of consumers are not met through the market mechanism. For example, it has long been recognised that universal free education is a good thing that will benefit both individuals and the society in which they live. However, a system consisting only of private educational provision would result in a significant proportion of the population remaining either uneducated or at best poorly educated. Therefore, in such circumstances it is felt that government has a legitimate role to play in providing education *en masse*. This is a straightforward case of private sector market failure.

However, market failure can occur within the public sector also. Although a considerable amount of public sector activity has its origins in responding to private sector market failure, as the public sector itself expands, it too will be faced with resource constraints. For example, the welfare state is primarily designed to provide a safety net for disadvantaged and needy groups within society. However, such assistance can only be provided in blanket form. Should the requirements of a particular group, for example, the elderly or disabled become too high maintenance and costly, the welfare state cannot always assist completely in satisfying the needs of such individuals.

This is one of the areas where social enterprises can play a vital role within society. An important niche they fill is to provide particular goods or services that slip through the cracks of both the public and private sectors, e.g. child care in a deprived community where no other provider wishes to become involved. Therefore, a new organisational form needs to intervene. This is the cue for social enterprise. As a result of this unique frame-work, social enterprises have frequently been referred to as the Third Way. That is, they are ostensibly another means of delivering goods and services that are distinct from those organisations operating within the public and private sectors. However, this distinction of the Third Way can be exaggerated. It will be seen that social enterprises are highly dependent upon the public sector for their funding requirements. In addition, those social enterprises that are particularly successful and create much employment can be ranked alongside the most successful entrepreneurial businesses found within the private sector. This is an important point to make because proponents of Third Way-type arguments fre-quently portray social enterprise as a unique sector. Such arguments also frequently dis-play an anti-capitalist bias, which is unfortunate as this merely serves to deflect attention away from the unique and constructive contribution that social enterprises make within all types of societies and economies.

Social enterprises are best viewed as a dynamic and innovative response to meeting many of the needs of individuals in a twenty-first century context. They possess different aims and ambitions to organisations more typically found in both the public and private sectors. This diversity is an aspect of social enterprises that will be the legitimate focus of our attention. Such organisations are usually wrestling with challenges that other organi-sations are not prepared to take on. They do not need the burden of apparently spearhead-ing some extravagant agenda whether it is the Third Way, the New Economics, or the Support Economy, which in reality has little to do with their specific functions.

Limitations on the Development of Social Enterprises

As with all SMEs, social enterprises face many difficulties. Finance is the most severe restriction on both the establishment and expansion of social enterprises. To begin with, due to their distinct mission they are normally not seen as good risks for commercial bank loans or for venture capitalists. There has been a tendency for more social enterprises to acquire bank loans and overdrafts but this is still very limited (Bank of England, 2003). Formal ven-ture capitalists are very reluctant to invest in this sector as they typically invest for the short term in order to achieve a quick and significant return on their investment. By their nature, social enterprises are nurturing organisations with a long-term perspective. Consequently, it is not surprising that social enterprises do not appeal to venture capitalists.

Social enterprises are therefore frequently forced to seek alternative means of finance most usually grants from government agencies, the EU and charitable trusts/foundations. Although grants are an important and valuable source of finance for social enterprises, they are not without problems. Seeking grants is a costly and time-consuming activity. Also, grant awarding bodies often have different aims and objectives to a social enterprise and can impose severe restrictions on the use of their awards. For example, such bodies can insist upon particular structures of board membership that may not be the most conducive towards achieving harmonious and entrepreneurial approaches. Consequently, the worst thing that can occur here is a situation of "mission drift" that deflects the social enterprise from successfully pursuing its objectives.

Another key problem for social enterprises concerns the frequent lack of a market for their product or service. We have already considered the issue of market failure within both the public and private sectors and how this acts as a stimulus for the establishment of many social enterprises. However, this is problematic in itself. In circumstances where both the public and private sectors do not supply specific goods or services, this implies that in many instances such provision is either unwarranted by the market or that it is uneconomic to provide. Consequently, this can render the environment for many social enterprises as distinctly unpromising. As a result many social enterprises face severe difficulties in making ends meet and this is why research has indicated that a high percentage of social enterprises would not be able to keep functioning without some form of subsidy (Watkins-Young et al., 2004).

Another major limitation on the development of social enterprises is a lack of quality/qualified staff to work in them. This is a major difficulty as social enterprises are often operated by well-meaning individuals who possess little or no business experience. Given the strong commitment to local ownership of such enterprises, it is frequently the case that outside assistance is not sought and a suspicion of outsiders is often prevalent. It is frequently the case that social enterprises cannot easily draw upon the type of skills that characterise entrepreneurial leadership.

There are serious constrains on both the establishment and development of social enterprises but they are not far removed from the type of difficulties faced by SMEs in general. As we will examine later, there are strategies that can be adopted to help social enterprises tackle such problems. However, a critical problem is what we can describe as "breakout". This is a concept that was first identified with respect to ethnic entrepreneurs. The argument being that if they are to grow they need to service the needs of a wider market than their own indigenous population. Hence, the term "breakout" was coined to describe this. With respect to social enterprises, and this will prove particularly relevant for tourism social enterprises, although legitimately possessing their roots within a particular community they will need to appeal to a much wider base of consumers than those to be found within that community.

Social Enterprise and Its Relevance for Tourism

When first encountering the notion of social enterprise, readers could be excused for wondering how relevant they are within the tourism industry. Tourism is typically viewed as a highly competitive and customer-oriented sector. However, when we begin to examine the types of social enterprise that operate within the tourism sector, it quickly becomes apparent that its contribution within this sector is significant. There are tourism social enterprises that represent all sizes within the SME sector. At one end of the spectrum is the hugely successful Eden Project in Cornwall. The Eden Project was one of the main

Millennium projects. It is set within a large crater where two huge greenhouses called Biomes house plants, crops and landscapes from both tropical and temperate climates. Visitors are encouraged not merely to view the items on display, but also to engage in education that emphasises the need to protect our fragile environment. Eden demonstrates how behaviour change can affect the environment as it occurs. The Project is about demonstrating our relationship and reliance upon plants. There are over 100,000 plants on display.

The Eden Project has been a phenomenal success. It is currently fourth in the UK visitor attraction rankings and hosts over a million visitors each year. It was founded primarily upon £86 million worth of grants from bodies such as the Millennium Commission and the EU. The Project is an excellent example of how a dynamic, but very capable group of individuals can make things happen. The economic and social benefits are immense. It now employs 500 permanent staff, 95% of these were recruited locally, and 50% were previously unemployed. The Project effectively injects several hundred million pounds and nearly 2,000 jobs into the economy of the South West of England.

The Eden Project is a good example of how a social enterprise can "breakout" of residing within a market niche that is narrowly community based only. This is a good illustration of why social enterprises within the tourism industry possess great potential for ultimately becoming financially self-sufficient. Furthermore, the Eden Project possesses a dynamic team, which avoids the problem of too many social enterprises, i.e. they are run by committees and consequently there is a tendency for the decision-making to be inflexible. As a result, such organisations can too easily possess little or no entrepreneurial flair and cannot, on our definition, be regarded as social enterprises.

At the opposite end of the spectrum of tourism sector social enterprises, we find the Rookhope Inn in County Durham. The Rookhope Inn is more than a pub. It provides bed and breakfast, a bicycle-hiring scheme and has created five jobs in the village. It has become an important focal point for community activities such as the use of IT facilities and courses run under the auspices of a local college. It also serves as a forum for local youth and as a meeting place. The pub had been closed for some time and the local community wanted to reopen it as a means of serving some of their needs. The trustees obtained £240,000 in loans from the Unity Trust Bank, the North East Community Loans Fund and the Northern Rock Foundation. This enabled the trustees to acquire the freehold and undertake much of the renovation work needed. Further grants enabled them to complete the refurbishment. This example illustrates how a community-based social enterprise can prove welcoming to outsiders. This is a significant point. Many social enterprises are so community focused that they can become suspicious of outsiders. This can prove a recipe for disaster as outside interest is most likely to provide the income necessary to prolong the life of the social enterprise.

Another important aspect of both the Eden Project and the Rookhope Inn is their location in rural areas, which have recently become the focus of greater attention of policy makers in the EU and national governments. Remote rural areas can be as deprived as the worst inner city areas.

These two examples of successful tourism-related social enterprises reflect only a fraction of the activities that such businesses cover. Theatres, ranging from the nationally acclaimed Crucible in Sheffield to the multitudes of smaller theatres in rural settings form an important contribution towards the cultural well-being of an area as well as encouraging tourists to spend time in those areas.

There are also several examples of successful bed-and-breakfast social enterprises. Six Mary's Place in Edinburgh being a particularly good example that is an award winning facility that provides employment for several local people including some who are disabled.

Visitor/heritage centres are another good example of social enterprises that provide employment for local communities but offer a valuable service for tourists.

Owing to insufficient data, it is impossible to estimate the extent of the contribution of social enterprises to the UK tourism industry. However, it is apparent that it plays a far greater role than we previously envisaged. A particularly important aspect of social enterprises is their contribution towards sustainable tourism. According to Inskeep (1991), sustainable tourism is geared towards protecting and enhancing the environment, meeting basic human needs, promoting current and inter-generational equity and improving the quality of life for everyone. It concentrates on how resources are managed in such a way that social, economic and aesthetic needs are met whilst preserving cultural integrity and encouraging broadness and maintaining life-support systems. The examples that we have considered fit neatly into this definition of sustainability. The Eden Project is primarily geared towards promoting enhanced environmental awareness that will benefit future generations. Furthermore, the contemporary economic benefits that it bestows upon the local economy enables many people to earn a living. The range of other identified tourism social enterprises also contribute towards aesthetics and preserving our cultural heritage and providing employment and business opportunities that would otherwise have not existed.

Conclusions and Recommendations

We have seen that social enterprises do play a role that is valuable within the UK tourism industry. It is a sector that is worth encouraging. This can be achieved in the following ways.

Firstly, we have seen that finance is the biggest single problem facing social enterprises. Their heavy dependence upon grant finance is particularly problematic. It can distract the enterprise from following its declared mission as well as engendering a grant dependency culture that does not necessarily encourage entrepreneurial activity. We have seen that tourism social enterprises, due largely to the nature of the market, frequently possess an ability to perform well entrepreneurially. This is important, as we have defined social enterprises, for our purposes, as being an organisation that is market oriented, community based and striving for financial surpluses that ultimately result in a sustainable venture. Therefore, if there is a genuine attempt to develop an entrepreneurial culture within an enterprise, they are more likely to become self-sufficient financially. As a result there should be greater emphasis upon awarding grants to tourism social enterprises that can demonstrate that they have a well-researched and viable business plan and experienced and capable individuals to implement it. This is a deliberate attempt to select the best organisations to invest in which will eventually be sustainable and generate employment. One of the difficulties with the social enterprise sector is that public money is often wasted in endeavouring to develop a business that has not undertaken market research and does not have the support of capable individuals. Such organisations are doomed to fail before they start. An encouraging aspect of tourism social enterprises is their ability to "breakout" of the confines of their immediate locality and attract visitors on a national and even international scale.

Another problem we identified with social enterprises was skill shortages. In the UK through the Small Business Service, Business Links and Enterprise Agencies anyone wishing to start their own business can access free training in marketing, accounting, IT, and writing business plans. However, when it comes to social enterprises specialist business advice is more limited. Considering social enterprises that are located within the tourism sector such specialist training and advice is virtually non-existent. Given the importance of social inclusion and the tourism industry in developing regional economic activity an opportunity for joined-up policy making has been missed. Both of these important issues should be integrated. This can be achieved by a programme that develops specialist advisors who can offer expertise in both social enterprises and the tourism industry. Enterprises that receive good training at the start-up phase are more likely to be successful. Furthermore, such training will improve the prospects of individuals being involved in social enterprises who, if not already possessing business acumen, can acquire it. The important thing about the type of initiatives mentioned above is that they will go a long way to create an enabling environment for social enterprises that will make them better businesses.

We referred earlier to the phenomenon of clustering through the formation of networks that help to generate social capital due to the mutual support generated by such associations. Indeed, for tourism destinations to compete they require a good clustering of SMEs that contribute significantly to the destination tourism product. The merging of the social capital that is found within the social enterprise sector with the private capital that the private sector possesses offers far more potential within the context of the tourism industry. Although both types of enterprises have different objectives, their target market is similar. This provides the relevant policy-making bodies with an excellent opportunity to establish a framework for more co-operation and strategic alliances between social and private enterprise. For example, in Shropshire, a social enterprise provides economical broadband services for all types of enterprises. From a destination perspective, the more co-operation that can be fostered could generate more business opportunities for both sectors.

At the European level, our consideration of social enterprises within the tourism industry is particularly pertinent. Many of the newly acceded EU member countries still find their economies in a transitional stage from having been command economies towards acquiring a more market-oriented framework. However, this is a slow and painful process as not only do mindsets need to be changed, but also fundamentally, there is often a serious lack of resources and personal wealth available to stimulate such transitions. The new member states will be looking towards the EU for significant funding to aid this process. However, this is a wonderful opportunity for social enterprises within the tourism sector to play a vital role. Given the recent history of many new member countries, social enterprises may represent a welcome transitional form of economic organisation that involves an element, at least initially, of public funding and the possibility of engaging in entrepreneurial activity. Furthermore, given the tremendous potential for tourism development and the remoteness of many of the regions ripe for such initiatives, social enterprises could form an attractive and meaningful contribution within such countries.

References

Bank of England (2003). *The financing of social enterprises. A special report.* London, UK: Bank of England.

DTI (2002). *Social enterprise: A strategy for success.* London, UK: Department of Trade and Industry.

EU (2005). *Social economy enterprises.* Online available at: http://europa.eu.int/comm/enterprise/entrepreneurship/coop/index.htm (last updated 19/01/2005).

Inskeep, E. (1991). *Tourism planning. An integrated sustainable approach.* New York, NY: Van Nostrand Reinhold.

OECD (1999). *Social enterprises.* Paris: Organisation for Economic Co-operation and Development.

SITF (2000). *Enterprising communities. Wealth beyond welfare.* A report to the Chancellor of the Exchequer from the Social Investment Task Force, London, UK.

Smallbone, D., Evans, M., Ekanem, I., & Butters, S. (2001). Researching Social Enterprise. *Small Business Service Research Report.* RR004/01

Watkins-Young, L., Jackson-Read, C., & Niel, A. (2004). *Switch on social enterprise — the state of social enterprise development in shropshire.* A report prepared by Collaborative Advantage for Shropshire County Council, Shropshire County Council, Shrewsbury, UK.

Chapter 7

Scottish Rural Tourism Enterprises and the Sustainability of Their Communities: A Local Agenda 21 Approach

David Leslie

Introduction

Tourism — at least for the foreseeable future — will see continuing growth in demand and worldwide expansion. Similarly, awareness and concerns over the importance of the quality of our environment will increase. Correlating with this will be an ongoing shift towards policies and practices intended to reduce negative human impacts and towards sustainable development. The substantial growth in tourism demand witnessed over the last decade has been influenced by a combination of the increase in number of international visitors and continuing expansion in the range and choice of destinations, fuelling a highly competitive marketplace. As the choice of destination for traditional forms of tourism activity has increased, so too has the diversity. Opportunities have arisen which hold potential for development in other hitherto less popular localities, particularly in rural areas, to promote tourism and the associated economic benefits.

Across Europe, the countryside has been shaped and managed by agricultural practices for centuries. But agriculture as the main bulwark of rural economies has been in decline whilst tourism has grown, generating substantial visitor spending. It is now the biggest sector of the economy in many rural areas, overtaking such established land uses as farming, forestry, fishing and field sports in terms of both employment and GDP. Often such development in one way or another has been supported by both national government and the EU, as such tourism enterprises, directly and indirectly, have gained substantially from the EU measures (of which there are many, see EC, 2004) aimed at rural development and regeneration. For example, promoting tourism to a region through a thematic approach based on related elements of an area's cultural heritage (see McKercher & du Cros, 2002; EC, 2003a). Furthermore, demand for rural locations is accelerating owing to the growing orientation to more adventurous and diverse activities. Evidently no rural area is 'safe from rash assault'. Today, such is the significance and pervasiveness of tourism activity in these areas that a downturn in demand for any one area, or more widely, has potentially serious implications for the local economy and the community. Witness the impacts of the Foot and Mouth Disease epidemic in the UK (Leslie & Black, 2006).

Throughout Europe there are myriad tourism enterprises dominated by hospitality operations but they also include diverse attractions, crafts and so forth. As discussed below, the vast majority of these businesses are small and medium-sized enterprises (SMEs); predominantly small and within which category micro-businesses (less than 10 employees) account for the majority. In many ways they are quintessential to the area; the essence of tourism supply in any rural locality and their presence fundamental to and a major influence on visitor demand and related expenditure. Therefore, it is these tourism SMEs that are the central focus of this chapter, set in the wider context of sustainable development — increasingly referred to as 'sustainability' — and the role that these SMEs play in terms of the local economy and community. Such a role should not be understated; one that is all the more significant given their actual and potential interrelationships with the local community through, for example, employment and purchasing practices. However, tourism is not a 'smokeless' sector. It is not only, '. . . one of the least regulated industries' (Mastny, 2002, p. 101), but also in comparison with most other sectors of consumer services, it has the most substantial negative impacts (Gossling, 2002, see Blair & Hitchcock, 2001; Hillary, 2000). Conversely, it has been argued that tourism: '. . . has the potential to bring about substantial environmental and socio-economic improvements . . .' and '. . . make significant contribution to the sustainable development of communities . . .' (WTTC, WTO and Earth Council, 1996, p. 4). To realise such potential requires recognition of not only the need '. . . to develop systems to assess the environmental performance of individual operations — enterprises' (Welford & Starkey, 1996, p. xi) but also the wider context and the objectives of sustainable development, which are encapsulated in the following:

- *social progress which recognises the needs of everyone;*
- *effective protection of the environment;*
- *prudent use of natural resources;*
- *maintenance of high and stable levels of economic growth and employment.*

(SDC, 1999, p. 1)

These objectives bring into question the development of tourism, and particularly a focus on the value of tourism enterprises to rural economies and related benefits amongst host communities. Basically, this requires that an enterprise contributes as much as possible to maintaining the quality of the environment — the product — and thus the quality of the resources, the community and their social cultural capital and the equitable distribution of the associated benefits (Hunter & Green, 1995). In effect, this requires a holistic approach within which tourism enterprises are not treated in isolation but in the context of the local economy, environment and community: an approach that is recognised in European rural development policy (see Hontelez, 2004; Nylander & Hall, 2005). In this way tourism is considered and integrated in an overall strategy for the area that aims to promote diversity and local added value (see Hummelbrunner & Miglbauer, 1994; ITP, 2004).

This attention to the wider context and the need to address the level and equity of the interrelationships between tourism and the local or regional economy, communities and the environment reflects the objectives of sustainable development and brings into focus local Agenda 21 (LA21). Local Agenda 21 is Chapter 28 of Agenda 21, a weighty document and major outcome of the Earth Summit of 1992, which sets out a comprehensive agenda and framework designed to stimulate and guide progress throughout the globe towards sustainable development in the 21st century. Chapter 28 explicitly calls for all local authorities to apply this agenda to the development of a local Agenda 21 plan for their area. The importance of these plans to encompass explicitly tourism planning and development is now widely recognised (see ETC, 2001; EC, 2003b; UNEP, 2003). A key factor of LA21 planning is the requirement to promote awareness of LA21 among all sectors of the community and seek their participation in the formulation of such plans (Leslie & Hughes, 1997; Aronsson, 2000; ICLEI, 2003). Thus LA21 planning holds the potential to raise attention to the environmental performance of businesses, i.e. issues of resource and waste management. This approach reflects the view that: 'If people are enabled to respond to local environmental imperatives, they are more likely to grasp the issues of conservation and move towards more sustainable lifestyles' (CC, 1993, p. 4) and potentially, therefore, influence their own behaviour and their business practices. In effect, LA21 planning includes the aims of addressing and promoting progress towards the 'sustainability' of tourism enterprises, which is not without problems (Ko, 2005). Reinforcement of this, and the presence of sustainable development on the political agenda of Europe, in terms of tourism, is not difficult to identify, for example, witness the European Union's (EUs) aim to '. . . promote sustainable development of tourism activities in Europe by defining and implementing an Agenda 21.' (EC, 2003b, p. 4). This further reinforces the role of local Agenda 21 planning and local governance. Indeed, a major outcome of the EUs recently established Tourism Sustainability Group is projected to lead to an 'Agenda 21 for European Tourism by 2007', which, it has been proposed, must include some form of business impact assessment (EC, 2002). This recognition of LA21, coupled with a plethora of non-sectoral specific policies and Directives germane to sustainability reinforces not only the advocacy of environmental management systems (EMS) and related practices but also the need to attend to the wider aspects involved in maximising the role and contribution of rural tourism enterprises to a sustainable future for the communities involved.

Evidently, the sustainability of tourism is not just about the physical environment on which so much of tourism demand depends but also the overall environmental performance of tourism enterprises and thus their connections with the community and the economy. However, before we consider these enterprises and their environmental performance, it is important that we establish the direction of the EU policy in this area. The attention then turns to rural tourism enterprises, in the process bringing to attention the plethora of policies and initiatives, literature and advice aimed at promoting environmental management (EM) practices and environmental performance that has developed since the 1980s. Subsequently, key findings of extensive studies into the environmental performance of rural tourism enterprises are presented and discussed. The outcomes of which lead onto to consideration of the implications of those findings, given the overall direction of the EU policy in support of progress towards sustainable development.

Key Aspects of EU Policy for Tourism and Sustainability

There is no question that the EU has substantial influence on tourism development and enterprises. Whilst indirect influences are well covered by Thomas (1996), Welford, Ytterhus, and Eiligh (1999) identify '. . . key elements of the EU strategy to manage the impacts of tourism on the environment (p. 171). A key theme of many of these, and subsequent, programmes pertinent to the tourism arena is the EUs commitment '. . . to promote . . . harmonious, balanced and sustainable development of economic activities . . .' and '. . . a high level of protection and improvement of the quality of the environment.' (Connelly & Smith, 2003, p. 261). This is gaining more explicit attention in the EU policy for tourism; for example, encouraging rural tourism enterprises to adopt 'responsible behaviour' and address their environmental performance (see EC, 2000). Steps taken to further this approach include the integration of sustainable development objectives into structural funds projects and other support initiatives; for example, the principles of the LEADER programme include: Principle 5 — Sustainability — 'Any rural area seeking to deliver quality must be concerned with managing the impact of tourism' and Principle 15: '. . . monitoring and evaluation of impacts (of tourism) on the visitor, enterprises, the environment and the local community' (EC, 2000, p. 63). Tourism is also one of the main sectors identified in the EUs 5th Environmental Action Plan (EAP) — 'Towards Sustainability' a cited aim of which is to reconcile tourism with development (Diamantis, 2000). This theme of seeking to progress the objectives of sustainable development has continued to grow in significance, heralded in the sixth EAP (2001–2010), which includes the objective: '. . . working with business and consumers to achieve greener forms of production and consumption and, in general, greening the market' (Connelly & Smith, 2003, p. 284). In this context, of more significance is the attention to enterprises: 'Business must operate in a more eco-efficient way, in other words producing the same or more products with less input and less waste, and consumption patterns have to become more sustainable' (EC, 2001, p. 3).

Essentially, the EUs approach is based on reinforcing the existing framework and maximising the initiatives involved; more specifically better '. . . monitoring and reporting of the sustainability of tourism, activities that further tourism consumption patterns by European citizens, and promoting sustainability in the tourism value chain and destinations.' (EC, 2003c, p. 3). This objective leads to establishing the Tourism Sustainability Group. To further this approach, they are: ". . . increasingly seeking to use policy instruments that tap into market dynamics such as taxation, eco-labelling . . ." (Johnson & Turner, 2003, p. 289); an approach also being used by national member states, e.g. the 'Hospitable Climates' initiative in the UK or the 'Balearic ecotax' (Palmer & Riera, 2003). Overall, not only is the EU continuing to further policy and directives aimed at progress towards sustainable development but also the steps they are taking are becoming more focused, more specific (see EEA, 2005). Indeed, SMEs are very much in the frame, such that now '. . . engaging them in environmental improvements is viewed as vital by the EU' (Hillary, 2004, p. 561).

Rural Tourism Enterprises

Recognition of the role of tourism enterprise in rural areas is perhaps most manifest in the EUs encouragement and support available to farms to diversify into tourism (Hjalager, 1996) particularly provision of accommodation (Sharpley, 2002; Chaplin, Davidova, & Gorton, 2004). But, the interrelationships of agriculture and tourism in these rural areas have gained little cognisance. Witness the Foot and Mouth Disease epidemic in the UK that was initially treated as just an agricultural problem, without the realisation that the domino effects, particularly the actions taken to control and contain the Foot and Mouth disease outbreak, would have potentially substantial effects on rural economies and tourism especially (Leslie & Black, 2006). An outcome that reinforces the need for not treating tourism in isolation of either the local economy or the community.

Collectively, SMEs account for approximately 99% of European tourism supply — over 2m businesses accounting for some 8m employees (EC, 2003c). By far the majority of these enterprises are micro-businesses (employ less than 10 persons); accounting for as many as 96% of hotels and restaurants (Vernon, Essex, Pinder, & Curry, 2003). Their significance lies in the following factors:

- Collectively they powerfully influence the perceived quality of nearly every visitor's experience — for better or worse.
- The money earned by micro-businesses tends to stay in the local community.
- Micro-businesses are the lifeblood of local communities; they often provide employment to people with lower skills/poor qualifications.
- Micro-businesses communicate and create the local character of a destination.
- Their actions impact daily upon sustainability issues.

(Becker, Dunn, & Middleton, 1999, p. 1)

Thus, rural tourism enterprises are very much part of the local community, especially as they are predominantly owner managed. Their role in promoting and supporting visitor demand is essential in any rural area. These visitors per se generate substantial expenditure; for example, spending on food and drink, walking, cycling, wildlife watching and field sports in Scotland has been estimated at £1038m (SE., 2001). This expenditure involves a range of enterprise categories, although the major proportion is accounted for by hospitality operations (see Table 7.1).

Table 7.1: General visitor expenditure (%) by category.

Sector	Day visitors	Domestic tourists
Accommodation	–	37
Retail	12	11
Catering	60	26
Attraction	13	5
Travel	16	20

Source: Leslie (2005).

What is important here is that these enterprises seek to spread the benefits arising from visitor expenditure, for example employing local people, using local services and purchasing local produce (see Boyne, Hall, & Williams, 2003; Leslie & Black, 2006), the latter of further significance in terms of 'food miles' and energy consumption. Purchasing local products is also important, manifest in the EU support for the production and marketing of local arts and crafts, particularly LEADER I and II, which recognises the connection between promotion of handicrafts and rural tourism services and the need for rural diversification (Crawley, Gaffey, & Gillmor, 1999; Goodwin & Francis, 2003). Enterprises potentially also have a wider influence in terms of sustainability by adopting 'Supply chain management' with the aim of selecting those suppliers that are addressing their own environmental performance (see Tapper & Font, 2003; Font & Carey, 2005).

As discussed earlier, whilst these enterprises may have little environmental impact individually, their collective impact is substantial. Therefore, any study of tourism enterprises must address the extent to which the tourism product is interconnected with the local community and in particular linkages with the economy and the relationship with the physical environment. This is all the more important in rural areas where the quality of the physical environment is integral to demand. Thus, tourism enterprises should recognise and accept that they have a responsibility for the impacts of their operations, including their customers. Furthermore: '. . . private interests, as they benefit from visitor spending, should invest in protecting and enhancing the local environment . . .' which is considered to be one of the critical areas '. . . on which a sustainable countryside will ultimately hinge.' (CC, 1993, p. 6)

In effect, this aims for progress towards sustainable development, any achievement towards which requires a substantial reduction in the consumption of resources (see Erdmenger, Burzacchini, & Levett, 2000). Essentially, tourism enterprises need to operate within the natural capacity of the destination. In other words, there should be no diminution of the natural capital. A first step to progress in this is to introduce environmental friendly management practices and subsequently an EMS (for a comprehensive analysis of EMS see Barrow (1999) and applications to tourism enterprises see Webster (2000)). But, a weakness with such a system is that it does not address broader social, cultural and community aspects of sustainability; hence the attention given to the overall environmental performance, which we take to include these aspects.

In the UK, the government and related rural agencies have been promoting aspects of EM to tourism enterprises since the late 1980s (Leslie, 2002). Further, there have been schemes designed to promote this and related practices by National Tourist Organisations and local authorities (Leslie, 2005; Font & Buckley, 2001). Leading organisations involved in the tourism sector have also been promoting voluntary schemes with emphasis on role of certification programmes such as Green Globe and eco-labels. For example, the undertaking of environmental auditing, considered to be an integral aspect in the management of an enterprise committed to addressing their environmental performance (see Diamantis, 1999; Goodall, 2003), by tourism enterprises was being advocated by the WTTC as early as 1991. In 1994 they established Green Globe, the aims of which are to promote and provide guidance to enterprises, which are seeking to introduce EM practices. Such has been the response by organisations and associations across Europe that today there is an extensive number of schemes, often categorised as ecolabels, relating to improving the environmental performance of tourism enterprises (see Hamele, 2001). Many of these arguably have arisen, directly or indirectly, as a result of EU initiatives, notably the fifth EAP (Hamele, 2001). A comprehensive collection of such schemes and practices is encompassed in UNEPs report on the progress of tourism towards sustainable development and is also evident in the Tour Operators Initiative for Sustainable Tourism, supported by a host of leading tourism associations (see WTTC, IFTO, IHRA, & ICCL, 2002). Furthermore, national and international hotel groups have also been responsive with an array of initiatives (see Goodwin & Francis, 2003).

The Environmental Performance of Rural Tourism Enterprises

It is clear from the foregoing that much has and is being done across the EU and specifically in the UK to promote and support tourism enterprises to address their environmental performance. But the majority of this is led by government and international groups and associations. But how much of this filters down to the myriad small and micro-enterprises involved in rural tourism? To what extent are the owners/managers of these enterprises addressing the environmental performance of their operations?

To address these questions, substantive empirical research designed to investigate the environmental performance of rural tourism enterprises was undertaken. This study involved the development of an extensive range of sustainability indicators reflective of the scope of local Agenda 21 (see Bell & Morse, 2000; Ceron & Dubois, 2003; UNEP, 2003) with due attention given to such factors as the profile of the business, employment, resource and waste management, owner-management attitudes and participation in community projects. Two areas were involved, namely the Lake District National Park (LDNP) in Cumbria and rural Scotland. Tourism in the LDNP is substantial; estimates suggest that in terms of the area's economy it is worth £1bn arising from some 5m tourists and 10m excursionists (CTB, 2005). Employment in tourism in Cumbria is estimated at 10% of the population (compared with about 6% nationally), 50% of which is located in the LDNP (Leslie, 2005). Significantly, the Cumbria Tourist Board (CTB) has been promoting sustainability in tourism since the early 1990s. In comparison, Tourism in Scotland's rural areas is considered to account for the majority of the 70% of jobs in the service sector and is seen as a bulwark of the rural economy (Anon, 2001). VisitScotland (VS) has also actively been promoting the sustainability of tourism enterprises, in support of which it launched the Green Business Scheme — an accredited EMS for tourism enterprises — in the 1990s. By reference to a range of sources such as accommodation guides and promotional literature databases (of approximately 900 and 1000 respectively) of tourism enterprises, the major proportion being accommodation operations, were established for the two areas. The postal survey of these enterprises in the LDNP and across rural areas of Scotland gained a response of 699 completed questionnaires, approximately equally divided between the two areas (see Table 7.2), with the majority of enterprises in the hospitality sector; processed using SPSS.

The substantial range of data so gathered provides a comprehensive profile of the contribution of tourism SMEs to rural economies and raises a range of significant issues. However, it is not possible given the constraints of space to present and discuss all the

Table 7.2: Categorisation of survey returns.

Category	LDNP (%)	Scotland (%)
Serviced accommodation, e.g. hotels, inns, guest houses, bed and breakfast (B&B)	230	224
Other sectors, e.g. restaurants, inns, attractions, caravan and camping sites	106	139
Total	336	363

Table 7.3: Ownership category.

Category	LDNP	Scotland
Ownership		
Owner managed	83	75
Manager	7	9
Local group	3	3
Regional group	1	3
National group	5[a]	8[a]
Length of time in current ownership (years)		
1–5	28	14
6–10	14	19
11–15	19	27
16–19	5	11
20–30	17	13
31+	19	16

[a]Includes National Trust properties.

data, and thus we will focus here primarily on key aspects relating to the profile of these enterprises, aspects of environmental performance such as the introduction of EMS and the awareness and attitudes of the owners/managers to the environmental agenda. Further, as the area samples are similar the opportunity is present to compare the findings of the two areas as well as drawing comparisons with those of similar studies. By far the majority of these enterprises are independently owned and owner managed (see Table 7.3). Scotland has slightly more enterprises that are part of a group, which might be expected given the larger geographic area and higher proportion of large hotels. Scotland also evidences longer average ownership and lower turnover of ownership compared with the LDNP (which is at par with the average for hotels and inns in England) and slightly the opposite for long-term ownership. Whilst this turnover of properties may raise questions over the sustainability of ownership there is evidence of the continuity of most of the enterprises involved. An important factor to emerge was that 'younger owners' are more likely to be environmentally aware and, comparative with long-term owners, more responsive and supportive of environmental initiatives.

Of particular significance within these samples is the diversity of the enterprises; ranging from a farmhouse bed and breakfast operation of two rooms to a 40-bedroom 5-star hotel to a small attraction receiving less than 10,000 visitors per annum. Further, within any one category there is potential for segmentation based on capacity or turnover or type of locality and also reason for ownership, e.g. lifestyle (see Thomas, 2000). In total this in itself brings into question the effectiveness of policy directed at tourism enterprises *per se*, policies which all too often appear to see tourism as a homogenous activity (Thomas, 2000). However, there are indications that the EU is gradually recognising that for SMEs, the 'one size fits all', is not applicable (EC, 2002).

The sample affirms that by far the majority of these rural tourism enterprises are micro-businesses and evidence none in the medium-size category based on employment, i.e. micro — less than 10; small 10–49 (Thomas, 2000), as the figures in Table 7.4 demonstrate. At the individual level, these enterprises offer little employment, but collectively, it is substantial; furthermore, part-time employment presents opportunities for local people for whom full-time work might not be suitable — or even available. For example, and for a variety of reasons not least of which is available resources and access, comparatively larger operations, particularly in the LDNP, employ 'overseas' staff who 'live-in'.

The attitudes of owners to the impact on the environment of their category of enterprise and also to 'going green' are important influences on their response to the environmental agenda. Thus, they were invited to grade a range of statements on the basis of 1 = 'strongly disagree' to 5 = 'strongly agree'. The statements and support for 'strongly agree' are presented in Table 7.5. These findings indicate some degree of recognition of their sector's impact and imply positive support for the introduction of some form of EMS. However, in contrast when they were asked to rank in degree of importance a range of management activities regarding the enterprise 'addressing customer complaints', 'maintenance/improvement of profitability' and 'achieving budgets' were considered most important to owners. 'Environmental reporting' and 'achieving environmental targets' were considered far less important; outcomes similar to Revell and Blackburn (2004), Barnett (2004), Leidner (2004) and Hobson and Essex (2001).

Table 7.4: Employment.

Number of Staff	LDNP		Scotland	
	Full-time	**Part-time**	**Full-time**	**Part-time**
None	46	44	31	30
1–2	16	27	28	25
3–5	13	15	22	17
6–9	6	7	10	10
10–18	8	5	5	5
19+	10	2	12	15

Table 7.5: Perceptions of the sector's impact and related aspects.

Question	Strongly agree (%)	
	LDNP	**Scotland**
The "x" sector has an impact on the environment.	38	32
The "x" sector's impact on the environment is significantly less than that of the manufacturing sector.	33	33
Operators in the "x" sector who claim to be 'green' are using it as a marketing ploy.	18	23
Most owners/managers do not have time to worry about the environment.	16	12
Customers are not interested in whether an operation is environmentally friendly.	18	10
It is not possible to be profitable and environmentally friendly.	7	4

Note: "x" = category of enterprise, e.g. accommodation and attractions.

Environmental Policy and Environmental Management System

Across the samples a substantial variance between the two areas was found with regard to whether the enterprise had a written environmental policy and had undertaken an environmental audit. However, it is noted that the absence of a written policy in itself does not mean the enterprise does not have a policy but rather that it has not been formalised.

	LDNP	**Scotland**
Written policy:	12%	25%
Undertaken an audit:	10%	20%

This variance between the two samples is hard to explain. However, a significant difference between the two areas is that VS has been actively promoting an EMS called the Green Business Scheme (GBS) since the late 1990s, which includes specific attention to promoting those enterprises that gain GBS accreditation. In contrast, until recently the LDNP did not have a localised scheme but rather the CTB has been promoting the Green Audit Kit. The CTB has now introduced its own system, very similar to the GBS, known as the Responsible Business Scheme. A second factor is that it is more likely that enterprises in both areas, which are interested and committed to 'going green', will have responded to the survey leading to a bias in the data. Even so, the findings indicate some progress since the 1990s (see Vernon et al., 2003; Carlsen, Getz, & Ali-Knight, 2001; Hillary, 2000).

Table 7.6: Awareness of range of 'green' initiatives.

Factor	Aware (%)	
	LDNP	**Scotland**
Green Flag International	22	15
BS 7750	18	23
Ecolabelling	18	15
Local Agenda 21	14	6
ISO14001	10	17
The Green Audit Kit	8	4
Green Globe	8	6
BA Environment Awards	8	7
Green Business Scheme	n.a	27
IHEI	3	4

The introduction of some form of EMS will be influenced by the owners/managers' awareness of such a system. Thus, respondents were invited to indicate whether they knew of a range of 'green' initiatives. As Table 7.6 shows, the general levels of awareness were found to be low. The most recognised initiative was that of the GBS, which correlates well with the above-mentioned finding. To an extent, so does the level of awareness of the Green Audit Kit which might be considered surprisingly low given this has been promoted by the CTB since 1995. In contrast, Hobson and Essex's study (2001) found that 39% of their sample was aware of the Green Audit Kit. This variance might be explained by the fact that this 'Kit' was developed in the area of their study and, as such, reinforces the point of the need for schemes if they are to be effective to 'connect' with enterprise owners/ managers. This finding is equally applicable across Europe (see Bendell & Font, 2004; Halma & Fadeeva, 2001). On the basis of earlier discussion, owners/managers could be aware of EM practices through membership of tourism organisations and/or a conservation or environmental group. To explore this, respondents were asked to indicate if they were a member of any one or more of a range of such organisations (see Table 7.7).

Cross analysis of the data drawn from membership of trade associations such as the HCIMA, Tourism Society or the Tourist Board did not find a definitive correlation between membership and awareness with the exception of the GBS. This finding supports Clarke (2004) who argued that many national trade associations are not promoting the need to address environmental performance and Mastny (2002) who argued that many efforts to promote green initiatives fail to reach the small operators. However, awareness of a 'green' initiative does not automatically mean that the appropriate responsive action will be taken as their involvement in a number of such initiatives demonstrates (see Table 7.8). The participation in Scotland in the GBS and/or ISO14001 supports Bendell and Font (2004) who found that whilst many such schemes have less than 2% accredited enterprises in the relevant sector a small number have gained a greater participation. However, the limited participation in more general environment initiatives reinforces the internal focus of EM on operational practices and costs. Furthermore, it affirms the point that attention

Table 7.7: Membership of a range of organisations.

Organisation	LDNP (%)	Scotland (%)
CTB/VS (ATB)	65	84
The National Trust	32	15
Chamber of Commerce	31	15
RSPB/SRSPB	12	10
HCIMA	11	8
Local Community Group	8	15
Local Agenda 21 Group	1	<1
A Tourism Forum	6	14
The Tourism Society	5	3
WWF	7	2
Greenpeace	4	1
Friends of the Earth	2	1

Table 7.8: Involvement in selected 'green' initiatives.

Initiative	Involvement: YES (%)	
	LDNP	Scotland
Made in Cumbria/Made in Scotland	7	4
Village of the Year	3	2
Tourism and Conservation Partnership (TCP)	12	n.a.
Local Agenda 21	1	4
Business Environment Network	2	2
Green Business Scheme (**GBS**)	n.a.	11
IHEI	1	2

to the adoption of an EMS alone is not sufficient when addressing the environmental performance of an enterprise and therefore the sustainability of tourism enterprises *per se* and their contribution to the local economy and community.

The limited support for the TCP, a visitor payback scheme established in 1993 that involves, for example, the voluntary addition to an accommodation account of a donation of £1 and even lower support for other 'environmental groups/projects', reflects the findings of other studies (e.g. Hobson & Essex, 2001). The difference between awareness and involvement also bears witness to the argument that: '. . . environmental education of consumers and increasing environmental awareness does not stimulate environmentally responsible behaviour.' (Sasidharan, Sirakaya, & Kerstetter, 2002, p. 172). The findings overall regarding EM practices are similar to those found in other studies not only undertaken in the UK (see Revell & Blackburn, 2004; Dewhurst & Thomas, 2003) but also across Europe (see Warnken, Bradley, & Guilding, 2005 Vernon et al., 2003; Donovan & McElligott, 2000).

Influential Factors

To gain insights into what enterprises consider to be influential to encouraging addressing their environmental performance, respondents were invited to rate a range of factors on the basis of 1 = least important to 5 = most important (see Table 7.9). The data are remarkably similar across the two areas with the exception that owners/managers in Scotland ranked 'cost savings' as more important. This supports the traditional paradigm of 'go green, save money' and implies attention to the adoption of EM practices that save on cost and not necessarily those practices that may increase costs, e.g. purchase of local products and produce (Carter, Whiley, & Knight, 2004). This argument is supported by the data on purchasing practices. Evidently, in common with most other owners/managers of enterprises, owners' purchasing patterns are influenced by the same factors: cost, availability and accessibility of suppliers. As regards support for other sectors of the local economy it was found that the convenience of the purchaser is often the main consideration in purchasing decisions, and as such, local suppliers are often overlooked due to competition (for example, from supermarkets and wholesalers) and more evident costs savings. Purchasers may be less inclined to look at the long-term value and benefit of buying locally in terms of supporting the local community and favour short-term gain. Such outcomes are very similar to those of Barnett (2004), Revell and Blackburn (2004) and Revell (2003).

The findings presented in Table 7.9 rather bring into question arguments that 'greening' the enterprise will give a competitive advantage and perceptions that customers generally are interested and thus this will influence their choice, for example, of accommodation, albeit it is recognised that it can influence some customers (Fairweather, Maslin, & Simmons, 2005; Leidner, 2004; Masau & Prideaux, 2003). This is perhaps surprising given the regularity with which consumers indicate their concern for the environment (EC, 2003c). Also, and of particular significance, is that in combination with other data, it was identified that the least likely influence would be international and national role models

Table 7.9: Factors potentially influential to addressing environmental performance.

Factor	Most important (%)	
	LDNP	**Scotland**
Customer care	53	52
Cost savings	48	59
Health and safety	50	49
Care for the environment	47	48
Customer demand	37	39
Personal beliefs	37	35
Quality management	31	32
Public relations	28	29
Potential legislation	19	22
Industry standards	17	14
Competitors' actions	7	6

and voluntary environmental reporting. Yet it is just such hotels and leisure groups that are adopting EMS, largely due to corporate influence (Chan & Wong, 2006). This further affirms the need for localised, locally owned, initiatives.

Barriers to Progress

The foregoing findings indicate some degree of progress in the adoption of EMS and, albeit to a lesser extent, addressing the wider aspects of the environmental performance of the enterprise. However, given the extensive promotion of attention and related policies and initiatives to EM practices, linkages with the local economy and community why are not more enterprises taking the appropriate responsive action? Clearly, the values and attitudes of owners/managers are factors but there are also other barriers. From this study and similar studies, as noted above, there is a consistency in factors considered to be hindering further progress. These are as follows:

- Lack of interest, inertia and ambivalence on the part of owners/managers;
- Limited awareness and understanding;
- Lack of time, too busy;
- Lack of resources, costs involved, e.g. for 'green products' and/or participation in a formal EM scheme;
- Lack of information;
- Lack of supporting infrastructure;
- Lack of availability and/or awareness of local products and produce.

The noted lack of awareness brings into question the efficacy of government lead efforts, especially where such effort neither is localised nor takes account of the practical realities of the enterprises involved (Leslie, 2005; Vernon, Essex, Pinder, & Curry, 2005; Thomas, 2000). This factor of awareness is also increasingly being recognised by the European Union (EU, 2004). But, as the findings attest, awareness is not in itself sufficient; this needs to be accompanied with appropriate support. Promotion and action must be manifest and championed at the local level (Levett, 2001).

Conclusion

Growing concerns over the quality of the environment and the impact of economic development in the latter part of the last century catalysed myriad-policy initiatives of wide diversity in scope and application intended to reduce negative human impacts and progress towards more sustainable forms of development. The EU has been notably responsive to this sustainability agenda, manifest in EAPs and a raft of Directives. Significantly in the recent years there has been a shift to a more focussed approach with more attention to less traditional sectors of the economy and particularly SMEs. Tourism is no exception. Thus, attention to the sustainability of tourism enterprises and their role in contributing to more sustainable communities in the long term not only is being promoted now but will also become more important as the century unfolds.

Collectively these tourism enterprises comprise the backbone of tourism supply in rural areas. Quintessentially, they are managed by people who predominantly live and work in the locality. Thus, they are very much part of the community and as such hold potential to contribute towards achieving a better balance within the local economy, environment and community. Tourism enterprises need to response appropriately to meet this environmental agenda. It is therefore essential for all operations to address issues of resource usage, consumption and waste, and thus introduce EM practices and address their overall environmental performance. Further, they should develop and promote linkages with other sectors of the area's economy, with the community more generally, and support local environmental/conservation initiatives. This will contribute to diversity within the local economy and more employment opportunities.

In light of not only the EUs 'sustainability' agenda but also the UK policy and related initiatives and those of professional associations in the tourism sector coupled with a plethora of sector and non-sectoral specific guidelines on 'greening' one might expect that many tourism enterprises have introduced an EMS. To explore this hypothesis substantive research into rural tourism enterprises found that progress in the adoption of EM practices has been made since the 1990s. But, as the results presented here attest, the awareness specifically of leading UK policy on tourism and promotion of 'green' initiatives and EM practices is very low — findings which, as identified, are not singular to this study and reflect those of other studies undertaken in the UK and other member states of the EU Such outcomes bring into question the effectiveness of the EU and national policies and of those agencies charged with taking forward such policies; especially when these have not been translated into action at the local level. Furthermore, it was found that 'being aware' is not a strong indicator of subsequent positive action, as the even lower levels of involvement in a range of initiatives/activities demonstrated.

Constraints on progress identified from the research, recurrent in similar studies, of lack of information, time, money/cost and infrastructural support need to be overcome. This requires greater cooperation between the organisations involved and the provision of: '. . . hands-on tools for integrating environmental and social concerns in day-to-day business, and establish economic conditions that reward such efforts.' (Von Geibler & Kuhndt, 2002, p. 63). Clearly, obvious and more direct encouragement and promotion is needed. A more effective communication process for LA21 plans by local (municipal) authorities may help to improve this situation, while also acting as a lead body in addressing and consolidating the wide range of issues being promoted by a proliferation of environmental organisations at regional, national and supranational levels. Furthermore, there is a need in each locale for an organisation to take forward 'the message'. In effect, a 'champion', respected by the 'tourism community', promoting and supporting a locally based and accredited system if it is to be effective. This system needs to be flexible to accommodate the different categories of, and variances within, tourism enterprises.

That more progress has not been made serves to reinforce the view that the availability of literature and/or advice is not in itself sufficient to assume awareness and to engender positive action, a factor now recognised by the EU (EC, 2003b). However, there is clear evidence of good practice across a range of environmental performance indicators, which is laudable. But this is neither that extensive nor representative of the majority of owners. Though it appears that whilst many owners evidence some commitment to environmental management, such commitment is often overshadowed by greater attention to short-term financial returns and far less to the wider aspects of the enterprise's environmental performance.

Evidently there is substantial scope for enhancing the role and contribution of rural tourism enterprises through developing their environmental performance. As Mastny argued: '. . . while many industry efforts embrace a shift toward environmental sustainability, they are less willing to incorporate social and cultural needs, including addressing labour and employment issues, protecting cultures, and maximising linkages with local economies and communities' (2002, p. 120). To achieve this requires change. As, Farrell and Twining–Ward argued, to overcome counter forces such as conservatism in tourism, prevailing ideologies and myopia: 'Above all, it requires an entirely new outlook on the world, building on what has already been learned' (2005, p. 119).

Overall, these findings are not unexpected and, partly at least, are a result of the emphasis to date on tourism in planning and regional development, which has been short term in focus, driven by economic objectives with a failing to recognise the interrelated dimensions of the environment, social capital and the economy. To overcome this there is a need for more creative planning in order to maximise these cross-sectoral links. A comprehensive, integrated approach needs to be adopted, a key facet of which is that tourism is not treated in isolation of the rest of the local economy and particularly of the community who are the oft-cited key beneficiaries of tourism. Thus, a holistic, locally and regionally focused approach founded on a basis of sustainable development is required.

A better balance between the environment, tourism and the host community is achievable if tourism enterprises improve their environmental performance, in the process playing a more constructive role in contributing to the sustainability of local communities. However, the voluntary approach to this whilst evidencing progress is not being taken up by the majority of enterprises. This is despite a raft of policy initiatives and myriad guidelines and advice. The oft-cited reasons for adoption, such as economic benefit/cost savings, competitive advantage and consumer demand, appear to hold, at best, limited sway. Arguably, further progress will only happen through increased awareness and understanding of the 'why', 'what' and 'how' involved in addressing environmental performance, as well exemplified by the findings. In other words, it is the attitudes and values of the individual — in many, many instances the owners of these enterprises — which, combined with their knowledge and understanding of environmental issues and related practices, is the key influence which needs to be addressed, a factor increasingly recognised by the EU (EU, 2004).

A continuing failing on the part of many enterprises to respond appropriately to this agenda holds potentially significant implications given the EUs drive towards addressing the EM and environmental performance of tourism enterprises. Witness the EUs recent stance on tourism, which makes the point that tourism in Europe cannot expand indefinitely and should be in tune with objectives of sustainable development; furthermore the sustainable development of tourism is now seen as a priority (EC, 2003b). There can be little doubt that the EUs agenda on sustainability is increasingly being translated into actions that directly or indirectly impact on tourism enterprises, for example regulations relating to waste disposal, recycling and energy consumption. It is arguable, therefore, that these enterprises must start putting environmental concerns to the forefront of business operations and strategic decisions. The implication is that in the absence of such voluntary action regulation will follow to enhance the role and contribution of rural tourism enterprises in the sustainable development of rural communities and their economies.

References

Anon (2001). *Agriculture's contribution to the Scottish society, economy and environment.* Aberdeen: University of Aberdeen, Dept. of Agriculture & Forestry and Macaulay Land Use Research Institute.

Aronsson, L. (2000). *The development of sustainable tourism.* London, UK: Continuum.

Barnett, S. (2004). *Perceptions, understanding and awareness of Green Globe 21: the new Zealand Experience.* State of the Art Conference II, Glasgow.

Barrow, C. J. (1999). *Environmental management — principles and practice.* London, UK: Routledge.

Becker, H., Dunn, S., & Middleton, V. T. C. (1999). *Think small — Think local — think micro-businesses.* A First Report for Consultation and Endorsement,

Bell, S., & Morse, S. (2000). *Sustainability indicators: Measuring the immeasurable.* London, UK: Earthscan.

Bendell, J., & Font, X. (2004). Which Tourism rules? Green standards or GATS. *Annals of Tourism Research, 31*(1), 139–156.

Blair, A., & Hitchcock, D. (2001). *Environment and business.* London, UK: Routledge.

Boyne, S., Hall, D., & Williams, F. (2003). Policy, support and promotion for food-related tourism initiatives: a marketing approach to regional development. *Journal of Travel & Tourism Marketing, 14*(3/4), 131–154.

Carlsen, J., Getz, D., Ali-Knight, J. (2001). The Environmental attitudes and practices of family business in the rural tourism and hospitality sectors. *Journal of Sustainable Tourism, 9*(4), 281–297.

Carter, R. W., Whiley, D., & Knight, C. (2004) Improving Environmental performance in the Tourism Accommodation Sector. *Ecotourism, 3*(1), 46–68.

CC (1993). *Sustainability and the English countryside — position statement.* Cheltenham: Countryside Commission, CCP 432.

Ceron, J.-P., & Dubois, G. (2003). Tourism and sustainable development indicators: The gap between theoretical demands and practical achievements. *Current Issues in Tourism, 6*(1), 54–75.

Chan, S. W. E., & Wong, C. K. S. (2006). Motivations for ISO 14001 in the hotel industry. *Tourism Management, 27*(3), 481–492.

Chaplin, H., Davidova, S., & Gorton, M. (2004). Agricultural adjustment and the diversification of farm households and corporate farms in Central Europe. *Rural Studies, 20*(1), 61–77.

Clarke, J. (2004). Trade assocations: An appropriate channel for developing sustainable practice in SMEs. *Journal of Sustainable Tourism, 12*(3), 194–208.

Connelly, J., & Smith, G. (2003). *Politics and the environment: From theory to practice* (2nd ed.). London, UK: Routledge.

Crawley, M. E., Gaffey, S. M., & Gillmor, D.A. (1999). The role of quality tourism and craft SMEs in rural development: Evidence from the Republic of Ireland. *Anatolia, 10*(1), 45–60.

CTB (2005). *Cumbria county tourism data.* Windermere: Cumbria Tourist Board.

Dewhurst, H., & Thomas, R. (2003). Encouraging sustainable business practices in a non-regulatory environment: A case study of small tourism firms in a UK national Park. *Journal of Sustainable Tourism, 11*(5), 383–403.

Diamantis, D. (1999). The importance of environmental auditing and environmental indicators in islands. *Eco-management and Auditing, 6*(1), 18–253.

Diamantis, D. (2000). Ecotourism and sustainability in Meditteranean Islands. Thunderbin International. *Business Review, 42*(4), 427–443.

Donovan, T., & McElligott, B. (2000). Environmental management in the Irish hotel sector — policy and practice. In: M. Robinson J. Swarbrooke, N. Evans, P. Long & R. Sharpley (Eds.), *Environmental management and pathways to sustainable tourism* (pp. 55–80). sunderland, UK: Business Education.

EC (2000). *Towards quality rural tourism: Integrated quality management [IQM] of rural destinations.* Brussels, UK. DG XXIII Tourism Directorate.

EC (2001). *Executive summary from: E.C. environment 2010: Our future, our choice.* 6th A. P. COM (2001) 31 Final Brussels. Comm of the European Communities.

EC (2002). *Agenda 21 — Sustainability in the European Tourism Sector.* Brussels, UK: Enterprise Directorate-General.

EC (2003a). *Using natural and cultural heritage to develop sustainable tourism.* Brussels, UK: European Commission, Directorate-General Enterprise — Tourism Unit.

EC (2003b). *Basic orientations for the sustainability of European tourism.* Brussels: Enterprise Directorate — General. COM (2003) 716 final.

EC (2003c). *Structure, performance and competitiveness of European tourism and its enterprises.* Luxembourg, UK: European Communities.

EC (2004). *EU Support for tourism enterprises and tourist destinations: An Internet guide.* Brussels, UK: Directorate D — Unit D3.

EEA (2005). *Environmental policy integration in Europe.* Technical Report 2 Copenhagen. European Environment Agency.

Erdmenger, C., Burzacchini, A., & Levett, R. (2000). *Local loops — how environmental management cycles contribute to local sustainability: Proceedings of the European Commission advanced study course on local instruments.* Brussels, UK: European Commission.

ETC (2001). *National sustainable tourism indicators: Monitoring progress towards sustainable tourism in England.* London, UK: English Tourism Council.

EU (2004). *Strategy for integrating the environment into industry.* europe.eu.int/scadplus/leg/en/lvb/128093.htm accessed 5/11/2004.

Fairweather, J. R., Maslin, C., & Simmons, D. G. (2005). *Journal of Sustainable Tourism, 13*(1), 82–98.

Farrell, B., & Twining-Ward, L. (2005). Seven steps towards sustainability: Tourism in the context of new knowledge. *Journal of Sustainable Tourism, 13*(2), 109–122.

Font, X., & Buckley, R. C. (Eds.) (2001). *Tourism ecolabelling: Certification and promotion of sustainable management.* Wallingford, UK: CAB International.

Font, X., & Carey, B. (2005). *Marketing sustainable tourism products.* Nairobi, Kenya: United Nations Environment Programme and Region Toscana.

Goodall, B. (2003). Environmental aduting: A means to improving tourism's environmental performance. In C. Cooper(Ed.), *Classic reviews in tourism* (pp. 192–226). Clevedon, UK: Channel View.

Goodwin, H., & Francis, J. (2003). Ethical and responsible tourism: Consumer trends in the U.K. *Journal of Vacation Marketing, 9*(3), 271–284.

Gossling, S. (2002). Global enviromental consequences of tourism. *Global Environmental Change, 12*(4), 283–302.

Halma, M., & Fadeeva, Z. (2001). Networking towards sustainability — value added? In: K. Green, P. Groenewegen & P. S. Hofman (Eds.), *Ahead of the curve: Cases of innovation in environmental management* (pp. 143–164). Dordrecht, The Netherlands: Kluwer.

Hamele, H. (2001). Ecolabels for tourism in Europe the European ecolabel for tourism? In X. Font & R. C. Buckley (Eds.), *Tourism ecolabelling: Certification and promotion of sustainable management* (pp. 175–184). Oxon, UK: CABI.

Hillary, R. (Ed.) (2000). *Small and medium-sized enterprises and the environment*. Sheffield, UK: Greenleaf.

Hillary, R. (2004). Environmental management systems and the smaller enterprise. *Cleaner Production*, 12, 561–569.

Hjalager, A.-M. (1996). Agricultural diversification into tourism: Evidence of a European community development programme. *Tourism Management*, *17*(2), 103–111.

Hobson, K., & Essex, S. (2001). Sustainable tourism: A view from accommodation business. *Service Industries Journal*, *21*(4), 133–146.

Hontelez, J. (Ed.) (2004). *The future of rural development policy: A position paper*. Brussels: European Environment Bureau.

Hummelbrunner, R., & Miglbauer, E. (1994). Tourism promotion and potential in peripheral areas: The Austrian Case. *Journal of Sustainable Tourism*, *2*(1/2), 41–50.

Hunter, C., & Green, H. (1995). *Tourism and the environment*. London, UK: Routledge.

ICLEI (2003). *Tourism and local Agenda 21 — the role of local authorities in sustainable tourism*. Paris: UNEP.

ITP (2004). *Tourism and local economic development*. London, UK: International Tourism Partnership.

Johnson, D., & Turner, C. (2003). *International business — themes and issues in the modern global economy*. London, UK: Routledge.

Ko, T. G. (2005). Development of a tourism sustainability assessment procedure: A conceptual approach. *Tourism Management*, *26*(3), 431–445.

Leidner, R. (2004). *The European tourism industry — a multi-sector with dynamic markets. Structures, developments and importance for Europe's economy*. Brussels: EC, Enterprise DG (Unit D.3) Publications.

Leslie, D. (2002). The influence of UK government agencies on the 'greening' of tourism. *Tourism Today*, *2*(Summer), pp. 95–110.

Leslie, D. (2005). Rural tourism businesses and environmental management systems. In: D. Hall, I. Kirkpatrick & M. Mitchell (Eds.), *Rural and sustainable business* (pp. 249–267). Chapter 14, London, UK: CAB.

Leslie, D., & Black, L. (2006). Tourism and the impact of the foot and mouth epidemic in the UK: Reactions, responses and realities with particular reference to Scotland. *Journal of Travel and Tourism Marketing*, *19*(2/3), 35–46.

Leslie, D., & Hughes, G. (1997). Local authorities and tourism in the UK. *International Journal of Managing Leisure*, *2*(3), 143–154.

Levett, R. (2001). Sustainable development and capitalism. *Renewal*, *9*(2/3), 1–9.

Masau, P., & Prideaux, B. (2003). Sustainable tourism: A role for Kenya's hotel industry. *Current Issues in Tourism*, *6*(3), 197–208.

Mastny, L. (2002). Redirecting international tourism. In World Watch Institute. *State of the World* (pp. 101–124). London, UK: Earthscan

McKercher, B., & du Cros, H. (2002). *Cultural tourism: The partnership between tourism and cultural heritage management*. New York, NY: Haworth Hospitality Press.

Nylander, M., & Hall, D. (2005). Rural tourism policy: European perspectives. In D. Hall, I. Kirkpatrick & M. Mitchell(Eds.), *Rural tourism and sustainable business*. London, UK: CAB.

Palmer, T., & Riera, A. (2003). Tourism and environmental taxes. With special reference to the "Balearic ecotax". *Tourism Management*, 24, 665–674.

Revell, A. (2003). *The ecological modernisation of small firms in the UK*. Business Strategy and Environment Conference. Leicester, UK.

Revell, A., & Blackburn, R. (2004). *UK SMEs and their response to environmental issues*. Kingston, UK: Kingston University, Small Business Research Centre.

Sasidharan, V., Sirakaya, E., & Kerstetter, D. (2002). Developing countries and tourism ecolabels. *Tourism Management, 23*: 161–174.

SDC (1999). *UK Government's strategy for sustainable development*. London, UK Government: Sustainable Development Commission.

SE (2001). *A forward strategy for Scottish agriculture*. Edinburgh, UK: Scottish Executive.

Sharpley, R. (2002). Rural tourism and the challenge of tourism diversification: The case of Cyprus. *Tourism Management, 23*, 233–244.

Tapper, R., & Font, X. (2003). *Tourism supply chains*. Leeds: Leeds Metropolitan University, Business and Development Group.

Thomas, R. (Ed.) (1996). *The hospitality industry, tourism and Europe: Perspectives on Policy*. London, UK: Cassell.

Thomas, R. (2000). Small firms in the tourism industry: Some conceptual issues. *International Journal of Tourism Research, 2*, 345–353.

UNEP (2003). *Tourism and local agenda 21 — The role of local authorities in sustainable tourism*. Paris: United Nations Environment Programme, Division of Technology, Industry and Economics.

Vernon, J., Essex, S., Pinder, D., & Curry, K. (2003). The 'Greening' of tourism micro business: Outcomes of group investigations in south-east Cornwall. *Business Strategy and Environment, 12*(1), 49–69.

Vernon, J., Essex, S., Pinder. D., & Curry, K. (2005). Collaborative policy making: Local sustainable projects. *Annals of Tourism Research, 32*(2), 325–345.

Von Geibler, J., & Kuhndt, M. (2002). *Helping small and not-so-small businesses improve their triple bottom line performance*. UNEP Industry and Environmment, July–December, pp. 63–66.

Warnken, J., Bradley, M., & Guilding, C. (2005). Eco-resorts vs. mainstream accommodation providers: An investigation of the viability of benchmarking environmental performance. *Tourism Management, 26*(3), 367–379.

Webster, K. (2000). *Environmental management in the hospitality industry*. London, UK: Cassell.

Welford, R., & Starkey, R. (Eds.), (1996). *The earthscan reader in business and the environment*. London, UK: Earthscan Publications.

Welford, R., Ytterhus, B., & Eiligh, J. (1999). Tourism and sustainable development: An analysis of policy and guidelines for managing provision and consumption. *Sustainable Development, 7*, 165–177.

WTTC, IFTO, IHRA, & ICCL (2002). *Industry as a partner for sustainable development: tourism report*. Prepared by World Travel and Tourism Council, International Federation of Tour Operators, International Hotels & Restaurateurs Association and the International Council for Cruise Lines. Kenya: United Nations Environment Programme.

WTTC, WTO and Earth Council (1996). *Agenda 21 for the travel and tourism industry: Towards environmentally sustainable tourism*. Oxford, UK: World travel and Tourism Council.

Chapter 8

Tourism SMEs in the Context of Sustainability: A Case Study of Pomerania Voivodship, Poland

Barbara Marciszewska and Anna Staszewska

Introduction

The globalisation of the tourism industry influences the behaviour of small and medium-sized enterprises (SMEs), which function in many countries as traditional suppliers of tourist goods and services to consumers on the one hand and as distributors or suppliers or as both to large and multinational enterprises on the other hand. The dual nature of the supply side of the tourism market composed of both large enterprises and SMEs requires adopting new forms of co-operation that facilitate the effective supply and distribution of tourist goods, services and experiences. Most tourism enterprises operate in a global market but they also play an important role at the local level. This situation confronts SMEs with many challenges within the framework of both globalisation and regional or local socio-economic processes. The recently changing structures of the tourism-related sectors, the emergence of new destinations and the strong market power of multinational enterprises have created for tourism SMEs development opportunities but at the same time placed them in an increasingly competitive environment.

The Polish tourism sector is composed mainly of small tourism enterprises, which organise and sell tourism products and offer a range of tourism services. However, it also involves large companies (such as hotel chains or foreign tour operators) that provide a range of tourism services thus increasing the level of competition in the tourism market. Such competition theoretically becomes a factor that stimulates tourist development, but in practice it frequently creates new opportunities for foreign enterprises at the expense of weaker Polish tourism SMEs. Limited-financial resources, insufficiently educated personnel, a lack of systematic access to information and knowledge put Polish tourism enterprises at a disadvantage *vis-à-vis* their more experienced rivals, and encourage them to look for innovative strategies that will enable them to maintain their market position. However, not all approaches to gaining competitive advantage are sustainable and as Von Moltke (1996) stresses, some may damage the natural, social and cultural resources that primarily attract tourists to a destination. It is therefore essential that strategies and practices adopted by tourism SMEs that operate under such competitive pressures take into consideration the value of these unique and scarce resources and the need for their preservation. While such approaches are more common in established-tourism markets, this may not always be the case in the new market economies. Indeed, enterprises in such economies are frequently concerned with pursuing strategies that enable them to achieve their short-term financial goals without due consideration of the negative social and environmental effects that their strategies and practices might generate. Such negative effects could, however, be reduced if tourism enterprises recognise them and implement the principles of sustainable tourism. This, however, cannot happen without an appropriate level of knowledge of sustainability issues among tourism SMEs. Indeed, knowledge-based sustainable tourism management can provide the essential basis for creating an optimal relationship between the volume of tourism flows and its impact on the natural, social and economic environments of a tourism destination.

Within this context, the aim of this chapter is to discuss the results of a study into the level of knowledge and understanding of the concept and practice of sustainable tourism among tourism SMEs that operate in Pomerania Voivodship, one of the 16 regions in Poland. Some background consideration of the role of tourism SMEs in sustainable regional development is undertaken. Recommendations for the future practice and research in this area are made.

Tourism SMEs and Sustainable Regional Development

According to Job, Metzler, Muller, and Mayer (2004, p. 56) 'the tourism industry in Europe is an economic sector dominated by small and medium enterprises (SMEs)'. This means that such enterprises contribute considerably to both their national economies and regional development. Some authors stress that SMEs, which offer a wide range of services, are more flexible than large firms and stimulate competition (Job et al., 2004). The same characteristics describe tourism SMEs. The highly competitive environment within which tourism SMEs operate can be perceived as a threat to tourism SMEs. However, it is also an opportunity for becoming more innovative and for providing a product of high quality.

The importance of tourism SMEs in regional development is unquestionable. However, their impact upon socio-economic life of the destination within which they operate significantly depends upon the destination's tourism policy, which determines the levels of competitiveness for both the tourism enterprises and the region. Vanhove (2004) notes that issues of competitiveness have become central to regional tourism policy making. Examples of good practice in the area of regional tourism development indicate that tourism growth depends upon the quality of natural, cultural and economic resources on the one hand and cross-sector activity and co-operation between SMEs and other stakeholders on the other. Indeed, tourism growth depends upon a range of economic sectors, which offer the necessary and complementary tourism goods and services. Poon (1993) stresses the importance of ensuring that tourism is developed in such a way that it benefits the destination while Vanhove (2004) emphasises the importance of using tourism to stimulate the development of other sectors. Both of these aspects of tourism development need to be included in a regional tourism policy if an integrated approach to regional socio-economic development is to be ensured.

From a regional perspective, identifying and achieving socio-economic benefits from tourism is of greater importance than merely striving for growth in individual-tourism enterprises. The attainment of such a goal requires adopting an innovative approach to horizontal co-operation between the tourism industry and other sectors. Bieger, Baritelli, & Wainert (2004) note that despite the fact that co-operative work frequently generates more than one direction in development, the synergy effect associated with co-operative arrangements enables the achievement of the ultimate goal faster. The primary conditions for successful co-operation within the context of regional tourism are as follows:

- knowledge development and exchange,
- understanding of the importance of quality for the tourism sector,
- clear goals and objectives of co-operation,
- knowledge about the economy and its current requirements and
- common approach to the concept of sustainability and its implementation in tourism management.

Central to realising the opportunity of deriving the socio-economic benefits of tourism is a sustainable approach to tourism development. Weaver (2001, p. 300) defines sustainable tourism as 'tourism that meets the needs of the current generation without compromising the ability of future generations to meet their own needs'. Such an approach to tourism development requires maximising the benefits from tourism while minimising the costs and ensuring that social, economic, cultural and environmental resources of the destination are preserved (Bramwell, Henry, Jackson, & Van der Straaten, 1996). Indeed, sustainable development is perceived as a precondition for a long-term tourism development that enables tourism SMEs to remain competitive. Sustainable tourism destinations not only help tourism enterprises maintain their position in a global tourism market but they also contribute to the sustainability of the country's tourism industry.

The engagement of tourism SMEs in pursuing the goal of sustainability depends, however, upon their awareness of sustainability issues including gaining an understanding of the concept of sustainability, the benefits of sustainable development, the management practices that contribute to sustainability and the problems associated with pursuing the sustainability goal. Furthermore, tourism SMEs need to understand that while pursuing the commercial objective of profit making, they depend upon local resources and as such they should be serving both tourists and local communities and therefore fulfil the requirements of both these groups (Marciszewska, 1998). Indeed, sustainable tourism is a real chance to develop local economies, environment and communities while at the same time generate profits for tourist enterprises.

Given that the flexibility of small and medium-sized businesses frequently constitutes a source of competitive advantage within this sector (Mugler, 1997), pursuing the goal of sustainability should be relatively easy for tourism SMEs. However, an adequate knowledge of sustainability is a pre-condition for attaining such a goal, which will ultimately help minimise the social, economic and environmental costs of tourism development.

A study conducted by Richards (1996) indicates that there is a need for improving knowledge on sustainability. Indeed, he stresses that 'a wide range of views on the concept of sustainable tourism emerged from the interviews' (Richards, 1996, p. 10). However, the study did not indicate whether similar problems could be observed among Polish tourism SMEs. Given the fact that Poland has a relatively short tradition of adopting a market approach towards tourism development and the fact that issues of sustainable tourism currently dominate the national and regional tourism policy agendas, it is necessary to investigate the level of knowledge and understanding of the concept and practice of sustainable tourism among Polish tourism SMEs.

The Knowledge of Sustainability among Tourism SMEs in Pomerania Voivodship

The tourism sector in Poland is characterised by a dual structure, similar to that identified by Keller (2004) who identifies a group of travel-trade firms that includes tour operators and airlines, and which is dominated by large companies and the group of destinations-based firms (e.g. visitor attractions, accommodation and catering facilities, leisure facilities) that is dominated by small and medium-sized enterprises. Many Polish tourism SMEs are family-owned businesses that are characterised by a distinct form of management. According to Getz, Carlsen, and Morrison (2004, p. 2) the uniqueness of family businesses relates to the fact that '. . . ownership makes a huge difference and [. . .] many are small for very personal, deliberate reasons'. This may have implications for owner-managers' approaches towards the transfer and application of knowledge from the business environment into their own enterprises.

A study into the level of knowledge and understanding of the concept and practice of sustainable tourism among tourism SMEs that operate in one of Poland's 16 provinces, Pomerania Voivodship, was conducted by the authors of this chapter in 2004. Pomerania Voivodship was selected as a region suitable for this study for a number of reasons. Firstly, the region, located in the North of Poland, is rich in natural and cultural resources, including some of the most popular of Poland's seaside resorts and cities (e.g. Gdansk, Gdynia and Sopot). In 2004, 4.2 million tourists visited this region of which 0.7 million were foreign tourists. It was the fourth most visited region by Polish tourists, representing an 8.5% share in the domestic tourist market, and the ninth most visited region by foreign tourists, representing a 5% share in the foreign tourist market (The Institute of Tourism, 2005). Secondly, the regional tourism development strategy for Pomerania Voivodship (2004) identifies sustainability as the priority goal but the ways of achieving this goal are not identified. The role of SMEs in sustainable tourism development is not described. Finally, one of the researchers and authors of this chapter (B. Marciszewska) actively participated in public debates in Pomerania Voivodship as the chair and moderator. She is also a member of the Monitoring Committee for tourism development in Pomerania Voivodship. The long-term involvement in and observation of tourism development in

Pomerania Voivodship provided the researcher with an insight into sustainability issues in this region and enabled her to obtain a detailed understanding of the phenomena studied.

Based on literature on sustainable tourism, a questionnaire containing 12 closed questions was designed with a view to investigating the levels of tourism SMEs knowledge and understanding of the concept and practice of sustainable tourism. The questionnaire was distributed via e-mail in December 2004 to a sample of 54 travel agencies that operate in Pomerania Voivodship and that are members of the Polish Chamber of Tourism — Pomeranian Branch. Thirty (55.6%) useable questionnaires were returned. The majority of enterprises that responded to the questionnaire (76%) were micro businesses that employed fewer than ten people and 47 % of the enterprises employed not more than three people. Only 24% of the enterprises employed more than ten people. The average period of work of employees fluctuated between 1 to 5 years although for some enterprises (18%) the average length of employment was more than 10 years. In comparison, almost 60% of the enterprises studied had been in business for more than 10 years, which seemed a relatively long time considering the rapidly changing business environment in Poland in the last decade and the high rate of SME failure in Poland.

How Do Tourism SMEs in Pomerania Voivodship Understand the Concept and Practice of Sustainable Tourism?

The results of this survey indicate that almost 71% of the respondents did not know what the concept of sustainable tourism was (Figure 8.1). Those who did (29%) could not define the concept of sustainable tourism correctly. Examples of some definitions of sustainable tourism that were provided by the respondents included the following:

- 'Tourism which, whilst developing, does not influence the environment negatively'.
- 'The development of tourism based on the natural environment which does not destroy it at the same time'.
- 'The preservation of the heritage for future generations'.
- 'The development of tourism which takes into consideration the conservation of the natural environment'.

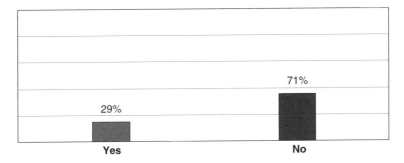

Figure 8.1: Do you know what the concept of sustainable tourism is?

- 'The association of the attraction between the natural environment and the tourist infra-structure (hotels, restaurants and monuments)'.
- 'The use of natural and cultural resources of destinations by tourists and local people at the same time'.

While all these statements contain an element of truth, they are not complete definitions of sustainable tourism, which may indicate that the respondents do not understand the concept fully. What seems to be common among the respondents is a reference to the natural environment. There are also some statements mentioning future generations and the negative influence of tourism, but there are not many references to the social environment of the destination. This may be because the negative environmental impacts of tourism are more visible than the social ones and consequently the respondents were more aware of them. It may also have been caused by the environmental focus of other questions included in this survey.

The research also assessed the respondents' attitudes towards environmental management in relation to tourism. A five-point Likert scale was used for this purpose. The majority of respondents agreed with most of the statements and 75% of respondents agreed that humankind is responsible for the Earth's resources and is obligated to bequeath it to future generations (Figure 8.2).

A quite high percentage of respondents agreed with the statement concerning the link between tourism and the environment and the dependency of successful tourism on the natural environment. Nonetheless, the fact that 58% of the respondents agreed with the statement (Figure 8.3) appears to fully support the assumption of awareness of the relationship but the respondents did not see sustainable approach being implemented in Poland.

Figure 8.4 shows the respondents' beliefs concerning the relationship between the number of visiting tourists and the attractiveness of the place. Almost 83% of respondents agreed with the statement that large numbers of visitors make the destination less attractive. However, people working in the tourism sector have to generate economic benefits for their enterprises and this can only happen when the numbers of tourists are increasing. This dilemma creates potential conflict between the need for tourism development and the need for destination sustainability.

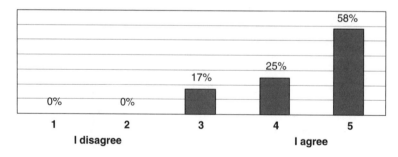

Figure 8.2: Attitudes to sustainability: We manage the natural environment and the resources of this country and we are obligated to bequeath it to the future generations in good condition.

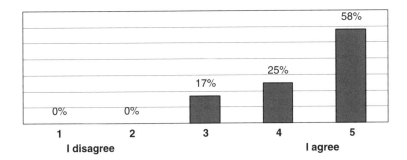

Figure 8.3: Tourism and the environment: Success of tourism and the environment are incontrovertibly linked. Without a clean environment tourism cannot be developed and be sustainable at the same time.

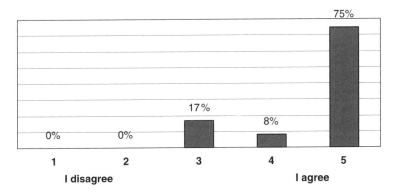

Figure 8.4: Environmental damage: The more attractive the site, the bigger the threat of large number of visitors, who make the site less attractive.

On the other hand, however, around 75% of respondents highlighted the importance of developing such a tourism industry that could be used either now or in the future (Figure 8.5). It is interesting to note, however, that 8% of the respondents used value 2 on the Likert scale, which shows disagreement with this statement, which may indicate that these respondents are primarily oriented towards achieving short-term gains from tourism.

Many respondents also agreed that everyone can protect the environment, for example, through changing their everyday activities (Figure 8.6). However, there was no indication as to what activities could contribute to attaining such a goal.

The respondents agreed to a lesser degree with the statement that the possibility of 'being green' is an achievable goal because it can provide many benefits for their business, their customers and staff and can help preserve the environment (Figure 8.7). This may suggest insufficient understanding of the relationship between the concept of a 'green environment' and the future opportunities and threats for tourism development.

The respondents were also asked whether they would be prepared to develop a sustainable tourism product for which they would charge more but spend part of the income on ecological, social and economic stabilisation. As Figure 8.8 shows, almost 60% of respondents

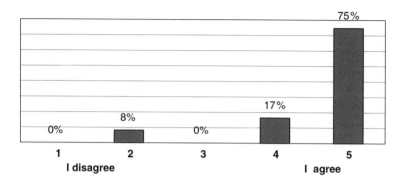

Figure 8.5: Business actions: It is very important for all tourist businesses to encourage such a development of the tourism sector, which can serve the needs of both contemporary and future generations.

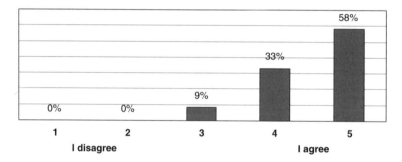

Figure 8.6: Environmental activity: We can all protect the environment, for example, through changing our everyday activities in the firm.

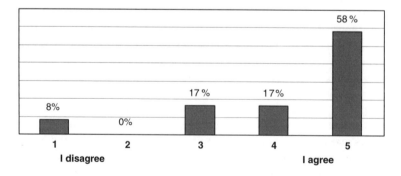

Figure 8.7: Environmental business goals: The possibility of 'being green' is an achievable goal because it can provide many benefits for your business, your customers and personnel and can help to preserve the environment.

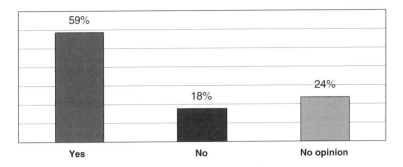

Figure 8.8: Sustainable tourism products: Would you be willing to create a sustainable tourist product, which would be higher in price with part of money being spent on ecological, social and economic stabilisation?

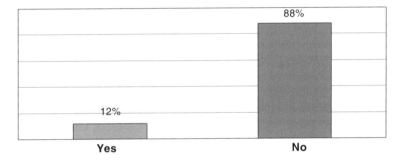

Figure 8.9: The Polish context: In relation to the previous questions, did you see such an approach being adopted in Poland?

are ready to create such new tourism products. However, only 12% have already seen such an approach being adopted in Poland (Figure 8.9).

The data suggests that there is a gap between the respondents' knowledge of sustainability and their attitudes towards sustainable tourism management. Furthermore, the respondents seem to have been oblivious to the signs of sustainable tourism in projects and investments in Pomerania Voivodship.

On the other hand, however, the respondents made interesting suggestions about what could be done in the area of sustainable tourism. Some of the respondents pointed out the necessity for a more active involvement of local communities and other tourism stakeholder representatives. Others, in line with their view of sustainable tourism being closely linked to environmental issues, said that it was necessary to co-operate with environmental protection organisations. There were also voices underlying the necessity of co-operation among various institutions in the process of introducing Agenda 21. Generally, the majority of respondents felt that the focus should be placed upon building bridges between various bodies and facilitating their co-operation for a common aim. Many respondents emphasised the need for an engagement of all interested parties but none of them mentioned that such activities should be initiated by the public sector tourist offices.

Discussion: Knowledge, Tourism Education and Management

The results of the study into the levels of understanding of the concept and practice of sustainable tourism among tourism SMEs in Pomerania Voivodship indicate that most respondents within the sector of tourism SMEs do not possess any knowledge about sustainable tourism or possess only superficial knowledge in this area, mainly oriented towards the issues of protecting the natural environment. They therefore do not seem to understand all dimensions of this concept. For many of them, this research was the first contact with the subject of sustainability. The data also suggests that there is a gap between the respondents' awareness of the issue of sustainability and their attitudes towards sustainable tourism management. It is therefore necessary to change both managers' and employees' attitudes towards managing their organisations so that both sustainability and economic criteria are addressed in their strategies and practices. Although this study established tourism-SMEs opinions concerning the relations between natural environment, its preservation and tourism, more sophisticated research should be conducted with a view to identifying the existing practices aimed at sustainable development and possible activities that tourism SMEs could introduce.

The significant lack of knowledge and understanding of what sustainable tourism is, among the respondents, can be viewed as evidence that sustainability is a relatively new concept and is not very popular among Polish tourism SMEs. This is, however, surprising as there are organisations in Poland that offer direct help and show how to introduce the concept of sustainability into the everyday practice of enterprises.

There are several potential reasons why there is a relatively low level of awareness and knowledge of the issues of sustainability among Polish tourism SMEs. Firstly, there may be insufficient promotion of sustainable tourism development by the Polish public sector bodies. Secondly, there may be a lack of co-ordination and information exchange between all tourism stakeholders (the public sector, NGOs and the private enterprises). Thirdly, the respondents may not monitor current trends in the tourism industry, as there is a range of tourism web pages that contain plenty of information concerning sustainable tourism development. Fourthly, people working in the tourism sector may not be able to implement sustainable approaches because they are often led in their activities by short-term financial considerations or they do not know how to efficiently implement sustainable practices.

Whatever the main reason for such a low level of understanding of the issues of sustainable tourism, awareness campaigns, training and wider access to information about sustainable tourism may be a good starting point in remedying this situation. If well designed, such support programmes may result in tourism SMEs introducing innovative products and practices that take into consideration rules of sustainable development in tourism. Indeed, results of another similar study conducted by Richards (1996, p. 18) indicate that 'raising awareness of sustainable tourism issues among those working in the tourism industry' is seen by the tourism industry as crucial in achieving the goal of sustainable tourism.

While the research conducted among Polish tourism SMEs that operate in Pomerania Voivodship indicates a lack of adequate knowledge in the field of sustainable development, the respondents demonstrated a positive attitude towards the subject and were ready to learn more. The findings clearly suggest that there is a need for greater information and development of knowledge in the area of sustainable tourism among Polish tourism SMEs.

To close the gap between the respondents' awareness of the issue of sustainability and their attitudes towards sustainable tourism management, a new educational approach with a focus on both sustainability and specific management concepts concerning the use of natural, human, social and economic recourses in the tourism production and consumption processes could be developed. Indeed, the above findings suggest that there is room for a new management concept in the SMEs giving priority to sustainable development that can fulfil the needs of current and future generations. Furthermore, as there are indications of respondent's willingness to develop sustainable tourism products, training and the exchange of good practices from other regions or countries could be introduced.

Central to the process of improving the knowledge of the concept of sustainable tourism and practices that support such a development of tourism is appropriate education. A question can be asked, however, whether the existing educational programmes meet the needs of the industry. As part of a recent research programme co-ordinated by Pomeranian Regional Tourism Organisation (PRTO) and led by four Pomeranian higher education institutions that educate students for the tourism sector, namely the Maritime Academy in Gdynia, the Academy of Physical Education and Sport in Gdansk, the Higher School of Tourism and Hotel Management in Gdansk and the Sopot Higher School of Physical Education and Tourism, one of the authors of this chapter (B. Marciszewska) was chairing a project aimed at investigating the quality and vocational value of tourism higher education. A questionnaire has been prepared and a survey carried out by Wojdakowski (2005). Among other issues, the study investigated the level of utilisation of employees' knowledge and skills by middle management. Both managers and employees were asked about the practical utility of the subjects taught during their studies. These findings confirm the value of knowledge of psychology and sociology as factors contributing towards improving staff self-assurance, communication with clients and service quality. The results of the survey show a gap between the content of tourism higher-education programmes and the needs of the tourist industry. Given the results of Wojdakowski's survey and considering the relatively low level of knowledge of issues pertinent to sustainability that was found in the study of Pomeranian tourism SMEs, it can be suggested that people working in the tourism sector are not sufficiently prepared to manage tourism SMEs in an effective, efficient and sustainable manner. To address this problem, it is necessary to adopt a new philosophy in Polish tourism education and management. Indeed, as Cioccarelli, Denicolai, and Francesconi (2005, p. 138) stress, 'a better understanding of local resources and competences leads to the rethinking of strategic and organisational structure of the destination, as well as the exploration/exploitation of information and communication technology; the aim is to support the sharing and the generation of knowledge at the inter-firm level. On the other hand, this perspective can suggest the appropriate approach to the tourism-sustainability problem; in fact, the resources appraisal — such as tangible natural capital, intangible local culture or individual knowledge and experience — can address the design of sustainable policy'.

Conclusions

Taking into account that 'the new market dynamics call [. . .] for more co-operation (e.g. on innovative business models or on human resource skills and competences), amongst

SMEs and other stakeholders' (OECD, 2005, p. 5), it is important to improve knowledge of the issues associated with sustainability among the employees of tourism SMEs. Such knowledge constitutes a pre-requisite for future sustainable tourism development. This is particularly true for new market economies such as Poland where enterprises are driven by short-term gains and the issues of sustainability are not sufficiently appreciated by the tourism industry. Tourism SMEs are constantly in search for new approaches towards rejuvenating tourism products but they need to realise that the quantity and quality of these products depend upon the quality of natural resources that the destinations offer to tourists and the socio-economic development of local communities. In the long term, therefore, the only way for creating new values for tourists is through adopting a sustainable approach to the natural, social and economic environments. The findings of the study into the level of knowledge and understanding of the concept and practice of sustainable tourism presented in this chapter indicate that tourism SMEs that operate in Pomerania Voivodship need to adopt a new management approach; the approach that ensures sustainable tourism development within this region. This, however, requires the appropriate education of existing and future tourism employees. Traditional higher education curricula in the subjects such as tourism and recreation do not stress sufficiently the sustainability issue within the context of its role in both tourism and economic development.

In view of the fact that tourism SMEs in Pomerania Voivodship are not sufficiently aware of the importance of ecological, social and economic threats, they cannot actively participate in creating a sustainable tourism policy. Short-term economic goals often become the leading criterion in the development of their strategies, which can create serious future threats for the tourism industry. Appropriate education seems to be the obvious starting point in enhancing knowledge of sustainability among Pomeranian tourism SMEs. Horizontal co-operation between all stakeholders within the tourism industry, including SMEs, policy makers and higher education institutions, should be seen as another possible way towards ensuring sustainable tourism development in this region. A greater understanding of goals and limitations of tourism SMEs and the environment within which they operate will not only aid in the improvement of this important economic sector, but will also provide benefits for local economies and communities.

References

Bieger, T., Baritelli, P., & Wainert, R. (2004). Do co-operations really pay? Contribution based on strategy process theory for the case of small and medium sized ski area companies. In: P. Keller & T. Bieger–(Eds.), *The future of small and medium-sized enterprises in tourism* (pp. 151–162). St. Gallen, Switzerland: AIEST. .

Bramwell, B., Henry, I., Jackson, G., & Van der Straaten, J. (1996). A framework for understanding sustainable tourism management. In: B. Bramwell, I. Henry, G. Jackson, A. Goytia Prat, G. Richards & J. van der Straaten– (Eds.), *Sustainable tourism management: Principles and practice* (pp. 23–72). Tilburg, The Netherlands: Tilburg University Press.

Cioccarelli, G., Denicolai, S., & Francesconi, A. (2005). Local resource-based sustainable development and tourist core — competences for innovation. In P. Keller & T. Bieger– (Eds.), *Innovation in tourism — Creating customer value* (Vol. 47, pp. 131–141). St. Gallen, Switzerland: AIEST.

Getz, D., Carlsen, J., & Morrison, A. (2004). *The family business in tourism and hospitality.* Wallingford, UK: CABI.

Job, H., Metzler, D., Muller, M., & Mayer, M. (2004). The contribution of tourism SMEs to regional economic development. In: P. Keller & T. Bieger (Eds.), *The future of small and medium-sized enterprises in tourism* (pp. 55–75). St. Gallen, Switzerland: AIEST.

Keller, P. (2004). Introduction: The future of SMEs in tourism. In P. Keller & T. Bieger – (Eds.), *The future of small and medium-sized enterprises in tourism* (pp. 7–21). St. Gallen, Switzerland: AIEST.

Marciszewska, B. (1998). Selected problems of sustainable tourism in Gdansk region. *Journal of European Business Education*, Buckinghamshire Business School. 8(1), 23–31.

Mugler, J. (1997). Strategic management of small and medium-sized businesses in the light of globalization of markets. *Journal of European Business Education*, Buckinghamshire Business School, 7(1), 69–78.

OECD (2005). *Increasing the role of SMEs in the global tourism industry.* In-progress draft report. 9–10 November, CFE/TOU(2005)3, Paris: OECD.

Poon, A. (1993). *Tourism, technology and competitive strategies.* Wallingford, UK: CAB International.

Richards, G. (1996). Sustainable tourism management education: Educational, environmental and industry perspectives. In: B. Bramwell, I. Henry, G. Jackson, A. Goytia Prat, G. Richards & J. Van der Steaaten (Eds.), *Sustainable tourism management: Principles and practice* (pp. 7–22). Tilburg, The Netherlands: Tilburg University Press.

The Institute of Tourism (2005). *Poland. Tourism in figures 2004.* Warsaw: The Institute of Tourism.

Vanhove, N. (2004). Introduction to section 2: SMEs and tourism policy. In: P. Keller & T. Bieger (Eds.), *The future of small and medium-sized enterprises in tourism* (pp. 109–124). St. Gallen, Switzerland: AIEST.

Von Moltke, H. (1996). Foreword. In: B. Bramwell, I. Henry, G. Jackson, A. Goytia Prat, G. Richards & J. Van der Steaaten (Eds.), *Sustainable tourism management: Principles and practice* (p. VII). Tilburg, The Netherlands: Tilburg University Press.

Weaver, D. (2001). Sustainable tourism: Is it sustainable? In: B. Faulkner, G. Moscardo & E. Laws (Eds.), *Tourism in the 21st century. Lessons from experience* (pp. 300–311). London, UK: Continuum.

Wojdakowski, P. (2005). Analiza jakości kształcenia dla turystyki w województwie pomorskim. Ekspertyza wykonana na zlecenie PROT. Gdansk: PROT.

Chapter 9

Developing Rural Tourism in Finland through Entrepreneurship

Raija Komppula

Introduction

Rural tourism typically refers to tourism outside densely-populated areas and tourism centres. In some countries, the term 'farm tourism' (agritourism, agrotourism) is synonymous with rural tourism. Wilderness tourism and forest tourism can, in some contexts, be included in the concept of rural tourism, whereas in some other circumstances these terms can be considered as separate (Hall, 1999, p. 73). In many countries, rural tourism is understood to be more or less synonymous with nature tourism or at least travelling in nature, and the 'framework' for rural tourism is usually offered by national parks and other publicly-owned land areas (Telfer, 2002, p. 135, see also Tyrväinen, Silvennoinen, & Nousiainen, 2002).

This chapter examines the objectives of developing rural tourism from two different perspectives. Firstly, the development of rural tourism is examined in the context of Finnish rural-development policy. According to Siiskonen (2002), rural policy is commonly seen as holistic, extensive development and it is described as coordinative and integrative. There is no established division between rural policy and rural development. Siiskonen (2002, p. 69), however, considers the strengthening of the economic activities and peoples' welfare in rural areas as the most-central objectives of this rural policy. The second perspective in this chapter relates to rural entrepreneurs. These two perspectives are considered because the former seeks to create conditions that influence the behaviour of the latter. By appreciating the dynamics of both aspects, there is greater likelihood of developing effective policy interventions.

The Rural-Development Perspective

Rural tourism is often seen as one significant means of developing livelihoods particularly in areas with negative population growth. It is believed that rural tourism creates new jobs, decreases migration and helps to maintain the local level of services. According to international research, rural tourism also seems to particularly improve the position of women, as the majority of the tourism businesses in farms are family businesses (Garcia-Ramon, Canoves, & Valdovinos, 1995). Equally, tourism has also increased local demand for primary-production businesses, particularly farm products, in rural areas. (Page & Getz, 1997; see also Leader European Observatory, 1996). Rural-development strategy objectives generally aim towards the creation and maintenance of new jobs, the expansion of business activities, the support of public services and the creation of new free-time opportunities for travellers (Sharpley & Sharpley, 1997, p. 117).

The development of rural tourism often specifically involves the economic and social development of a rural area. Rural tourism is a relatively small sector of the tourism industry from a global perspective, yet it still has great significance for local economies at many destinations. When the benefits yielded by tourism are generally examined in an area as gross income and person work years, many economic, social and environmental benefits with wider significance receive less attention. Tourism increases an awareness of, for example, a need for the preservation and development of local culture and can strengthen the local cultural identity. Many services, which also benefit the local population, stay alive with the help of tourism. The success of rural tourism is dependent on an attractive environment, which is why tourism often enhances the protection of nature and culture (Sharpley & Sharpley, 1997, pp. 40–41).

The rural-support programmes targeted inside and also outside the European Union have generated not only large-scale national, but also local rural-tourism development programmes (Telfer, 2002, pp. 136–137, see also e.g. Koscak, 1998). According to Clarke, Denman, Hickman, and Slovak (2001), the development of rural tourism is most successful when it is based on national strategy and co-ordination and strategy with local commitment and local actors (Clarke et al., 2001, p. 201). The success of tourism-development plans is dependent on both the administration's ability to support-development projects and the entrepreneurs' desire and ability to commit themselves to the development plans (Komppula, 2000).

According to Telfer (2002), the developers of rural tourism should also take into account the negative effects of its growth. These negative effects are related to, for example, ecological, cultural and social sustainability and capacity. One central question, according to Telfer, is who ultimately benefits from the growth of rural tourism, is it only a small local-elite group or can a rural-area gain influences that benefit the entire community through the growth of rural tourism (Telfer, 2002, pp. 146–147)? There may also be conflict over areas whose the national tourism and recreation value is high, but for whose resources the local population may have other simultaneous needs, for example in reindeer husbandry, forestry, other agriculture or industry (see e.g. Nilsson, 2000).

The Rural Policy Committee in Finland has been founded by the government and is appointed by the Ministry of the Interior. This committee's task is to harmonise rural-development measures and to enhance the efficient use of resources targeted for rural areas. This committee has appointed a theme group on rural tourism in order to promote an overall development of rural tourism. After its first term, the committee apparently proved its necessity and will continue its term at least until the end of 2005 (http://www.mmm.fi/maasmatk/enggroup.htm, Nylander & Martikainen, 2003, p.3, Maaseutumatkailun teemaryhmä, 1996, Maaseutupolitiikan yhteistyöryhmä, Maaseutumatkailun teemaryhmä, 2000).

The first tasks of the Theme Group on Rural Tourism were ambitious: to draft a long-term rural-tourism strategy and action programme, to compile basic information on rural tourism, to help compile the sections relevant to rural tourism for a national rural-development plan and the EU programmes, to start national-development projects on rural tourism, to develop a national booking system for rural-tourism products in co-operation with local organisations and to expand the marketing of rural tourism. A significant challenge for their second term is to consider how to proceed in the development of rural tourism after the first term of structural funding (http://www.mmm.fi/maasmatk/enggroup.htm, Nylander & Martikainen, 2003, p. 3).

The development programme of the Theme Group on Rural Tourism mentions, for example, family and small businesses, local- and independent-development works and collaboration within the field as its strengths. Its weaknesses include, for example, a lack of efficient and long-term marketing, earlier investments in buildings, poor profitability, the mixed level of services and production-based service culture. The increasing demand caused by urbanisation, the peace and quiet and space in the countryside have been seen as opportunities, and the diminishment of the countryside as a threat (http://www.mmm.fi/maasmatk/kokonaisohjelma.htm). According to Martikainen (2001), the most-central problems in the rural-tourism business are the small size of the businesses and the subsequent amateurish approach towards entrepreneurship. There are also seen to be shortcomings in the professional competence of the leaders of the development programmes of rural tourism (Martikainen, 2001).

According to the vision of the theme group, rural tourism in 2007 will be an essential and solid part of tourism and rural areas in Finland as a source of livelihood, employment and cultural advocacy: 'The financially successful continuously developing networks of family and small businesses produce tourism services for all four seasons by making the most of the intrinsic resources offered by the countryside for domestic and foreign customers who demand high-quality experiences and respect the principles of sustainable development'. The theme group emphasises that rural tourism is not a unified line of business, but the services that it offers can be divided, like other tourism services, into catering, accommodation, programme and additional services. According to the theme group, the most-important underlying values when developing rural tourism are: responsibility towards the environment, health and a high appreciation of the cultural heritage of the countryside (www.mmm.fi/maasmatk/kokonaisohjelma.htm).

The quantitative objectives for developing rural tourism by 2007 is to achieve at least a 50% utilisation rate for accommodation, to increase the yearly turnover in the field to over two billion FM (app. 335 million) and to provide employment equal to about 6000 person work years. With the current utilisation rate of the whole capacity this means a growth of about 8% annually, for the turnover and employment about 30% per annum. These growth objectives are based mainly on the growth of turnover in existing businesses.

The focal strategic points in order to reach these goals will be placed on the enhancement of product-development work and marketing, the development of the quality-control system, an increase in know-how and the targeting of public funding towards these areas of emphasis (www.mmm.fi/maasmatk/kokonaisohjelma.htm).

The public funding, targeted at the development of rural tourism, is mainly channelled through the rural sections of the Employment and Economic Development Centres, which means that the development projects are mainly local or regional. There have been some cross-regional projects, for example, the *Aavan meren tällä puolen* — joint marketing project (see http://www.matkamaalle.com/ajank/lomalaid2.html). According to Martikainen (2001), local and regional decision-making leads an undermining of national objectives due to an inefficient and fragmented support policy.

There are plenty of actors to develop rural tourism. If rural tourism is understood to be part of the tourism product, the Finnish tourism policy guidelines should also obviously be applied in the development projects related to rural tourism. The Ministry of Trade and Industry bears the main responsibility for the tourism policy. Regional policy, which is ruled by the Ministry of the Interior, affects the development of tourism on regional development. According to the guidelines of the rural-policy programme of the Ministry of Agriculture and Forestry, the opportunities from tourism for the development of rural areas are enhanced by the promotion of rural, village and nature tourism based on small businesses and network co-operation.

According to the tourism policy guidelines of Finland, the objective is to use the public funding targeted at tourism as efficiently as possible. The funding decisions should primarily concentrate on improving the supply of services in the existing tourism destinations and on the development of the business activities of tourism. When supporting new activities, special attention should be paid to developing tourism services that are innovative and create new demand. The funding should primarily support specialisation in certain products, the creation of top products and themes, the development of tourism services in off-peak seasons, hub-firms and the networks supporting these theme-based development activities, stronger and versified tourism conglomerations and the development of products based on the greater area concept that aims at foreign marketing (www.ktm.fi/print_page.phtml?menu_id=63&lang=1&chapter_id=5515).

The Rural-Tourism Entrepreneur's Perspective

Rural-tourism businesses in Finland can be divided into three groups: basic production farms, diversified farms and other rural businesses, which are small rural (non-farming) businesses. Farming is the most-important rural livelihood. In 2000, there were 79,800 farms in Finland of which 27%, that is 21,838, were diversified farms (Niemi & Ahlstedt, 2002, pp. 14–15). According to the small-enterprise register of rural areas, 3.8% of the farms (3032) offer tourism services. In Sweden, the corresponding figure is 0.6% (Gössling & Mattsson, 2002, p. 29 www.mtt.fi/mttl/liik/yristysrekisteri/matkailu1.html).

Altogether, 1753 businesses leased holiday cottages, 509 businesses offered other accommodation, 330 provided restaurant and café services, 471 offered catering or other food services and 963 gave programme services. It is difficult to estimate the number of rural businesses outside agriculture, because some of the small businesses registered in the business register (turnover more than 8400, but employ less than 20 people) operate in connection with a farm (Niemi & Ahlstedt, 2002, p. 16). In other words, they are registered as both businesses and farms in different statistics. In the small-enterprise register of the rural areas, there were a total of 3248 businesses that offered tourism and recreation services in the whole country in 2000. These employed a total of 5736 persons work years and their turnover adjusted according to the wholesale price index was a total of 410 million (www.mtt.fi/mttl/liik/yritysrekisteri/matkailul.html). In the capacity report of the Theme Group on Rural Tourism, it was estimated that there are 3600 rural-tourism businesses (Markkola, 2003a,b).

The start of other business activities is often timed with the change of generation on farms. In a large number of farms, agriculture and other business activities complement each other, and the plan is to continue such diversified activities in the future. On the other hand, on some of the farms, diversification is considered a transitional stage either from agriculture to other business activities or there may be a return back to agriculture after an experimental stage (Niemi & Ahlstedt, 2002, p. 15). The most-important reasons for diversification are the balancing of the annual income, creating extra income and growth by distributing the risks to several lines of business (Rantamäki-Lahtinen, 2002).

According to a report on the accommodation capacity of rural areas, published by the Theme Group on Rural Tourism, the average age of the entrepreneurs is 50.5 years. Only one-quarter of the entrepreneurs know who will continue their business. Approximately 69% of the businesses operate round the year, but only one-quarter considers tourism as their main form of livelihood. Each enterprise employs approximately 1.5 person work years. The turnover of 44% of the businesses is under the limit of VAT (8400) and only 12% of the businesses have a turnover of over 84,000. Half of the businesses have some kind of a quality-control tool at their disposal. (Markkola, 2003a). According to Puurunen (2001), the profitability of the businesses in the field is, in general, poor.

The occupancy rate of accommodation services varies considerably according to seasons: in summer, it is over 50% but during other seasons under 15% (Markkola, 2003b). In 2000, the average-utilisation rate for beds was 17% and of accommodation facilities it was an average of 25% (Martikainen, 2001, p. 21). Ninety per cent of the businesses offer accommodation services, 58% food and two-thirds also offer different types of programme services. The year round accommodation capacity in an enterprise is about 16 beds; it can be estimated that there are approximately 42,000 beds in total in the whole country within rural tourism (http://www.mmm.fi/maasmatk/enggroup.htm). Rural-tourism entrepreneurship, hence, typically consists of micro-businesses, family businesses, businesses run by couples and often also portfolio entrepreneurs.

Tourism entrepreneurship is often called 'opportunity entrepreneurship'. On farms, tourism activities may start, for example, in such a way that the owners want to preserve empty buildings and other facilities for posterity. By using the old buildings and yards for their own benefit, the funds used for their renovation can at least be partly recovered (Gössling & Mattsson, 2002). In Eastern Finland, many businesses offering rural-cottage accommodation have come about without any plan; perhaps when the farmer has built a cottage primarily for family use, using wood from the forest acquired after the winter's cuttings.

In the countryside, agriculture and forestry create a positive general attitude towards entrepreneurship. The desire to not leave the area encourages people to find alternatives to wage labour, which may not be available in the neighbouring municipalities, either. The tradition of independent work creates a general-positive attitude towards one's own entrepreneurship, even though the image of an entrepreneur's work reflects the work done by an agricultural entrepreneur (Niittykangas, 1999, p. 124, see also Virtanen, 2000). A suitable opportunity to start activities, earn extra income, the challenge offered by tourism industry and the independence of an entrepreneur's work are the most-important reasons to become an entrepreneur, according to a study on rural-tourism entrepreneurship in North Karelia (Lassila, 2003).

Indeed, according to studies conducted by Komppula (2000, 2002, 2004) and Lassila (2000a,b, 2003), rural-tourism entrepreneurship at its most typical is lifestyle entrepreneurship, where the entrepreneurial objective is to guarantee the family a reasonable income, to keep the family and extended family's farms and buildings inhabited. The growth of the enterprise is most-commonly understood to mean the growth of the capacity or number of the work force. The objective is not to expand the enterprise so greatly that a full-time labour force outside the family is needed. Profit on the invested capital and turnover are, of course, aimed at, but only within the previously mentioned limits. In a study by Komppula (2002), it was apparent that growth is particularly aimed at in relation to quality: customer welfare, loyal customer relations and close contact with the customers are the most-important meters of success. Therefore, the success of a company is measured with meters related to quality of life rather than economic factors. The results obtained by Komppula and Lassila are parallel to those found in international rural-tourism research (see. Ateljevic & Doome, 2000; Busby & Rendle, 2000; Carlsen & Getz, 2000; Clarke et al., 2001; Dewhurst & Horobin, 1998; Getz & Carlsen, 2000; Grolleau, 1996; Hall & Rusher, 2002; King, Bransgrove, & Whitelaw, 1998; Lynch, 1998; Morrison, Rimmington, & Williams, 1999; Thomas, 2000; Walker, 2000). Juutilainen's study (2001) on the strategy and success of small family-owned hotels also obtained similar results.

Hence, from the entrepreneur's point of view, the development of rural tourism means, in general, the development of one's own enterprise, particularly the technical, functional and interactive quality of the product. The entrepreneurs are also involved in local- and regional-development projects, or those related to some theme through different projects. There are also numerous educational and training projects available for the entrepreneurs, but they are not always convinced of the effectiveness of training in the development of an enterprise; they rather expect concrete measures, such as product development, networking, market development and, in particular, the creation of sales (Komppula, 2000, 2002, 2004).

Development of the Rural Area or Rural Tourism?

The perspectives of the development of rural areas and tourism business are, at least to some extent, clearly contradictory in the development of rural tourism. Support for the diversification of farms encourages part-time small-scale tourism entrepreneurship, whereas the development guidelines for tourism aim at the growth and development of existing businesses, particularly in tourism centres. If the business operates on a part-time basis, this does not necessarily mean that its operations would not be professional, but often it does mean, unfortunately, that there is no time, money and skills left over from the other forms of livelihoods for the professional development of the tourism business. From the point of view of the entrepreneur, income derived from many lines of business certainly diminishes the economic risks, but at the same time it disperses the scarce resources.

The growth objectives regarding this line of business of the Theme Group on Rural Tourism, therefore, seem overly optimistic compared against the general-development trends of the tourism business in Finland, or the study on rural-tourism entrepreneurship. The average-occupancy rate of hotel rooms in Finland has remained slightly under 50% for the past five years (Statistics Finland, 2002), and considering that particularly in towns and in winter occupancy is raised by business travel, the objective of the Theme Group to raise the utilisation rate of the accommodation capacity to over 50% in a couple of years seems idealistic.

When the growth objectives of companies are moderate but the national employment and turnover objectives high, it may be asked if the national growth objectives mean that more new businesses are being encouraged to be founded in addition to the existing ones, even though the utilisation rates of the old businesses are extremely low, and the companies' wish to employ staff outside the family is very limited.

Owing to development measures in rural areas, new tourism businesses that are small and operate on a part-time basis are continuously emerging in the tourism industry, though their location does not always correspond to the market expectations. Accommodation services are, in many cases, developed at incorrect locations: where there is land and wood available, people may build in locations with no demand for accommodation. The development of rural tourism is frequently scattered, small-scale and unplanned. Anecdotally, there are plenty of development projects, the professional know-how of project leaders within tourism is often lacking and the objectives are local short-term objectives. The perspective of development of rural areas represents in many areas, in marketing terms, a production-oriented way of thinking. The attention is focused on the resources of the service provider with no consideration on the demand and the customers' needs.

Despite the previously described criticism, it must be stated that the development of rural tourism, even if implemented from the point of view of the development of the rural area, may be in harmony with the guidelines of the tourism policy. The development measures of the rural policy regarding rural tourism are mainly implemented by the rural departments of the Employment and Economic Development Centres and there are great regional differences between their respective operations and customs. Therefore, the central question is how the different parties see rural tourism in relation to other forms of tourism, and how they define rural tourism overall. In such areas where the prerequisites of actual agriculture are good, rural tourism and particularly co-operation between tourism businesses have developed slowly. In regions where the traditional agriculture has no more operational preconditions, it has been necessary to invest towards a more professional approach in the development of other sources of livelihood, such as tourism business. In the faster developed rural-tourism areas, both the developers of the regional policy and tourism feel that rural tourism is part of other tourism industry. Therefore, there is no contradiction between the development of the rural area and tourism.

Rural-tourism policy emphasises the significance of larger geographic tourism regions in foreign marketing, the creation of tourism centres, supporting the hub-firms and networks, specialisation and theme or activity-based products. The Employment and Economic Development Centres and also partly the Regional Councils implement the national tourism policy at the regional level. Owing to this, the development projects are usually based on administrative and geographical region. National-level projects or projects concerning several regions, have been extremely hard to be financed or implemented.

Harmonising the Perspectives?

Based on the results of several studies conducted among rural tourists in Finland, it is seen that customers value the traditional country scenery, a living countryside, nature, opportunities for activities, easy accessibility and personal service. The entrepreneurs, for their part, aim to keep their units fairly small, emphasising personal service, offering services near nature, and emphasising the rural lifestyle. The entrepreneurs' willingness to maintain a small firm size hence seems to support the fulfilment of the wishes of the customers.

The main emphasis in the development of rural areas is in a location. In policy terms, the region and the strengthening of its economic activity and the welfare of the people in the countryside is the main focus instead of being on the customer and his or her needs. The development is based on existing 'productive' resources in each location. If these conditions lack an innate appeal for tourists, for example a lake, which is fundamental for a Finnish tourist, lots of resources would have to be invested in order to create compensatory appeal. If enough attention is not put into considering which tourism segments and what kinds of customer needs could be served within the framework of the existing resources, the investments in rural-tourism development may have minor-economical effects.

The integration of rural tourism as a part of the regional tourism businesses requires an active and professional organisation to act as the co-ordinator of the development, long-term planning and, in particular, commitment to a development strategy, including most-central financiers. Seamless co-operation and division of labour with this organisation and the local tourism organisation will secure the development of rural tourism as part of the overall offering of an area. At best, organisations could be nested within each other, where the use of resources could be optimal. Marketing would then focus on the service entities offered by the area based on the customer's travelling motives, and not based on the regional boundaries or location of villages.

Customer-oriented development orientation requires tight co-operation amongst the developers and researchers of rural tourism. A national survey that predicts the quality and amount of tourism demand would serve all forms of tourism, not only rural tourism. It would also be interesting to examine amongst regional financier and development parties how significantly the guidelines of the tourism policy, the national strategy on rural tourism and the results of tourism studies steer the planning and decisions of financiers and developers.

References

Ateljevic, I., & Doome, S. (2000). Staying within the fence: Lifestyle entrepreneurship in tourism. *Journal of Sustainable Tourism, 8*(5), 378–392.

Busby, G., & Rendle, S. (2000). The transition from tourism on farms to farm tourism. *Tourism Management, 21*(2000), 635–642.

Carlsen, J., & Getz, D. (2000). *Relatively speaking: Business goals and operating issues for rural, family owned/operated tourism and hospitality businesses.* (pp. 1–20). Paper presented at ICSB Brisbane, Queensland, June 2000.

Clarke, J., Denman, R., Hickman, G., & Slovak, J. (2001). Rural tourism in Roznava Okres: A Slovak case study. *Tourism Management, 22*, 193–202.

Dewhurst, P., & Horobin, H. (1998). Small business owners. In: R. Thomas (Ed.), *The management of small tourism and hospitality firms* (pp. 19–38). London: Cassells.

Garcia-Ramon, M. D., Canoves, G., & Valdovinos, N. (1995). Farm tourism, gender and the environment in Spain. *Annals of Tourism Research, 22*(2), 267–282.

Getz, D., & Carlsen, J. (2000). Characteristics and goals of family and owner-operated businesses in the rural tourism and hospitality sectors. *Tourism Management, 21*(2000), 547–560.

Grolleau, H. (1996). Putting feelings first. In: Marketing quality rural tourism: The experience of LEADER I. Bruxelles: LEADER European Observatory.

Gössling, S., & Mattsson, S. (2002). Farm tourism in Sweden: Stucture, growth and characteristics. *Scandinavian Journal of Hospitality and Tourism, 2*(1), 17–30.

Hall, D. (1999). Rural, wilderness and forest tourism: Markets, products and management. In E. Arola & T. Mikkonen (Eds.), Tourism industry and education symposium Jyväskylä, Finland: Symposium proceedings. Reports from the Jyväskylä Polytechnic, 5. Jyväskylä, pp. 69–85.

Hall, M. C., & Rusher, K. (2002). A risky business? Entrepreneurial and lifestyle dimensions of the homestay and bed and breakfast accommodation sector in New Zealand. In:E. Arola, J. Kärkkäinen, & M.-L. Siitari (Eds.), *Tourism and well-being* (pp. 197–210). The 2nd tourism industry and education symposium May 16–18, 2002, Jyväskylä, Finland.

Juutilainen, A. (2001). Entrepreneurs' perceptions of strategy and success in small firms of the tourism and hospitality industry. Licentiate Thesis: University of Lappeenranta (unpublished data).

King, B. E. M., Bransgrove, C., & Whitelaw, P. (1998). Profiling the strategic marketing activities of small tourism businesses. *Journal of Travel & Tourism Marketing, 7*(4), 45–59.

Komppula, R. (2000). Matkailuyrityksen sitoutuminen verkostoon — tapaustutkimus Pohjois-Karjalan maakunnallinen matkailuverkosto. Acta Universitatas Lapponiensis 30. University of Lapland.

Komppula, R. (2002). Definitions of growth and success — Case studies in finnish rural tourism industry. 12th Nordic Conference on Small Business Research. Creating Welfare and Prosperity Through Entrepreneurship. Kuopio, May 26–28. 2002. CD-ROM proceedings.

Komppula, R. (2004). Success and growth in rural tourism micro-businesses in Finland: Financial or life-style objectives. In Thomas, R. (Ed.), *Small firms in tourism: International Perspectives* (pp. 115–138). Boston: Elsevier Ltd.

Koscak, M. (1998). Integral development of rural areas, tourism and village renovation, Trebnje, Slovenia. *Tourism Management, 19*(1), 81–86.

Lassila, H. (2000a). Factors affecting the success in rural tourism businesses. A case study. Paper presented in the Finnish National Symposium in Tourism Research, May 2000, Rovaniemi (unpublished data).

Lassila, H. (2000b). Problems in developing tourism entrepreneurship in a rural region: A case study. In M. Robinson et al. (Eds.), *Developments in urban and rural tourism.* Gateshead, UK: Atheneum Press.

Lassila, H. (2003). Maaseutumatkailuyrittäjyys Itä-Suomessa. Pohjois-Savon ammattikorkeakoulun julkaisu A4: 2003. Savon kopiokeskus Oy, Kuopio.

Leader European Observatory (1996). Marketing quality rural tourism: The experience of LEADER I (2nd edn). Bruxelles.

Lynch, P. (1998). Female micro-entrepreneurs in the host family sector: Key motivations and socio-economic variables. *Journal of Hospitality Management, 17*, 319–342.

Maaseutumatkailun teemaryhmä (1996). Suomen maaseutumatkailun kehittäminen; suuntaviivat vuoteen 2005. Helsinki.

Maaseutupolitiikan yhteistyöryhmä, Maaseutumatkailun teemaryhmä (2000). Maaseutumatkailu. Strategia ja kehittämisohjelma vuoteen 2007. 4/2000 (julkaisematon).

Maaseutupolitiikan yhteistyöryhmä, Maaseutumatkailun teemaryhmä (2003). Selvitys maaseudun matkailukapasiteetista 2002. Pohjois-Karjalan, Kainuun ja Pohjois-Savon erillisraportit.

Markkola, S. (2003a). Selvitys maaseudun matkailukapasiteetista vuonna 2002. MaaseutuMatkailu kevät, 2003, 6–9.

Markkola, S. (2003b). Maaseutumatkailun majoitustilojen käyttöasteet 2002. MaaseutuMatkailu kevät 2003, 10–13.

Martikainen, R. (2001). Maaseutumatkailu. Toimialaraportti 2001. Toimiala infomedia. KTM:n ja TE-keskusten julkaisu.

Morrison, A., Rimmington, M., & Williams, C. (1999). Entrepreneurship in the hospitality, tourism and leisure industries. Bath: Butterworth-Heinemann.

Niemi, J., & Ahlstedt, J. (Eds.) (2002). Suomen maatalous ja maaseutuelinkeinot 2002. Maa- ja elin-tarviketalouden tutkimuskeskus. MTT Taloustutkimus MTTL Julkaisuja 101. Agrifood Research Finland Economic Research. Publications 101.

Niittykangas, H. (1999). Väestön piirteet ja yrittäminen. In H. Niittykangas (Eds.), *Yrittäjyys ja maaseutu* (pp. 112–127). Kuopion yliopiston selvityksiä E. Yhteiskuntatieteet 9. Kuopion yliopisto. Kuopio.

Nilsson, P. Å. (2000). Tourism's role in new rural policy for peripheral areas: The case of Arjeplog. In F. Brown & D. Hall (Eds.), *Tourism in peripheral areas* (pp. 133–151). Aspects of Tourism 2. Clevedon: Channel view publications.

Nylander, M., & Martikainen, R. (2003). Maaseutumatkailun teemaryhmä jatkaa työtään. Toimeksianto vuodelle 2003–2005. MaaseutuMatkailu, Kevät 2003, 3.

Page, S., & Getz, D. (1997). The business of rural tourism: International perspectives. London, UK: International Thomson Business Press.

Puurunen, J. A. (2001). Majoitus- ja ateriapalveluja tarjoavien päätoimisten maaseutumatkailuyritysten kannattavuus. Agricultural Economics Research Institute, Finland. Working Papers 2/2001. Helsinki.

Rantamäki-Lahtinen, L. (2002). On-farm diversification from the management perspective. CD-proceedings of 12th Nordic Conference on Small Business Research. Creating Welfare and Prosperity through Entrepreneurship (pp. 1–14). Kuopio Finland May 26–28, 2002.

Sharpley, R., & Sharpely, J. (1997). Rural tourism. An introduction. Oxford, UK: International Thomson Business Press.

Siiskonen, P. (2002). Maaseutupolitiikka ja maaseututkimus etsivät oikeutettua asemaansa. Maaseututkijatapaaminen 22.-23.8.2002 Vaasassa. Maaseudun uusi aika 2/2002, 68–70.

Statistics Finland (2002). Tourism statistics 2002. Statistics Finland,. SVT. Transport and Tourism 2002:10. Helsinki 2002.

Telfer, D. (2002). Tourism and regional development issues. In R. Sharpley & D. J. Telfer (Eds.). *Tourism and development*. Concepts and issues. Channel view publications, Aspects of Tourism 5, pp. 112–148.

Thomas, R. (2000). Small Firms in the tourism industry: Some conceptual issues. *International Journal of Tourism Research, 2*, 345–353.

Tyrväinen, L., Silvennoinen, H., & Nousiainen, I. (2002). Luontomatkailusta yritystoimintaa. Loppuraportti 31.5.2002. Joensuun yliopiston metsätieteellinen tiedekunta.
Virtanen, J. (2000). Maaseutumatkailuyrittäjäksi ryhtyminen. Turun kauppakorkeakoulun julkaisuja. Sarja C-1: 2000.
Walker, E. (2000). An empirical study of measures of success in micro businesses. (pp. 1–14). Paper presented at ICSB Brisbane, Queensland. June 2000.

Internet References

www.mtt.fi/mttl/liik/yritysrekisteri/matkailu1.html
www.mmm.fi/maasmatk/kokonaisohjelma.htm
www.ktm.fi/chapter_files/vn_periaatepaatos.htm
www.ktm.fi/print_page.phtml?menu_id=63&lang=1&chapter_id=5515
http://www.matkamaalle.com/ajank/lomalaid2.html
http://gis.joensuu.fi/research/matkailu/yr-ma-ka.htm
http://www.mmm.fi/maasmatk/enggroup.htm

Chapter 10

Linking Rural Heritage and Traditions with Tourism SMEs in Slovenia

Sonja Sibila Lebe

Introduction

In the first part of this chapter, Slovenia and its SME sector will be presented to the reader, and the consistence of its SME policy with the directives of the DG Enterprise will be discussed. The main expectations of the SME sector will be explained. The problems of the post-communist economies will be shown, including the lack of family firms in the tourism and hospitality sectors.

Slovenia is one of the countries to have joined the European Union (EU) in May 2004. It reached the Maastricht convergence criteria by December 2005 and is going to introduce the Euro as its currency in January 2007. Slovenia's GDP is comparable with Portugal, Greece and Spain. It is often described as the most-successful newcomer out of the Central- and Eastern European countries to the EU (Dun and Bradstreet's country ratings since 1995, http://www.dnb.co.in/RMSolution.htm).

Today, SMEs in Slovenia are considered as the source of good ideas, as being extremely flexible and adjustable to new circumstances on the market, and as being the source of many innovations launched on the market. Yet, several potential problems relating to SME development are apparent: low knowledge and skill levels of entrepreneurs, lack of advantageous financing possibilities and limited possibilities for human resource development. Currently, entrepreneurship tends to be seen as the best solution for bridging the gap between science and the market (Antoncic et al., 2002) and bringing benefits in the form of employment and GDP growth to the region.

The European tourism industry is an SME-dominated sector, with over 99% of firms having fewer than 250 employees, and about 94% employing fewer than ten persons. On average, European tourism SMEs provide jobs for six employees (micro-enterprises). There are several SMEs without any employees, as officially only the owners work there (some kind of legal grey economy: part-time employment of students to avoid paying social services for them).

They significantly contribute to individual countries' GDP. On average, 6.5% of the total turnover generated by SMEs in Europe (http://europa.eu.int/comm/enterprise/services/tourism/index_en.htm) is sustained by tourism SMEs.

Small businesses are a traditional form of entrepreneurship in rural areas of the EU-19 countries (i.e. EU members prior to the accession of the additional ten countries in 2004, plus four Eastern European members of the OECD, namely Czech republic, Hungary, Poland and the Slovak republic) and play a major role in providing jobs for the local population. SMEs dominate rural communities in the USA as well, and are vital to its economic prosperity (Shields, 2005). This allows us to conclude that establishment of SMEs proves to be the most-appropriate way of bringing development into a country's rural areas in economically medium- and well-developed countries.

After becoming independent in 1990 and having changed its political order, a market-based economy could be introduced in Slovenia and measures for the development of SMEs. In only 15 years, the number of SMEs per 100 inhabitants can now be compared to the average of the EU. What cannot be compared is the economic efficiency, which is lagging considerably behind traditional European market economies, as is demonstrated later in the chapter.

Statistics for 2004 show that within Slovene tourism firms the micro-enterprises prevail (93.5%) followed by small (5%), medium (1.2%) and large (0.3%) enterprises. Value-added per employee in micro-enterprises reached only half of that in the EU-19 and is still lower in large enterprises: it reaches the level of only 1:4 (Dekleva, 2005; Hocevar, 2005).

Tourism as a labour-intensive sector is an important source of employment but only competitive businesses are able to grow and create additional employment (http://europa.eu.int/comm/enterprise/). Therefore, the enterprise policy at European and state levels should assure conditions of competitiveness. In order to address the competitiveness of SMEs, Slovenia has adopted its national development programmes for the SME sector according to EU guidelines (http://europa.eu.int/comm/enterprise/services/tourism/tourism_forum/documents/2005/summary_report.pdf). To be able to measure the progress of entrepreneurship growth in Slovenia, a conference is organised each year where Slovene entrepreneurs and academicians discuss possible ways of further improvement of the sector; it is embedded in the Global Entrepreneurship Monitoring (GEM) research (http://www.gemconsortium.org).

There are neither specific measures nor any additional incentives for the SME sector in the field of tourism. This means that tourism SMEs have to search for their competitive advantages and competitiveness individually. In this chapter, we limit the discussion on these topics to just rural areas.

The Communist Past and Its Consequences

Almost all tourism enterprises in well-known European traditional tourism countries are family or micro-businesses: in Switzerland 99% of enterprises employ less than 250 employees, and out-of-tourism SMEs only 1% employs more than 250 people (figure for Austria: 0,1%) (Kohl, 2002). Family SMEs can be considered as proof that small- and medium-sized businesses have a much better chance of being successful if their business is based on tradition (Frehse, 2001). The latter is missing thoroughly in former communist countries, because over a period of about half a century any kind of self-initiative, often based on innovation (i.e. considered in all market economies as the most valuable outcome of entrepreneurship), was systematically hindered or even forbidden.

In post-communist countries, entrepreneurship was a new lesson to be learned after the breakdown of the system in Europe. In some countries, such as the former Soviet Union republics of Georgia or Moldova, where entrepreneurship has been slow to develop, unemployment has been high (http://europa.eu.int/comm/enterprise/), whereas in other countries with a lively small-business sector (e.g. Czech Republic, Hungary and Slovenia) this percentage has been considerably lower, and was so even during the period when collapsing national-industry giants were on their downfall.

The breakdown of the communist system has forced the Central- and Eastern-European countries into a complete economic re-orientation and re-organisation of national economies. The service sector was getting more and more important, and in new development plans, tourism was proclaimed one of the key economic sectors. The main expectations concerning tourism have changed compared to the communist era: its main task is now not primarily to deliver foreign currency, but provide new jobs; and in rural areas its development belongs to measures that should prevent further depopulation.

Development of Entrepreneurship in Slovenia

Attention now turns to a description of the development of SMEs in Slovenia since 2000 and to a comparison of the SME sector in Slovenia with the situation in the EU-19 and in other GEM countries. Key problems are exposed, such as a very low level of value-added, low productivity and the absence of risk capital. The final part of this chapter examines the situation in rural areas, where additional economic challenges exist for tourism enterprises.

In 1988, the first private enterprise was established in Slovenia. One year later, there were 35,000 active private enterprises (Turk, 2000); and by the mid-1990s, entrepreneurship as well as tourism, were considered as two key development factors in Slovenia. A special ministry for small businesses and tourism has now been established in order to support development.

Several state-aid programmes have been launched (http://www.mg-rs.si/); all of which conform to the EU programmes of the DG Enterprise. Examples include incentives for women entrepreneurs and youth, education programmes for the long-term unemployed and subsidised voucher-consulting systems. No systematic measures for SMEs in tourism have been launched. Moreover, since 2000, no extra research has been done to investigate the state of tourism SMEs, though the hospitality sector is mentioned separately in all GEM publications concerning Slovenia.

In terms of productivity, the relative value-added per employee in Slovene SMEs differs considerably between economic sectors. A level high above the average was obtained by electricity, water and gas suppliers (194.3%), followed by military services, social security, traffic and financial mediators (by 124.5%). Beneath the Slovene average other personal services (99%) can be found, and below this there are agriculture and hunting (76.7%), civil engineering (64%), education (65.7%) and hospitality (64%). Worse results (61.4) have been obtained only by fishery, but this sector forms only a marginal part of Slovene economy.

In 2003 the average labour costs per employee were around 3.4 million Slovene Tolars (about 14,240). The average has been surpassed by the mining sector (approximately 22,500), public sector and social security sector (approximately 22,430), followed by financial mediators. Beneath the average, we can find hospitality at the lowest point, with around 10 thousand Euros, followed by education and civil engineering (around 11,300), agriculture (around 13,160) and trade (Rebernik et al., 2004).

Hospitality is thus at the bottom of the productivity sector of the Slovene economy (which is normal for a sector with a very intense labour engagement), and at the same time at the bottom of the average labour costs, which can partly explain a very high fluctuation of personnel. To save labour costs, less-skilled persons are often employed in hospitality SMEs, and this has a negative impact on service quality and on the ability of acting innovatively. The innovation process does not function satisfactorily; a lack of staff and funding prevents the setting aside of funds for research and development, which is common for all European tourism SMEs. There are no patents that would compensate for the cost of innovation by providing monopoly profits. The reason seems to be the same all over the world: tourism SMEs are predominately concerned with their day-to-day needs (Keller, 2004).

According to GEM reports, in 2000, 99.7% of Slovene enterprises were SMEs and they gave employment to 65.9% of all employees in Slovenia (66.4% in EU-19). The dispersion of SMEs into micro-, small- and medium-sized enterprises was comparable between the EU-19 and Slovenia, as well as the share of labour costs in value-added, relative-employment share, number of employees per enterprise and the relative share of enterprises. Significant differences appear when comparing the turnover per enterprise with Slovenia having half of the EU average.

Typically, Slovene enterprises in 2001 had 63% of its labour costs in value-added. Below this average, mainly micro-enterprises with one to nine employees (16%) could be found, and above this there were large-sized (65%), medium-sized (73%) and small enterprises (66%). In 2001, there were around 100,000 enterprises registered in Slovenia, with an average of six employees per enterprise (same as the EU-19). The labour productivity reached in Slovenia was 88% and in the EU-19 it was 78%. (Mocnik & Rebernik, 2002).

The main two issues in the report for 2003 (Rebernik, 2004) were concerning firstly the average value-added per employee that was lagging considerably behind the EU (80,000 in the EU and only 23,000 in Slovenia)[1], and secondly the availability of attractive bank conditions for SMEs. 'Small is not beautiful' was the slogan chosen to describe the interest rates, which were too high for the SME sector to stimulate firm foundations.

The International Family Enterprises Research Academy (IFERA) research (IFERA, 2003) noted recently that family businesses prevail in several European countries (Germany 60%, France 60%, United Kingdom, Portugal and Belgium 70%, Netherlands 74%, Spain 75%, Sweden 79%, Cyprus, Finland and Greece 80%, Italy 93%). The main two problems in Slovenia were exposed as inheritance and ownership (trying to retain the firm as family property at any price) (Duh & Tominc, 2005). Additionally, the problem of very weak innovativeness in Slovene SMEs was identified. Innovations are still (world-wide)

---

[1]The difference became smaller in 2004: EU had an average value-added of 75,000 and Slovenia reached 24,180 (Kroslin 2005).

seen as something that has to do with industry (product and process innovations), direct-ing the attention to the cause-consequence process on the way from invention to innova-tion. Tourism is known as a sector that applies all kinds of innovations very swiftly after they appear (like the stream machine for travelling on land and water, aircrafts, computers, Internet etc.) but is weak in innovating itself.

The last European Innovation Scoreboard (EIS) research carried out in 2005 shows that Slovene enterprises lag behind the average of the EU. Networking is regularly disregarded as an innovation potential in tourism and hospitality enterprises: from informal collabora-tion (e.g. occasional joint promotional activities) to regular-business activities and firmer forms of co-operation, e.g. joining a tourism cluster or founding with partners in the des-tination of a destination management company (DMC). Joint reflections of skilled per-sonnel could bridge many gaps between the high expectations of guests on the one hand and the relatively low knowledge level of unique entrepreneurs on the other, which could be considerably improved in joint activities. This problem is particularly evident in rural areas because of the incapacity of SMEs to react and adapt to global trends and the inca-pacity to mitigate the extremes of life cycles through innovating the services.

In tourism, the fact that innovation cycles exist was ignored for a long time. Countries with established tourism markets have supported mainly big enterprises and have spent the last 50 years developing industrial methods to cope with the growing tourism demand. The globalisation process, including the internationalisation of tourism demand and the emer-gence of new competing regions, has surprised them. A typical example of the life cycle of innovations is the decline of tourism in the Alps (Keller, 2004).

One of the innovative ways of treating the tourism and hospitality sectors is supporting the development of SMEs. Small and medium providers of services are less sensitive to market changes and have a much higher ability to adapt to changes (even to life cycle changes) than the large ones. By comparing large tourism firms and SMEs we can see that in general the SMEs have clear disadvantages by achieving economies of scale and in the field of cost-reducing. More positively, can be seen in the possibility of their acting as per-sonalised service providers (Keller, 2002) or by linking these personalised services with local traditions as a possible clear point of differentiation and a quality factor of the service.

Data for 2004 were gathered from two different sources: from the Chamber of Commerce statistics (Dekleva, 2005) for companies (consisting of data from hospitality, tourist agencies, cable-ways, ski centres, casinos, marinas, sport facilities and leisure) and the Chamber of Crafts for handicrafts (mostly micro-enterprises based on self-employment) (Hocevar, 2005). In 2004, there were 5,433 tourism and hospitality enterprises: 15 large, 25 medium, 2,809 small and 2,584 micro-enterprises (951 out of the latter had no employ-ees). There were 36,544 people employed in the tourism and hospitality sectors (excluded the owners in the micro-sector): 6,388 in micro, 8,739 in small, 4,165 in medium and 5,464 in large enterprises. Tourism and hospitality made up about 5.6% of all SMEs and approximately 10% of SMEs in the field of services.

Although young, the SME sector in tourism and hospitality has developed an interesting trend: an above-average failure of enterprises can be observed after 1997. The annual rate of closure after that date was between 2.5% and 10%, affecting especially the micro-sector. The reason might be explained by the above-average success of larger enterprises that improved their market presence compared to previous years.

Comparing Slovene SMEs to Other GEM Countries, Especially to the EU-19

In all 41 GEM countries in 2002, the rate of men owning an enterprise was about ten times higher than that of women: on average 2.1 to 0.2 per 100, respectively. Slovenia's ratio is marginally more favourable (6.37 to 2.26) but still shows the predominance of men as entrepreneurs (Reynolds et al., 2003).

In around 90% of enterprise formations, the two main motives for start-up are a sudden opportunity (driven by the desire to take advantage of a market situation, of a business opportunity or of favourable financial conditions) and necessity (driven by the urgent personal need of a job, by the wish to be independent etc.). Investment out of opportunity prevails. Within the segment of 18 to 64 years old adults we can find at the lower-end France, Croatia, Japan and Hong Kong (very low: less than 3% per 100 adult inhabitants are employees); in the middle-section China (6%), Finland and Brazil (7%); at the upper end, with a very high willingness to start a business if the terms of investment are favourable, we can find the USA (9%), New Zealand (12%) and Uganda (17%) (Reynolds et al., 2003).

Taking necessity into account, the picture becomes very different—only six countries exceed 3%: China, Brazil and Chile (around 6%), Argentina (7%), Venezuela (11%) and Uganda (a good 13%). The quoted data are based on a three-year average, which means that the relative level of individual participation in entrepreneurship appears stable over time, and that the motivations that lead individuals to pursue entrepreneurship appear stable within the different countries.

If the trigger for start-up is a good opportunity, the probability of success is much higher. There are several forms of aids that can be described as opportunities in Slovenia: the voucher system for education with very high quotas for women entrepreneurs; attractive programmes for first job seekers and other measures specially created for young people; a variety of programmes offered to the long-term unemployed persons. An information point is available in all bigger cities (and a 24 hour-a-day Internet service), where all documents and information concerning start-ups and availability of micro-credits or special governmental incentives (like tenders) are available. All of them are available for tourism and hospitality firms.

One of the main burdens preventing further start-up in Slovenia is the almost non-existence of risk capital in Slovenia. The GEM report for 2004 shows that Slovenia was placed at the bottom of compared countries that have access to risk founds; Israel, Sweden and Finland were placed at the top of the scale (Rebernik, Tominc, & Pusnik, 2004). In Slovenia, a better availability of venture or even risk capital would doubtlessly cause a shift from the 'opportunity seekers' (ca. 3%) to the 'job seekers' (ca. 1%). To prevent false business decisions and loss of money, an obligatory counselling on starting up a business could be settled as a pre-requisite obligation when applying for such a grant.

Development of Rural Areas Through Tourism Entrepreneurship

All former communist countries were faced with severe ownership restrictions, deriving from the so-called 'land maximum'. The farmers in Slovenia were not allowed to own more than 5 ha of land (12.5 acres). After the fall of the iron curtain, former communist countries did change the laws and there are no longer ownership limitations but the problem of very small (and thus not profitable) farms persists. The reasons are: lack of money to purchase more land on the one hand and very low interest in staying at the farm (more and harder work for less money than in the industry or service sectors). Consequently, young people are leaving the rural areas that retain only a sparse population, have limited access to transportation and have restricted labour market, which all creates adversity for small businesses (Shields, 2005) and causes further abundances of small farms.

To survive as small farms, they urgently need to carry out some additional economic activities. The Slovene government has recognised that state aid will have to be organised at several levels to prevent them from dying. Several governmental measures, meant to keep the rural environment populated, are thus oriented towards creating new jobs in the rural areas and to provide favourable conditions for founding small businesses. Tourism is considered as one of the most-important sectors to help realise these programmes.

Many problems occur with the realisation of local initiatives. The government has failed in transferring its authority to the local and regional levels. Additionally, the Slovene public finance system does not secure budgets for municipalities (leading to the lack of funds), which additionally discourages initiatives (Verbole & Verbole, 2004). In the context of the development of entrepreneurship in the countryside, so-called rural development cores played an important role. A programme called 'Self-Employment in Rural Areas' was jointly started by the Ministry of Labour, Family and Social Affairs, the Ministry of Economy and the Ministry of Agriculture, Forestry and Food to address the economic problems and to create new employment opportunities in rural areas. The programme's priority target groups are young people, especially women, living in rural areas. The programme tries to operate by organising joint workshops combined with individual visits from experts. This is done with a view to help develop business ideas for self-employment projects in the area.

One method to promote tourism would be to generate new ideas on what can be done in a rural destination and to list local attractions on a data bank for tourists. Keller agrees that the economic success of a destination depends on several independent variables, including innovativeness (as a point of differentiation from emerging destinations) and its accessibility (as transport and time factors). The challenge for the local entrepreneur is, therefore, not only in rejuvenating the products and services but predominately in creating additional customer value with new products; the solution is to invest in new economic activities (Keller, 2004).

In Slovenia — as in other post-communist countries — mergers can be observed in rural spaces. Farms are becoming bigger, consequently gaining the possibility of becoming more competitive. Yet, farms are closing: 2800 ceased to trade in the last 10 years, an average of 2.5% per annum. Further reductions from the current 86,000 to around 60,000 is expected by 2010, with swift depopulation of rural spaces and overgrowing of fields by woods (more than 60% of Slovenia are covered by woods or are in the process of being overgrown) (Kulovec, 2004).

A permanent and planned co-operation between two ministries is required — one for agriculture and another for economy — responsible for the SME policy and for tourism. About 50% of all Slovene farms will need an additional challenge (and chance!) in the next 10 years in order to assure a farmer normal family life. Additional possibilities are sought for in the sectors of food manufacturing and selling — especially 'healthy' foods like biologically-dynamically gained crops, traditional farm handicrafts, wood economy (heating by biomass) and (eco) tourism.

Rural Destinations

The development of rural areas in Europe has been considered problematic for quite some time. Most job opportunities can be found in cities, which causes permanent migration (predominately of young people) from the countryside towards urban areas. To prevent further depopulation, attractive job opportunities have to be created in the countryside, as well as social services that are relevant for young families including medical care, kindergartens and schools. Several possibilities for providing them can be created within a sophisticated rural DMC.

To achieve this, a rural destination has to take two steps. First, it needs to establish a DMC that permits employment of professional personnel and clustering of all tourism and tourism-related businesses into an integral tourism offer. Then, secondly to actively incorporate the destination's cultural heritage into its tourism offer and base the destination's unique selling proposition on local heritage and traditions.

Cultural Heritage

In any period of human history a culture is partly sustained by the tension between that which is thought to be of value, inherited from the past, and that which is the product of energetic, dynamic and deliberate innovation (Corner & Harvey, 2001). Modern tourism tries to combine both. Burnett (2001) argues that heritage as a concept has expanded onto the global stage and permeates the local, regional and national spheres.

The philosophy of global corporations is based on adapting the same product to different national preferences and selling practically the same services everywhere, which makes them operate the selling as to a few standardised markets rather than as many customised markets. On the other hand Robins quotes that many commentators talk about the renaissance of locality and regions (Robins, 2001).

Heritage occupies a high-moral ground, as the heritage attractions tend to concern themselves with ethical approaches, sustainable practices and with authenticity claims, which are often used in promotional slogans like 'the oldest buildings' or even 'the most authentic'. Beside the wish to get a touch of history, there are clear consumerist tendencies; beside a good historic value, there are the desires to be entertained, to be educated and to be provided with an enhancement to one's very sense of self (Burnett, 2001).

The notion 'local' has several specific understandings, depending on the segment of people being considered. It is mostly present in the consciousness of people as something that has to do with authenticity, with national pride and thus has emotional value. When talking about heritage, these emotions are even stronger. It is often understood as something precious, something people can identify with, something that is worth mentioning and seeing and should be respected by locals and visitors. Such emotions can be best observed and experienced in rural areas, as these are spaces where globalisation has not made the world uniform (and thus simplified and poorer) to the same extent as in urban spaces.

Cultural heritage in rural areas is usually not spectacular: no big museums like the Louvre or London's National Gallery nor great theatres or concert halls; and yet there are often veritable cultural treasures waiting to be discovered. In all rural spaces, a part of local heritage is kept alive. This might be old guesthouses, majestic old farmhouses, a post office or even a manor, some lovely arranged flower gardens, a church or a chapel; or a quite different part of local tradition, such as delicious recipes for typical local dishes, special ways (occasions) of serving them or unique kind of vessels or materials they are made from, and local folklore dances or songs.

One of the appropriate ways of bringing such heritage goods into the consciousness of local inhabitants (as something that has to be prevented from disappearing or being destroyed) and into the consciousness of visitors (as something that is worth visiting, that enriches) is to integrate them into the tourism service offered in the destination. They can and should be the 'software/information' source for private businesses and may be the best guarantee that the owner of the enterprise is going to protect them and take care of them.

Linking Tourism Entrepreneurship with Rural Heritage and Traditions

There are many possibilities for establishing links between heritage and entrepreneurship. In the tourism and hospitality sectors this link provides the possibility of creating a unique and competitive offer. On the demand side, tourists get the possibility of buying not only typical, regional souvenirs but also goods that are somehow different and that cannot be found, like global brand items, in the centre of any city.

If taking the opportunity to make the heritage and the local traditions the starting point for a business, there are many possibilities in the arts and crafts sectors, usually bound to the traditional raw materials of the region. All kinds of such businesses are important for establishing a successful tourism destination. The more the tourist can visit, see and buy in a destination, the more it is different to what they know from their own countries, the more they have the feeling of getting to know the "real" destination, its origins and even its secrets.

An example of such practice is emerging in the northeastern part of Slovenia. The region Goricko (which means hilly) is rural and was proclaimed a nature park in 2003 because of its preserved nature and its rich biodiversity. One of the reasons for having remained untouched is the geographical position of the park. It lies between Austria and Hungary and was belonging to remote and somehow 'forgotten' places before the fall of the iron curtain in Europe. The same can be said for the area across both-mentioned borders, which gave the three countries a unique possibility of founding a three-lateral nature park Goricko-Orseg-Raab (Slovenia-Hungary-Austria).

Both the geographic and administrative centres of the Slovene part of the park are located in a village called Grad (which means castle). It obtained its name from the biggest castle in Slovenia (365 rooms), inexplicably immense for being situated 'in the middle of nowhere'.

Through an EU-Phare programme, the castle has been partly renovated. Further financing has to be assured to complete the renewal in the next decade or two. According to the Phare plans, the castle will host a visitor centre, a restaurant, guest rooms and several 'show-and-sell' rooms on the ground floor. Only one of these rooms is foreseen for souvenir selling. All others will be given to arts and craftspeople, who will demonstrate and explain their working practices to interested visitors. The visitors in turn will have the opportunity to try their hand at the production of typical, traditional crafts of the region. Something less usual will be one or two rooms for alternative medical treatments. The castle is known as a place of strong energetic sources, and in the surroundings of the castle there are two well-known natural energy fields, which attract several busloads of visitors daily, all coming in search of health or well-being.

All plans for unique handicraft businesses have been worked out within the European project (N(EuropeAid/112237/D/SV/SI) of establishing this natural park. The project's output was several project plans (including investment, marketing, human resource development and financial plans) for establishing tourism or tourism-related small businesses in the fields that have been chosen as best appropriate for the region. Vital parts of the project were courses for the local population, providing the attendants with the basic skills needed, by a successful entrepreneur. Courses were given in elementary computer skills and Internet use (e-mail writing and responding to them), basics of marketing, elementary language skills in German and Hungarian (as being a part of the three-lateral park), basics concerning a firm foundation, availability of state-aids, followed by communication training and some specific courses on handicraft skills and courses in alternative medicine.

An interesting attempt was made in 2005 to establish a DMC. The Slovene NTO (Slovenska turisticna organizacija, STO) decided to finance the elaboration of a strategy of oenogastronomy. It will consist of two main parts: the first will be the strategic part and the second part will be the marketing plan. The strategic part will be based on a SWOT analysis, and will be dedicated to identifying development possibilities. For the sake of research, hospitality providers will be clustered into three groups: (a) hotels, (b) restaurants and guesthouses and (c) tourism farms. The latter two are exclusively SMEs. The main stress will be on searching for possibilities on how to best incorporate some high-quality providers into STO's strategic plans. Gastronomy enterprises (regardless of their size) will be invited to co-operate closely (e.g. fairs, study tours and 'farm-trips' for journalists) with the STO provided that they permanently list a certain percentage of typical local foods on their menus and serve local, well-matching quality wines to these dishes. For such enterprises, the STO will co-finance trainings for their personnel and it will integrate the names and addresses of these enterprises in official publications.

Conclusion

In this chapter, some specific topics relating to SMEs in Slovenia have been discussed. The stress has been put on the search for possible ways tourism SMEs could help develop rural areas. For about half a century, all communist countries were faced with severe property restrictions. Public opinion was very unfavourable as private owners were looked upon as a kind of criminal (exploiter, capitalist), which made their social status rather difficult (Lebe, 2001; Shackleford, 2001). The problematic was similar in rural areas because of the 'land maximum'.

The consequence of 'communist equality' caused great damage to the cultivation of family traditions and valuable knowledge (e.g. during the communist regime of Yugoslavia, only three kinds of bread were baked). Together with traditions an important part of country's heritage and thus of its identity got lost. Communism was a system that did not respect (or even foster) values like inventiveness, tradition and boldness. There was scarcely a possibility to be inventive and creative in such a system.

To be especially attractive — a prerequisite for being successful in the market — rural areas have to find their point of differentiation from other, similar regions. The best way to do this is to combine rural businesses with regional culture and traditions and thus fill in some possible niches. SMEs can find their "raison d'etre" in offering — in contra to the big chains with globally renowned brands and globally unified offers — locally typical goods and services. To do this, they need locally accumulated knowledge and tradition, and have to recuperate their pride and affiliation about the value of rural culture and the possibilities it offers to visitors and to the local inhabitants.

The National Tourist Board, STO, is playing a very positive role in supporting SMEs. It intends in each region to link together the services of gastronomy, tourist farms, vintners, thematic paths (like wine- or fruit roads) and locally typical entertainment that is based on food, wine and gastronomy. This will be of considerable help, especially for SMEs, for a joint and highly professional promotion at an international level, leading to a rejuvenation of local rural economies via tourism SME development.

References

Antoncic, B., Hisrich, R. D., Petrin, T., & Vahcic, A. (2002). *Podjetnistvo*. Ljubljana: Zalozba GV.

Burnett, K. A. (2001). *Heritage, authenticity and history*. In S. Drummond & I. Yeoman (Eds.), *Quality issues in heritage visitor Aattractions*. Oxford, UK: Butterworth Heinemann.

Corner, J., & Harvey, S. (2001). *Great Britain limited*. In: Enterprise and heritage. Crosscurrents of national culture. London, UK: Routledge.

Dekleva, M. M. (2004). Poslovanje gospodarskih dru b sektorjev zdru enja turizma in gostinstva., Ljubljana: Gspodarska zbornica.

Duh, M., & Tominc, P. (2004). Pomen, znacilnosti in prihodnost druzinskih podjetij. In M. Rebernik, P. Tominc, & M.a Duh (Eds.), Tadej Kroslin, Gregor Radonjic: Slovenski podjetniški observatorij, 2. del. Ekonomsko-poslovna fakulteta Univerze v Mariboru, 2005 Maribor.

Frehse, J. (2001). Internationale dienstleistungskompetenzen. Erolgsstrategien fuer die europaeische Hotellerie. Gabler Verlag.

Hocevar, E., Obrt v stevilkah (2005). Statisticni pregled. 2005 Obrtna zbornica Lubljana.

IFERA: Family Business Dominate. (2003). *Family business Review*, *16*(4), 235–239.

Keller, P. (2002). Les PME face a la concurrence de l'industrie du voyage: Introduction au seminaire. Madrid: OMT.

Keller, P. (2004). Conclusions of the conference on innovation and growth in tourism. OECD. https://www.oecd.org/dataoecd/55/48/34267885.pdf

Kohl, M. (2002). The significance of SMEs in Europe's tourism supply. Madrid: WTO.

Kroslin, T. (2005). Inovacijski potencial podjetij in izzivi njegovega razvoja za doseganje vecje uspesnosti slovenskega gospodarstva. In M. Rebernik, P. Tominc, M. Duh, T. Kroslin, & G. Radonjic (Eds.), Slovenski podjetniški observatorij 2004, 2. del. Maribor: Ekonomsko-poslovna fakulteta Univerze v Mariboru.

Kulovec, M. (2004). Dopolnilna dejavnost — osnova podjetnistvu na podezelju. Proceedings from the conference Portoroz: Entrepreneurship — the best answer to the future, Ljubljana: Small business development centre.

Lebe, S. S. (2002). Government incentives for the creation of tourism SMEs. The future of small and medium-sized enterprises in European tourism faced with globalization. Madrid: UNWTO.

Mocnik, D., & Rebernik, M. (2002). Slovenski podjetniški observatorij 2002, 2. del. Maribor: Ekonomsko-poslovna fakulteta Univerze v Mariboru.

Project documentation Goricko: N(EuropeAid/112237/D/SV/Sim.

Rebernik, M. (2003, 2004). Executive summary. In: M. Rebernik, D. Mocnik, J. Knez-Riedl, P. Tominc, K. S. Rantasa, M. Rus, T. Kroslin, & S. Dajcman (Eds.), *Slovenian Entrepreneurship Observatory.* Maribor: Faculty of Economics and Business.

Rebernik, M., Knez-Riedl, J., Mocnik, D., Rantasa, K. S., Rus, M., Kroslin, T., & Tominc, P. (2002). Slovenski podjetniški observatorij 2002, 2. del. Maribor: Ekonomsko-poslovna fakulteta Univerze v Mariboru.

Rebernik, M., Tominc, P., Pusnik, K., & Psenicny, V. (2004). Global entrepreneurship monitor. Slovenija: Podjetnistvo na prehodu. Maribor: Faculty of Economics and Business.

Rebernik, M., Tominc, P., Rus, M, & Dajcman, S. (2004) Global entrepreneurship monitor. Slovenija. Part I. Maribor: Ekonomsko-poslovna fakulteta Univerze v Mariboru.

Reynolds, P. D., Bygrave, W. D, & Auito, E. (2004). GEM 2003 Global report. Reynolds, Bygrave, Aiuto and Babson College.

Robins, K. (2001). Tradition and translation. In: Enterprise and heritage. Crosscurrents of national culture. London: Routledge.

Shackleford, P. (2002). Conclusions. The future of small and medium-sized enterprises in European tourism faced with globalization. Madrid: UNWTO.

Shields, J. F. (2005). Does ural location matter? The significance of a rural setting for small businesses. *Journal of Developmental Entrepreneurship, 10*(1), 49–63.

Turk, M. (2000). Being an entrepreneur in Slovenia. Gea College International Conference 'Dynamic Entrepreneurship foe the New Economy' Ljubljana.

Verbole, P., & Verbole, A. (2004). Rural women entrepreneurs: A case in Slovenia. Proceedings from the Portoroz conference 'Entrepreneurship — the best answer to the future', Small business development centre.

Internet References

http://europa.eu.int/comm/enterprise/services/tourism/tourism_forum/documents/2005/summary_report.pdf

http://europa.eu.int/comm/enterprise/services/tourism/index_en.htm

http://europa.eu.int/comm/enterprise/

http://www.dnb.co.in/RMSolution.htm

http://www.gemconsortium.org

http://www.mg-rs.si/

http://www.world-tourism.org

Chapter 11

Strategies for Small- and Medium-Sized Hotels in the Slovak Republic

Marian Gúčik, Vanda Maráková and Ivana Šípková

Introduction

Tourism is a form of consumption that satisfies specific needs of people during travelling and staying away from home for either leisure or business purposes. Among a wide range of tourist services, the provision of accommodation and catering is vital to satisfying tourist needs. A combination of these services is delivered by the hotel industry, which includes hotels and similar facilities (e.g. motels and boarding houses). Apart from accommodation, hotel establishments offer catering and other paid and non-paid complementary services. The hotel industry constitutes an important part of a wider tourist accommodation sector that also includes holiday villages, campsites and hostels (Gúčik, Királová, Orieška, Patúš, & Vetráková, 1991).

The development of the hotel industry is one of the top priorities within the European Union (EU) member countries. Indeed, the growth of accommodation and catering services stimulates the development of the tourist infrastructure and thereby regional and local development in tourism destinations. According to Eurostat (2006), in 2002 accommodation services, which include short-stay lodging in hotels, motels, inns and camping sites, generated EUR 56.2 billion of value added in the EU-25 countries and had workforce of almost 2 million persons. The majority of the enterprises are represented by SMEs, in spite of increased concentration in the hotel industry. There are two major reasons why the process of concentration within the hotel industry is unlikely to cause a significant drop in the share of SMEs within this sector. Firstly, the establishment of a domestic chain requires developing a strong brand and a significant investment in technology, both of which are very costly. Secondly, many independent European hotels will be against joining global hotel chains regardless of the benefits they offer. Such hotels are elements of European culture and history, which actually constitute their competitive advantage, while global chains are just places to stay overnight. Nevertheless, European small and medium-sized

Tourism in the New Europe
Copyright © 2007 by Elsevier Ltd.
All rights of reproduction in any form reserved.
ISBN: 0-08-044706-6

hotels face increasing competition from the large, frequently global, hotel chains, particularly within the European transition countries, such as the Slovak Republic.[1]

The aims of this chapter are: (1) to discuss the current trends in the hotel industry in the Slovak Republic and the key challenges that the industry faces; (2) to indicate possible strategies for the Slovak small and medium-sized hotels that operate under the new conditions of accession to the EU; (3) to evaluate whether current public sector support of Slovak SMEs can facilitate pursuing the proposed strategies. The discussion presented in this chapter is based upon recent research work undertaken by the authors in relation to the Slovak tourism market under the conditions of the EU.[2]

Trends in the Slovak Hotel Industry

The first boom in the Slovak hotel industry dates back to the beginning of the twentieth century. It emerged mainly in response to factors such as the development of coach mail, railways, balneology and economic growth. The oldest Slovak hotels include those located in the capital city of Bratislava (hotel Carlton and hotel Blaha, later called Krym), in the spa town of Piestany (spa hotel Thermia Palace, spa hotel Pro Patria, and hotel Royal, later called Slovan), in the highest Slovak mountains, the High Tatras (hotel Grand, Grandhotel Praha, and spa hotel Hviezdoslav), in Trencin (hotel Tatra) and in Kosice (hotel Europa). The most significant Slovak hotels merged in 1925 and became part of a Slovak hotel company injected with capital from the Tatra bank, which owned 27 of the largest and highest quality hotels. Shortly before socialisation in 1947, there were 26,700 beds in accommodation facilities in the country. Out of those 12,800 beds were in hotels, boarding houses, villas and inns, 10,400 in spa facilities and 3500 in chalets and hostels. The communistic putsch of 1948 led to the nationalisation of all privately owned possessions and a transition to a centrally planned economy. A newly established company, The Slovak Hotels, owned by the government involved 50 hotels with a capacity of 5000 beds. Many hotels lost their original function and won it back only in 1956. The next wave of building new hotels came in 1963 in response to the development of foreign tourism. At that time, hotels in Slovakia were operated by a few organisations such as the Cedok, the Trust of Tourism Enterprises with headquarters in Prague through a company called Interhotely, the

---

[1]The Slovak Republic is situated in Central Europe (area 39,035 km^2, 5.4 m. inhabitants). Since May 1, 2004, it became a new member of the EU. Slovakia became a part of the joint state of Czechs and Slovaks — Czechoslovak Republic in 1918 after the breakdown of the Austrian-Hungarian monarchy. In 1939, it achieved autonomy, and during World War II, it was an independent state. After the war in 1945 Slovakia was incorporated into Czechoslovak republic again. The years 1948–1989 can be characterised as years of a centrally planned economy and the country was a part of the East Block. Transformation into a democratic country with a market economy started after the so-called Velvet Revolution in 1989. In 1993, the Czech and Slovak Federative Republic was terminally divided into two separate countries.

[2]The research work was conducted at the Faculty of Economics, Matej Bel University, Slovakia. The research team has taken part in the development of the national tourism strategy in Slovakia. Findings from the research are available for tourism associations. The researchers co-operate with the Slovak Association of Hotels and Restaurants. Information on the Slovak hotel market has been published in the journal *Ekonomicka Revue Cestovneho Ruchu*, which has been edited at the Faculty for 39 years.

Association of Slovak Co-operatives through local branches called Jednota, regional enter-prises Restauracie, a tourism company Javorina and others. After the political and social changes of 1989, most of the Slovak hotels have been privatised and a few large compa-nies were replaced by a number of private enterprises. Some hotels were returned to their original owners before nationalisation (Patúš & Gúčik, 2005).

In 1993, there were 578 accommodation facilities in Slovakia with 20,084 rooms and 47,843 beds. Since then, the number of accommodation facilities grew rapidly. In 2003, there were 2509 accommodation facilities with 47,693 rooms and 121,299 beds (see Table 11.1). Between 1993 and 2003 the number of these facilities grew four-fold, the number of rooms doubled and number of beds more than doubled. It should be noted, however, that these figures are partly influenced by change in statistical reporting.

Since 1993, the share of hotels in all accommodation facilities has been continuously dropping, and in 2003, it accounted for only 43% (see Table 11.2). In contrast, an increase in the number of boarding houses can be observed, which represented a share of 10% in 2003. A similar trend can be observed in relation to non-hotel accommodation facilities, which are highly seasonal in nature (tourist hostels, holiday villages, camp sites etc.).

Changes in the structure of rooms and beds broadly reflect changes in the structure of accommodation facilities (see Table 11.3). It is interesting to note that hotels of higher standard (5- and 4-star hotels) represented in 2003 only 6.9% of all rooms and 6.4% of all beds. Middle-class hotels offered 33.5% of all rooms and 33.6% of all beds. However, the current distribution of hotel rooms and beds does not match the demand and is not com-parable with other European standards. The above-mentioned circumstances impact upon room occupancy levels and the economic performance of accommodation facilities. The annual average occupancy of accommodation facilities in Slovakia is about 36%. The

Table 11.1: The development of accommodation capacity in Slovakia.

	1993	1995	2000	2003	(%) change 1993–2003
Accommodation facilities	578	1,027	1,928	2,509	4.3
Rooms	20,084	27,309	39,440	46,693	2.3
Beds	47,843	64,602	102,800	121,299	2.5

Source: Calculation based on the data of the Statistical Office of the Slovak Republic, 1994, 1996, 2001, 2004.

Table 11.2: Structure of accommodation facilities in Slovakia (%).

Accommodation type	1993	1995	2000	2003
Hotels (including motels)	58.1	56.1	42.4	43.0
Boarding houses	2.5	4.7	7.1	10.0
Other accommodation facilities	39.4	39.2	50.5	47.0

Source: Calculation based on the data of the Statistical Office of the Slovak Republic, 1994, 1996, 2001, 2004.

Table 11.3: Structure of rooms and beds in accommodation facilities in Slovakia (%).

	1993	1995	2000	2003
Rooms				
Hotels	65.1	64.0	47.6	48.6
5-Star and 4-star	—	10.3	3.7	6.9
3-Star	—	31.6	31.0	35.5
2-Star	—	37.5	42.6	35.9
1-Star	—	20.6	22.7	21.7
Boarding houses	2.2	4.4	7.2	9.9
Other accommodation	32.7	31.6	45.2	41.5
Rooms total	20,084	27,309	39,440	46,693
Beds				
Hotels:	58.0	56.1	42.4	42.9
5-Star and 4-star	—	9.3	3.3	6.4
3-Star	—	28.3	28.2	33.6
2-Star	—	38.7	42.3	36.2
1-Star	—	23.7	25.2	23.8
Boarding houses	2.5	4.7	7.1	9.9
Other accommodation	39.5	39.2	50.5	47.2
Beds total	47,847	64,602	102,800	121,299

Source: Calculation based on the data of the Statistical Office of the Slovak Republic, 1994, 1996, 2001, 2004.

highest occupancy rates are observed in spa destinations (Trencianske Teplice – 62%, Piestany – 51%) and mountain tourism resorts such as the High Tatras (39%).

Table 11.4 shows the number of guests and overnights in accommodation facilities in 2003. Almost 71% of guests were domestic visitors. The share was similar in terms of overnights. The average length of stay for each guest was 3.6 nights. The share of for-eigners staying in hotels was 67%, and the share of their overnights was 64%. The average length of stay per foreigner was 3.5 nights. Most of the foreigners (54.3%) preferred to stay in hotels of higher standard, while domestic visitors usually stayed in hotels of lower standard (55.7%).

In 2002, a new classification scheme for accommodation facilities was introduced (Vyhláška, 2001). It is enforced by law and contains requirements with regard to the stan-dards of equipment and services, and takes international criteria into consideration. In response to this law, many accommodation facilities have been modernised, which has led to an improvement of standards and the quality of hotel services.

Currently, hotels and restaurants represent approximately 4.5% of all businesses in the Slovak economy (Statistical Office of the Slovak Republic, 2004). By 1997, these facili-ties were privatised. In terms of their legal form, private limited companies dominate the

Table 11.4: Guests and overnights in accommodation facilities in Slovakia in 2003 (%).

	Guests total	Foreign guests	Overnights total	Overnights of foreign guests	Average length of stay per guest total	Average length of stay per foreign guest
Hotels:	58.4	66.8	53.3	64.5	3.3	3.5
5-Star and 4-Star	8.8	13.2	6.1	9.3	2.3	2.4
3-Star	35.7	41.1	37.9	43.9	3.5	3.7
2-Star	37.6	32.9	36.8	32.6	3.2	3.4
1-Star	17.9	12.8	19.2	14.2	3.5	3.8
Boarding houses	8.9	8.1	7.6	7.1	3.0	3.2
Other accommodation facilities	32.7	25.1	39.1	28.4	4.3	4.0
Total (thousands)	3,374	1,387	12,056	4,964	3.6	3.6
Share (%)	70.9	29.1	70.8	29.2	—	—

Source: Calculation based on the data of the Statistical Office of the Slovak Republic, 1994, 1996, 2001, 2004.

Table 11.5: Accommodation and catering facilities in Slovakia by number of employees in 2003 (%).

Number of employees	Accommodation facilities	Catering facilities
0	18.9	36.8
1–9	58.4	58.8
10–19	10.5	3.4
20–49	7.2	0.8
50–249	4.8	0.2
250 and more	0.2	0.0

Source: Calculations based on data provided by the Ministry of Economy, 2004.

sector. Only 3% of hotels and restaurants are owned or managed by foreign or international companies.

Accommodation facilities in Slovakia are provided by small and medium-sized enterprises. Almost 77.3% of accommodation facilities and 95.6% of all hospitality facilities do not employ more than nine people, and according to the EU classification, they are rated as micro-enterprises (Table 11. 5).

According to the Slovak criteria, a small-sized hotel is considered to have up to 100 beds while a medium-sized hotel should have between 100 and 250 beds. The minimum capacity

Table 11.6: Average size of accommodation facilities by hotel type in 2003.

	Number of rooms	Number of beds
Hotels:	49	113
5-Star and 4-star	60	128
3-Star	69	149
2-Star	48	110
1-Star	34	85
Boarding houses	12	32

Source: Calculations based on data of the Slovak Statistical Office, 2004.

of a hotel is 40 beds, which is equal to the capacity of a coach. The average size of hotels in Slovakia in 2003, as measured by the number of beds, was medium (see Table 11.6). Only 1-star hotels represented the category of small hotels, as measured by the number of beds.

The Slovak hotel sector is fragmented and dominated by small and medium-sized hotels, which is similar to other European countries. The majority of Slovak hotels are family businesses.

To describe the potential of Slovakia for offering accommodation services, the following indicators can be used — density of beds in hotels per 1000 inhabitants (12 beds per 1000 inhabitants) and density of beds in hotels per 100 km^2 (132 beds per 100 km^2). Both indicators show readiness for tourism development, although these figures are lower as compared with neighbouring countries, e.g. the Czech Republic (22.9 beds per 1000 inhabitants and 194 beds per 100 km^2).

Currently, there is only one domestic hotel chain in the Slovak market called SOREA, which was originally established as a company to provide recreation for the members of a trade union and which has been subsequently transformed into the largest local hotel chain focused on leisure travel. It consists of 15 hotels and 3 boarding houses with an overall capacity of 4500 beds. There are more hotel companies, which include three or more hotels, but they cannot be considered as hotel chains. Twelve hotels are operated by multinational hotel chains. These are InterContinental Hotels Corp., Holiday Inn., SAS Radisson, Best Western, Meydan, Kempinski, Atlific and Czech OREA.

Small and medium-sized hotels have to cope with low occupancy rates and low profitability. In order to raise profitability they try to rationalise and cut costs. Staff costs constitute a significant share in total costs. The average wage in the Slovak hotel sector is low and this affects the performance of employees. This is demonstrated by imperfections in service quality and consequently by the declining demand for accommodation services. It is necessary to improve this situation and search for appropriate strategies for small and medium-sized hotels in Slovakia.

Strategies for Small and Medium-Sized Hotels in Slovakia

The importance of independent small and medium-sized hotels in the tourism market is obvious. They offer a product that global hotel chains are not able to offer. However, there is a permanent change in the hotel sector in Slovakia caused by the globalisation processes. To ensure the survival of small and medium-sized enterprises, it is essential that (Gúčik & Šípková, 2004)

- each hotel elaborates its strategy focused on quality related to the requirements of its target group of customers,
- the process of privatisation in Slovakia is complemented by a process of concentration based on business integration and the establishment of national hotel chains,
- competitive hotels join multinational hotel chains to meet the challenges presented by increased European competition.

A traditional hotel catering for every occasion cannot survive in the current market. Efforts to offer something for everybody can lead to the collapse of the business. Certain actions need to be undertaken by the hoteliers themselves, as well as by the Slovak Association of Hotels and Restaurants (established in 1993). There are many strategic options open to small and medium-sized hotels and pursuing them under the right circumstances may help them succeed. These options include focussing on particular market segments, an active sale strategy, as well as co-operation within a tourism destination, the establishment of voluntary associations and franchising (Gúčik, 2000). The selected strategies need to conform to a range of environmental factors such as the trends in the tourism industry in Slovakia, characteristics of tourist demand and other socio-economic and political factors.

The strategy of focussing on particular market segments requires small and medium-sized hotels to build special facilities and products suitable for the needs of the chosen target segments. For example, a segment of families with children requires a family/children friendly hotel and appropriate activities. Holidaymakers keen to pursue sports require hotels offering opportunities for pursuing sports and appropriate facilities, e.g. tennis courses and golf courses. Holidaymakers oriented towards health and well being require a hotel with health, fitness, beauty facilities and an appropriate range of activities. Other groups of customers such as congress participants, business travellers and disabled people will also require facilities and activities tailored to their specific needs. Hotel specialisation clearly provides opportunities for gaining a competitive advantage by small or medium-sized hotels. It may also enable them to achieve higher occupancy rates.

Pursuing a strategy of focussing on particular market segments and the choice of the target segments depends upon the situation in the market (the external opportunities) and resources of a hotel. It may also require complying with the requirements of the Slovak hotel classification scheme, which distinguishes certain types of accommodation facilities by the market segments served and sets so-called facultative criteria that need to be met by a hotel that wishes to represent a specific type of a hotel. A minimum score has to be achieved for a hotel to be classified within a certain category. Facultative criteria refer to the building, equipment, complementary services, leisure and well-being facilities, equipment for conferences and seminars. Orientation towards particular target groups should be supported by differentiated marketing. Although at present undifferentiated marketing prevails in Slovak hotel industry, there are more and more hotels that respect customer focus.

As concerns the strategy of active sale, it should be noted that small and medium-sized hotels do not normally have a marketing department as part of their organisational structure. The process of sales takes a lot of time and effort. The owner of a small hotel has many duties and little time for marketing its products. Hiring a marketing manager would be too costly. If a hotel does not offer its own packages, co-operation with tour operators may be required. A tour operator is an important distribution channel performing functions such as promoting the hotel and its product, and conducting market research. Hotels own web sites or electronic distribution systems play a similar role. At present, most hotels place their web sites on the Internet and rarely use travel web companies and portals to intermediate the product due to costs. A hotel web site has to provide the opportunity to make bookings, while at present it is commonly used only as an information tool (Gúčik, 2005).

City hotels face problems of low occupancy rates at weekends. One way of reducing this problem is to offer weekend packages for groups through tour operators or other distribution channels. An essential aspect in adopting such an approach is to focus on certain theme and entertainment, e.g. a theatre weekend, an opera festival, folklore weekend or a craft market. The occupancy rate in resort hotels in low season might be increased by the improvement of amenities, complementary services and price policy.

The co-operation strategy assumes the association of hotels based on partnership. Co-operation should produce a synergy effect that should be greater than the sum of individual effects. Co-operation may occur at the local or regional level. Co-operation enables common use of human and material resources aimed at revenue growth and reduction in costs. Co-operation can be related to any aspect of hotel operation, e.g. centralised laundry, joint logistics, joint sales of product, building and the utilisation of complementary equipment (swimming pools, golf areas, tennis courts etc.). Furthermore, co-operation can include marketing, further education and training. It is essential, however, that the tasks are defined and divided between partners and a co-ordinating unit is established.

Co-operation in a tourism destination should involve tourism enterprises as well as other enterprises offering services for tourists (bowling, ski lifts, cultural facilities etc.) and local authorities. It is the only way to create a common product promoted in the market under one brand.

Voluntary associations are formed by hotels with similar products and a similar marketing concept. They merge to implement common marketing strategy focussing on a particular target group. In this case, synergy results from joint efforts in the market for similar products. Partners within this kind of partnership are usually geographically distant. Voluntary associations can act in various legal forms, which allow the maintenance of legal and economic independence of the associated partners. The main objective of such associations is to introduce professional marketing, raise the product market share and rationalise sales. This concept has been successfully applied in Austria (Osterreichische Kinderhotels) and in Switzerland (Swiss Kinderfreudliche Hotels, which is a family holiday specialist).

Franchising is a system for the commercialisation of products, services and technologies. Large hotel companies usually act as franchisors, e.g. Holiday Inn, Marriot, Ramada, Radisson, Accor. A franchisor justifies and at the same time remits the franchisee to operate a hotel based on defined standards. A franchisor provides a franchising package (known brand, access to central reservation system, know-how and relatively non-risky start-up) to an entrepreneur starting up in the hotel business.

Slovakia as a tourism destination can succeed in the global market only if individual hotels integrate into multinational chains or create national domestic chains, which will be competitive. However, an improvement of the external environment in which Slovak hotels operate constitutes a precondition for achieving competitive advantage by Slovak hotels. Key areas of improvement include transport links facilitating better access to Slovakia and to Slovak tourism resorts, tourism and tourism-related infrastructure, service quality, knowledge of foreign languages and intercultural skills of tourism workers.

In the process of pursuing the above-mentioned strategies by Slovak hotels many difficulties have been encountered. These are the consequence of a 50-year absence of private ownership in the period of centrally planned economy and limited know-how of new owners under the conditions of a market economy. Globalisation and internationalisation of tourism business after joining the EU have accelerated the changes in the approach and philosophy of hotelkeepers.

Support for Small and Medium-Sized Hotels

Support for small and medium-sized hotels in Slovakia includes financial and non-financial instruments, as part of government support for tourism enterprises. These support measures are examined generally within this chapter because the support of hotel industry is not monitored separately in Slovakia. Most of the programmes discussed below are not sector-based (Maráková, 2004).

Financial Support

The Slovak government offers a range of financial measures to tourism enterprises among which the most important ones include credit and interest rate allowances, provision of state guarantees, provision of loans, non-refundable grants and the investment of risk capital companies (Maráková, 2004).

Loan and credit programmes.   Provision of soft loans and credits is currently the most significant form of support for tourism SMEs. The aim of this form of support is to facilitate access to medium- and long-term loans under more favourable conditions than those offered by commercial banks.

Since 2000, interest rates in Slovakia have been falling down to between 7 and 9% per annum in January 2005. However, there are significant differences in interest rates varying by bank houses and bank products. Despite the high demand for credits and loans, the abundance of liquidity in the banking sector and the decrease in interest rates, the willingness to provide credits and loans for tourism sector was declining in the early 2000s. Other reasons that contributed to such a situation included the high level of cautiousness on the part of the restructured bank sector as well as the low efficiency of tourism enterprises. More recently, however, bank lending for the tourism sector has increased. Nevertheless, the share of bank credits to GDP of Slovakia is three times lower than that in the established EU member countries. Furthermore, there is a problem of imbalance, when banks prefer to offer higher loans while tourism entrepreneurs consider taking smaller loans.

Table 11.7: Support for tourism enterprises: The Micro-Loan Programme.

Year	Number of loans provided			Amount of financial resources (SKK million)		
	Total	Tourism	Share of tourism (%)	Total	Tourism	Share of tourism (%)
1997	35	–	–	8325	–	–
1998	21	–	–	4241	–	–
1999	100	–	–	31,146	–	–
2000	53	11	20.8	23,937	3425	14.3
2001	75	6	8.0	20,376	2300	11.3
2002	245	17	6.9	94,902	5526	5.8
2003	305	13	4.3	134,374	5660	4.2
Total	834	47	5.6	317,301	16,911	5.3

Source: National Agency for the Development of Small- and Medium-Sized Enterprises, 2004.

In recognition of the above difficulties in obtaining private finance for the development of tourism SMEs, the National Agency for the Development of SMEs in Slovakia has been authorised to use state budget finances to solve the problem of the limited availability of credits for SMEs. The Slovak government carried out credit programmes through selected state institutions, the state budget and in the past from the EU PHARE programme. Of particular benefit to tourism enterprises is the availability of smaller loans through the Micro-Loan Programme and Support Credit Programme.

The objective of the Micro-Loan Programme is to help small entrepreneurs who start their business to overcome a temporary lack of financial resources. Data on the number and the amount of micro-loans offered from the start of this programme are shown in Table 11.7.

As for the Support Credit Programme, it allows SMEs to obtain operating and investment capital in the form of a medium-term credit. It is currently the largest credit programme funded from the state budget (Table 11.8). Both the credit and the micro-loan programmes are implemented mainly by offering soft loans.

Guarantee programmes.   Guarantees have been offered through the Slovak Guarantee and Development Bank financed partly by the EU PHARE programme and partly by the state budget. Guarantees to tourism SMEs are offered through a programme for SME support in the form of bank guarantees for financial credits. So far tourism SMEs have obtained 79 guarantees worth SKK 395.8 million, which represents 3.6% of guarantees in total. The guarantees obtained stimulated the creation of 12,300 new jobs.

Grant schemes.   Two grant schemes of particular significance to tourism SMEs are the Support Programme for Tourism Development and the Pilot Grant Scheme. The Quality Programme is also important for entrepreneurs in tourism.

Table 11.8: Support for tourism enterprises: The Support Credit Programme.

Year	Number of loans provided			Amount of financial resources (SKK million)		
	Total	**Tourism**	**Share of tourism (%)**	**Total**	**Tourism**	**Share of tourism (%)**
1995	243	10	4.1	587.0	21.5	3.7
1996	223	29	13.0	745.0	112.5	15.1
1997	87	10	11.5	306.9	30.2	9.8
1998	109	5	4.6	403.4	20.6	5.1
1999	192	19	9.9	693.5	76.9	11.1
2000	186	20	10.8	652.8	63.6	9.7
2001	81	15	18.5	259.8	42.2	16.2
2002	38	3	7.8	139.0	1.7	1.2
2003	21	1	4.8	100.0	1.0	1.0
Total	1,180	112	9.4	3,887.3	370.2	9.5

Source: National Agency for the Development of Small and Medium-Sized Enterprises, 2004.

The Support Programme for Tourism Development represents direct support for tourism business. By the end of 2002, the volume of supported investments was SKK 5.3 billion, and direct contributions paid to entrepreneurs were SKK 602 million. The multiplier effect of this support was calculated as 1:9, which means that SKK 1 of provided grant generated investments in tourism worth SKK 9. More detailed data on the number of supported projects and the amount of grants are shown in Table 11.9. The most frequent applications for the grants related to proposals for building and modernisation of boarding houses, hospitality facilities, ski lifts, ropeways and the establishment of complementary services in mountain resorts. Since the beginning of the programme, 6261 new jobs were created, 11,133 beds were added to the portfolio of accommodation facilities and 38,907 seats were established.

The Pilot Grant Scheme for tourism development was established as part of the preparation for the use of structural funds and was conducted between 2001 and 2002. Projects needed to be focused on one of the following objectives: investment and non-investment activities, human resources development and regional and local co-operation. Supported activities should be related to one of the main problems of Slovak tourism especially the low diversity of the tourism product, lack of co-operation, undeveloped marketing and inadequate professional skills of tourism staff. Predominantly non-investment activities were supported. It is anticipated that 1.8 million from the grant scheme generated investments of 2 million.

The Quality Programme relates to the implementation of a quality management system. Tourism enterprises can receive a financial contribution towards the education, counselling, pre-certification and certification process based on norms ISO 9000, ISO 14000 and HACCP. Since the start of this programme in 2000, only two tourism enterprises (spa companies) were supported.

Table 11.9: The support programme for tourism development in Slovakia.

Year	Number of approved financial grants	Amount of approved financial grants (SKK thousands)	Average financial grant per project (SKK thousands)	Number of jobs generated	Number of beds generated	Number of seats generated
1991	3	351	117	95	86	140
1992	60	12,960	216	729	750	3,900
1993	60	19,620	327	700	600	4,100
1994	46	27,554	599	223	654	4,024
1995	31	18,786	606	268	337	1,475
1996	52	59,904	1,152	615	690	3,261
1997	60	79,080	1,318	770	1,751	3,873
1998	49	60,123	1,227	330	967	2,392
1999	28	14,538	519	258	291	1,177
2000	44	45,233	1,028	258	566	1,525
2001	105	91,665	873	404	1,000	2,741
2002	150	165,307	1,102	707	1,872	5,931
2003	145	57,557	397	904	1,569	4,368
Total	833	652,678	784	6,261	11,133	38,907

Source: Slovak Guarantee and Development Bank, 2004.

Table 11.10: Demand for capital and number of applications received by Seed Capital Company.

Year	Volume of demanded financial resources		Number of applications		
	Total (SKK thousands)	Total	Tourism	Share of tourism (%)	
1995–2000	2,793,869.7	372	42	11.3	
2001	153,950.0	23	1	4.3	
2002	116,790.0	18	6	33.3	
2003	341,241.0	41	10	24.2	
2004	216,097.0	28	4	14.3	
1995–2004	3,621,947.7	482	63	13.1	

Source: Seed Capital Company, 2005.

Risk capital.   Another form of support is represented by the Starting Capital Fund managed by the Seed Capital Company based in the National Agency for the Development of Small and Medium Enterprises. The main aim of the fund is to support start-up businesses by capital input (maximum amount of SKK 10 million). Table 11.10 presents data concerning the number of applications. The share of applications from the tourism sector was

13.1% for the period 1995–2004. Only six tourism enterprises out of 26 applicants were supported.

Non-financial support

In terms of non-financial support, consultancy and education are of particular importance. Costs related to these activities often exceed the financial capability of small and medium tourism enterprises. These activities are not primarily aimed at tourism enterprises, but tourism SMEs are involved in them. Topics of educational programmes refer to theoretical knowledge and practical skills in the operation of a market economy. These programmes are organised by the National Agency for the Development of SMEs through the network of Regional Consultancy and Information Centres and Business Innovation Centres. Certain support is available within the state policy on employment where creation and sustainability of jobs are encouraged.

Conclusion

The recent trends in the Slovak hotel industry indicate the decreasing share of hotel rooms and beds in favour of non-hotel accommodation facilities. The share of beds in high-quality hotels is low. This does not meet the demand requirements because up to 54% of foreigners prefer to stay in hotels of higher standard. The average occupancy rate of all accommodation facilities is about 36%.

The hotel industry in Slovakia is represented primarily by independent small and medium-sized enterprises. The only domestic hotel chain that operates in the Slovak market is SOREA with 4500 beds. Only 12 hotels are involved in multinational hotel chains.

The independent small and medium-sized hotels are of great importance to the Slovak hotel industry. They can be successfully run if they pursue an appropriate strategy that responds to current market challenges. Among various strategic options open to individual hoteliers, focus on a particular market segment, active sale, destination co-operation, establishment of voluntary associations and franchising may be of particular importance in the hotels' attempts to establish their competitive advantage.

Small and medium-sized hotels in Slovakia are supported by a range of financial and non-financial instruments. Loan and credit programmes, provision of guarantees, grant schemes and provision of risk capital are considered the most significant financial instruments. However, the current financial and non-financial support does not fully facilitate pursuing the strategies identified in this chapter. This is mainly due to the fact that the support relates only to certain aspects of these strategies.

References

Eurostat (2006). *European business. Facts and figures 1995–2004.* http://epp.eurostat.cec.eu.int.

Gúčik, M. (2000). Stratégie prežitia slovenského hotelierstva. *Ekonomická revue cestovného ruchu,* *33*(3), 139–148.

Gúčik, M. (2005). Možnosti maximalizácie výnosov v cestovnom ruchu z predaja cez internet. *Ekonomická revue cestovného ruchu, 38*(3), 187–188.

Gúčik, M., Királ'ová, A., Orieška, J., Patúš, P., & Vetráková, M. (1991). *Hotelový a reštauračný manažment*. Bratislava: ES VŠE.

Gúčik, M., & Šípková, I. (2004). *Globalizácia a integrácia v cestovnom ruchu. Knižnica cestovného ruchu 7*. Banská Bystrica: Slovak-Swiss Tourism.

Maráková, V. (2004). Formovanie podpory malých a stredných podnikov cestovného ruchu. *Ekonomická revue cestovného ruchu, 37*(1), 23–36.

National Agency for the Development of Small- and Medium-Sized Enterprises (2004). *Annual Report 2003*.

Patúš, P., & Gúčik, M. (2005). *Manažment ubytovacej prevádzky hotela. Knižnica cestovného ruchu 7*. Banská Bystrica: Slovak-Swiss Tourism.

Seed Capital Company (2005). *Annual report 2004*.

Slovak Guarantee and Development Bank (2004). *Annual report 2003*.

Statistical Office of the Slovak Republic (1994). *Statistical yearbook of the Slovak Republic 1993*. Bratislava: Veda.

Statistical Office of the Slovak Republic (1996). *Statistical yearbook of the Slovak Republic 1995*. Bratislava: Veda.

Statistical Office of the Slovak Republic (2001). *Statistical yearbook of the Slovak Republic 2000*. Bratislava: Veda.

Statistical Office of the Slovak Republic (2004). *Statistical yearbook of the Slovak Republic 2003*. Bratislava: Veda.

Vyhláška, Č. (419/2001). Z. z. o kategorizácii ubytovacích zariadení a klasifikačných znakoch pre ich zarad'ovanie do tried (Classification scheme for accommodation facilities).

Chapter 12

The Effectiveness of Promoting Package Tours by Polish Travel Agents

Jolanta Staszewska, Janusz Klisinski and
Izabella Sowier-Kasprzyk

Introduction

The growing significance of the service sector and the rapid development of tourism characterise many Central and Eastern European economies including Poland. The European integration process and the liberalisation of cross-border regulations make travelling within the EU easier. The higher standards of living in Poland and the rapidly developing foreign business contacts and activities constitute important factors that stimulate the growth of tourism trips abroad both for leisure and business purposes. Such growing demand strengthens the importance of tour operators and travel agents that organise and/or sell package tours. The huge potential for earning profits within this sector of the tourism industry, combined with low barriers to entry, has been quickly recognised both by Polish entrepreneurs and established foreign-tour operators. The number of enterprises operating within this sector has been growing rapidly and has led to increased competition among those firms leaving the less-experienced group of independent and small travel agents in a highly vulnerable position. In such an environment, competing on price alone is no longer sufficient for firms to maintain their market share. Similarly with other industries, marketing, and particularly promotional activities have become important ingredients for influencing and winning consumers and profit making. Not all types of promotional activities, however, facilitate the attainment of such objectives. Resources invested in designing and running promotional campaigns are frequently lost particularly by firms less experienced in using promotional tools such as the small independent travel agents. Furthermore, promotional activities of travel agents may also be influenced by the decisions of those tour operators whose packages travel agents sell and by the dynamic business environments, such as Poland's.

Tourism in the New Europe
Copyright © 2007 by Elsevier Ltd.
All rights of reproduction in any form reserved.
ISBN: 0-08-044706-6

The aim of this chapter is to assess the effectiveness of promoting package tours by Polish travel agents and to suggest a model for effective promotion within this sector. To this end, the chapter considers the changing demand for outbound tourism in Poland and for package tours in particular as well as the characteristics of the supply of package tours in Poland. Based on a literature review, conditions for the effective promotion of package tours are identified. The assessment of the effectiveness of promoting package tours by Polish travel agents utilises results of a primary study conducted in 2003 and 2004. The chapter concludes with suggesting ways for enhancing the effectiveness of promoting package tours by Polish travel agents.

Characteristics of the Demand for Package Tours in Poland

Tourism is an integral part of people lifestyles in many countries. In Poland, it is developing slowly and this process is connected with the evolution of Polish tourism consumption.

According to the Polish Tourism Organisation (Zawadzki, 2003), after dynamic growth in domestic travel in the 1970s, the decline in tourist activity among Poles had been observed until 1994. The growth in tourism activity in Poland occurred again between 1995 and 1999. From 1999, the overall participation of Polish residents in tourist activity has been declining in terms of the number of Poles over 15 who were undertaking such activity (The Institute of Tourism, 2005a). While in 1999, 63% of Polish residents over 15 participated in tourism, in 2004 only 48% did. However, the participation of Polish residents over 15 in trips abroad was more stable over the same period and decreased from 14% to 12% of Polish residents over 15 who undertook trips abroad. The number of domestic trips declined from 66 million in 1999 to 25 million for short breaks and from 25 million to 15 million for long trips (5 days and more). The number of tourist trips abroad has also declined from 7.5 million in 1999 to 6.3 million in 2004 (The Institute of Tourism, 2005a).

In 2004, the majority of Polish tourist trips abroad were undertaken to Germany (2.30 million). Other countries most visited by Polish tourists included the Czech Republic (0.55 million), Slovakia (0.55 million), Italy (0.50 million) and Austria (0.35 million). The next most-visited countries included Belgium, France, Ukraine and the United Kingdom. Within the top 18 countries most visited by Polish tourists in 2004 only two were non-European: Egypt and the United States, both receiving 0.10 million of Polish tourists (The Institute of Tourism, 2005a).

The main purpose of tourist trips abroad in 2004 was sightseeing, recreation and entertainment (38%) but its share has declined from 44% in 2002. Business and incentive trips were the second most popular type of tourist trips abroad and accounted for 33% of all tourist trips abroad in 2004, which represented a significant increase over 2002 where they accounted for 17%. The share of tourism trips abroad for visiting friends and relatives has also been declining from 28% in 2002 to 22% in 2004 (The Institute of Tourism, 2005b).

As for travel organisation, the majority of Polish tourist trips abroad were self-organised (52% in 2000 and 2002). However, the share of package tours has been growing from 28% in 2000 to 30% in 2002 (The Institute of Tourism, 2005b).

The evolution of tourism consumption in Poland is also characterised by a gradual move from traditional tourism to contemporary tourism. According to Alejziak (1999), the traditional model of tourism is characterised by group travelling, passivity of tourists, focus on the quantity rather than quality of trips, lack of preparation and knowledge about the culture and tourist attractions of the visited areas, lack of adjustment to the lifestyles of local communities in visited areas, noisiness of tourists, inability to speak the language of the visited country, curiosity, expectation of comfort and fast means of transport. In contrast, the contemporary model of tourism is characterised by individual travelling, longer holidays, making several trips a year, making individual and spontaneous itinerary decisions, undertaking physical activity, expecting high quality of the tourist experience, interest in acquiring general knowledge of the destination visited, adopting the lifestyle of the visited population, desire for calmness rather than comfort, buying small personal souvenirs and gifts and reducing the speed of moving around.

Understanding the characteristics of the demand for tourism trips abroad and the characteristics of the traditional and contemporary Polish tourists is crucial in designing desirable package tours and promoting the benefits that the tourists might expect from buying such tours. It is anticipated that the following types of package tours will be of particular interest to Polish tourists: sightseeing package tours (for tourists who want to see the main attractions of a country), pilgrimage package tours (for the people who want to see religious places), music package tours (combining participation in musical events), cultural package tours (including visits to historic monuments, galleries, meetings with outstanding persons form the world of culture), eco-package tours (for people who are interested in the natural environment) and incentive package tours (for specific groups of professionals) (Mazurek-Lopacińska, 2000).

Characteristics of the Supply of Package Tours in Poland

The legal requirements for undertaking business activity in the area of organising and selling package tours in Poland were first specified in the law on tourist services of 1997 (Dziennik Ustaw, 1997). The law identifies three types of tourist enterprises: the travel organisers (tour operators), the travel intermediaries and the travel agents. According to this law, a travel organiser plays the most important role in the package tours industry as it creates and sells such packages, that is inclusive tours that includes some components of a tour sold at an inclusive price (e.g. accommodation, transport, catering, other complementary services). With a view to protecting the tourists, the law requires all travel organisers to obtain a permit to run such a business activity. Some of the conditions that an entrepreneur needs to satisfy in order to obtain the permit include evidence of financial guarantees and evidence that the manager of the business possesses appropriate tourism vocational education.

The law also defines the role of a travel intermediary who is expected to make agreements with the providers of tourist services on behalf of the intermediary's clients. The client pays commission to the travel intermediary for his services. Travel intermediaries are also required to obtain a permit to run such a business and the conditions for obtaining such a permit also include financial guarantees and appropriate vocational education.

The travel agents act as intermediaries on behalf of travel organisers. As they sell package tours designed by the travel organisers, and as the travel organisers have to comply with the legal requirements for carrying out such activities, the travel agents are not obliged by law to obtain a permit to run such a business.

The Central Register for Travel Organisers and Travel Intermediaries lists all permits granted for running this type of activity. The number of all registered travel organisations in April 2006 was 2607 of which 557 (21.4%) were registered as travel organisers, 48 (1.8%) as travel intermediaries and 2002 (76.8%) as businesses conducting both travel organiser's and travel intermediary's activity. In terms of the legal form of these enterprises, most of them are private firms (70.62% of all registered enterprises in April 2006) followed by private limited companies (18.60%) and associations (3.11%) (Ministry of Economy, 2006). This may indicate that the majority of these enterprises are small and medium-sized. Indeed, in December 2001, 23% of those enterprises registered in The Central Register for Travel Organisers and Travel Intermediaries employed only one person, 22% — two and 14% employed three persons. Only 0.28% of these enterprises employed more than 100 people (The Institute of Tourism, 2002). It is also interesting to note that between 1999 and April 2006, as many as 2828 enterprises were removed from the register either because their permits expired (67%) or because they no longer fulfilled the conditions imposed by the law (32.6%) or for other reasons (0.4%) (Ministry of Economy, 2006).

The statistics showing the number of travel agents in Poland are, however, difficult to obtain, as travel agents are not required to obtain a permit to run such a business. The Central Office of Statistics in Poland includes the activities of travel agents under other, more generic economic sectors and categories. It is, however, estimated that in 2001 there were some 3500 travel agents in Poland, most of which were micro and small businesses (The Institute of Tourism, 2002). It should be noted, however, that this number does not include all travel agents in Poland as many travel organisers also run their own travel agencies and they do not register this type of activity as a separate business activity.

Despite an increasing concentration of capital and mergers among Polish travel organisers, intermediaries and agents, a tendency towards individualisation of selling and independent activity has been observed. These changes in the business environment facilitate the application of new technologies in designing and selling package tours. Of particular importance are modern communication systems (e-mails), modern reservation systems (Amadeus, Sabr) as well as modern presentation, distribution and promotion systems (CD presentations, e-commerce). It is expected, however, that the use of these technologies will differ depending on the requirements of the market segment that a particular enterprise is targeting. To enable tourism employees to understand and respond to the changing business environment, training and continuous professional development programmes are being developed (Mazurek-Lopacinska, 2000).

Conditions for the Effective Promotion of Package Tours

The declining demand for tourism trips abroad combined with the increased supply of tour operators and travel agents in the Polish market renders the business of selling package tours highly competitive. For small and medium-sized travel agents that sell package tours created by travel organisers, promotion becomes an important tool for influencing and winning consumers and profit making. Indeed, effective promotion can influence consumer preferences, motives, image and choices. This is particularly important in selling package tours, which are intangible and the consumption of which is distant in terms of time and place.

Organisations can view promotion in two ways. As a process of communication with a consumer, promotion requires the recognition of the importance of the message that is to be communicated between the sender and the receiver, message coding and decoding, the information channels and potential conflicts within them, and the factors that interfere with the appropriate transmission of the message (Sliwinska, 1999). In a systems approach (Wiktor, 2001) promotion is considered as part of the marketing activity and as such it should: benefit and satisfy the customer; respond to trends in the business environment; be integrated with other marketing instruments; and maximise the potential for synergy that the use of various promotional tools may create (Staszewska, 2004).

The promotion of package tours gives promises. If those promises are met during the consumption of the package tour and the tourists are satisfied, then the communication effect of promotional activities is achieved. A satisfying experience leads to consumer loyalty demonstrated by such behaviour as re-purchase or recommendations, which enables achieving the selling effect of promotional activities. It is therefore important for promotional activities to be designed in such a way that enables attaining both the communication and the selling effect of promotion (Staszewska, 2004).

Within the context of package tours, effective promotional activity requires adopting a variable integrated means of promotion. To be effective, promotional activities need to be integrated with other marketing tools, such as market research, market segmentation, product design and price. Internal integration requires using a unique variety of forms and means of promotion (promotional mix) that facilitates effective communication with the target market segment (Wiktor, 2001). Indeed, different market segments are susceptible to different promotional tools and messages. What is important in the choice of the promotional mix is its ability to generate a synergy effect; that is the result of using a promotional mix should be greater than the sum of results that the use of individual promotional tools would produce (Pabian, 2002). A well-designed promotional mix should enhance consumer awareness of and trust towards the product (the communication effect) and readiness to purchase the product (the selling effect) (Staszewska, 2004).

As tour operators create package tours, they play the main role in the process of the integrated promotion of these products. Indeed, the effectiveness of promotional activities undertaken by travel agents depends significantly upon the marketing activities of the tour operator whose package tours are sold. Therefore, marketing partnership between the tour operator and the travel agent is critical in ensuring the effectiveness of promotional activities. This is particularly important for independent travel agents that usually sell package tours created by various tour operators. Depending on the agreement between the tour operator and the retailer the level of participation of the travel agent in marketing activities varies. Frequently, tour operators design and finance their own promotional campaigns and all travel agents selling the tour operator's products benefit from them. Consequently, the techniques used for promoting package tours may differ depending upon the activities and the requirements of each tour operator. The messages included in the promotional material may also transmit a confusing image, particularly when a travel agency sells package tours on behalf of several tour operators (Staszewska, 2004). Indeed, the use of integrated marketing communication, which assumes integrating and co-ordinating all communication channels with a view to transmitting a coherent message about an organisation and its products (Staszewska, 2004) may assist travel agents in overcoming these problems. It requires integrating internal promotional activities, determining the role of each promotional tool and method and appointing a manager responsible for marketing communication.

Given the frequently limited influence upon the choice of promotional techniques and messages used by each tour operators, the independent travel agent also needs to develop its own unique approach towards communicating with the market; an approach that will integrate the diverse promotional approaches of each tour operator. The limited resources of travel agents constitute, however, a major barrier to adopting such a strategy.

In summary, the two major conditions for the effective promotion of package tours include: (1) the ability of the promotional activity to achieve the aims of promotion, including the communication and the selling aims; (2) the ability of the promotional activity to generate synergistic effects through the appropriate integration of promotional tools.

An Assessment of the Effectiveness of Promoting Package Tours in Poland

Research into the effectiveness of promoting package tours by travel agents in Poland was conducted by the authors of this chapter in 2003 and 2004. The study investigated the promotional activities of 25 travel agents in the region of Silesia, which has the largest number of travel operators and travel agents in Poland. All travel agents were independent, established businesses selling package tours for a range of tour operators including foreign tour operators. Some of them were also selling their own package tours created as part of their own travel-organising activity. The majority of the travel agents that were subject to this investigation were small (employing up to 50 people) but some of them were also micro enterprises (employing less then 10 people) or medium enterprises (employing less then 250 people).

In order to address the question of the effectiveness of promoting package tours by these organisations, three techniques of data collection were used:

- face to face semi-structured interviews with the directors of the travel agencies;
- a questionnaire survey conducted personally at the point of sale of the package tours with the clients of the 25 travel agencies (sample size: 600);
- structured observation at the travel agents' sales premises.

The semi-structured interviews contained questions concerning the travel agents' aims of promotion, their promotion-planning process, their promotional budgets, their methods of selecting promotional techniques and types of techniques used, their ways of evaluating the effectiveness of promotional activities and their perception of the levels of consumer satisfaction with the promotion.

The questionnaire contained a mixture of closed and open questions concerning the respondents' perceptions of the travel agent's promotional activities, their satisfaction with

Table 12.1: The questionnaire survey respondents' profile ($N = 600$).

Age (years)	Income per person per month (PLN)	Education	Gender	Place of residence	Family status
<20 (8%)	<2000 (40%)	Degree (32%)	Male (41%)	Urban (86%)	Single (45%)
20–40 (59%)	2000–3000	Diploma			
41–60 (25%)	(55%)	(63%)	Female (59%)	Rural (14%)	With family (55%)
>60 (8%)	>3000 (5%)	Primary–(5%)			

these activities, their perceptions of the effectiveness of the promotional communication, their purchase and re-purchase intentions and their preferences towards promotional tools. The respondents' profile is presented in Table 12.1.

The structured observation was declared and was conducted at the travel agents' point of sale. Areas observed included the attitudes of the sales assistants towards the clients; the level of their knowledge, professionalism, and communication skills; clients' behaviour; conversations between the sales assistants and the clients; the appearance of the sales premises; promotional materials; the way in which promotional materials were used by the sales assistants; the level of clients' interest in visual promotion within the sales premises. All data collected were analysed using statistical methods. The data analysis process and findings from this study identified certain relationships that constituted a basis for constructing a model for an effective promotional process.

Main Findings

The travel agents interviewed for the purpose of this study evaluated their promotional activities as rather effective and they were quite satisfied with their promotional activities. However, this view was not shared by the consumers who on average thought that the travel agents' promotional activities were poor. The major weaknesses of the travel agents' promotional activities that were identified in this study include the following:

- the promotional aims are short-term and concentrate purely on increasing sales;
- the promotional activities frequently try to achieve a one-off sale rather than repeat purchases;
- the promotional activities do not consider consumer expectations; market research is not conducted;
- the use of diverse promotional methods and tools is limited;
- the promotional activities are not co-ordinated, integrated or logically linked;
- the promotional activities do not vary in relation to the needs of specific market segments;
- the promotional promises are rarely kept;
- the promotion does not interest consumers and rarely stimulates a purchase;
- the consumers are willing to establish relations with the travel agents but the firms are not ready for this.

The results of the study indicate that the travel agents do not promote package tours in an effective manner. Their promotional activities are not integrated externally or internally and are mainly oriented towards increasing one-off sales. Consumers do not rate the promotional activities of package tours highly, which challenges the travel agents' beliefs regarding the effectiveness of their promotion. Indeed, the promotional activities of travel agents do not possess marketing features, are not comprehensive or integrated and thus are ineffective.

In terms of the types of promotional tools used, the study found that the most frequent forms of promotion included package-tours catalogues, newspaper advertisements and internet advertisements. Travel agents also used sales promotion, including concessions, discounts and first and last-minute offers. They also frequently participated in travel fairs. Furthermore, there were some examples of public relations activities including the organisation of events, meetings with consumers and study tours. One-to-one personal selling also occurred and in terms of direct marketing, most travel agents used direct mail.

However, the promotional tools used by the travel agents did not always match consumer expectations concerning travel agents' communication with them. Indeed, consumers preferred the individual approach and tangible benefits. In terms of sales promotion, they would prefer free testing of the package tours and free ancillary services. As for personal selling, they would prefer a group of sales assistants taking care of their individual requirements rather than the one-to-one arrangement. Preferred forms of direct marketing included personally addressed mail and electronic mail. They considered charity activities as good PR activities. Although they did value catalogues, internet promotion of package tours was also very important to them. The consumers surveyed also indicated that newspaper advertisements as well as first and last-minute offers were not as important in stimulating purchases as the travel agents thought.

It should be noted, however, that most of the promotional activities pursued by travel agents are decided upon and financed by the tour operators whose package tours are sold by the travel agents although tour operators usually allow travel agents to augment the promotional activities with methods that the travel agents feel might be more appropriate for the local market. Resource constrains on most travel agents do not, however, encourage such actions. The influence of tour operators on the effectiveness of promoting package tours by travel agents cannot therefore be undermined and further study is needed to determine this effect.

Both the travel agents and the consumers were asked to assess the effectiveness[1] of each of the promotional tools used by the travel agents. Sales promotion, personal selling and direct marketing were poor, both in the opinion of the travel agents and the consumers. While consumers thought that advertising was fair, the travel agents considered it poor. All respondents indicated that the reliability of information is the most important aspect in promotion.

The influence of both internal and external factors upon the effectiveness of promotional activities was estimated as poor. Travel agents believed that their promotional activities were mainly influenced by tour operators and by consumers as well as by the promotional activities of competitors.

---

[1]The level of effectiveness was measured on a scale: very good, good, fair, poor, none

While estimating the communication effect of promotional activities, the travel agents indicated that the consumers understood the promotional message, that promises were kept, and that dishonest information was not included in the promotion. They thought that promotion was the second-most important source of the interest in a package tour after personal factors that influence consumer choice. The travel agents assessed the attractiveness of their own promotional messages as good and suggested that promotional communication helped improve their image.

The views of travel agents concerning the communication effect of promotional activities were not entirely shared by consumers who were not aware of the fact that they were the intended recipients of promotion and who claimed that promises in promotional information were not always kept, particularly in the case of advertising.

As for the sales effect of promotional activity, most travel agents did not measure the effects of promotion on sales but some observed a moderate increase in sales that might be attributed to promotional activities while others observed a stabilisation in sales volumes. They believed that promotion raises consumers' interest in package tours and stimulates spontaneous purchases.

Nearly all the consumers surveyed stated that promotion stimulates their willingness to purchase but has a poor influence on their actual purchase. The consumers thought that the most important factors that influence their purchase of package tours are: quality; personal factors; opinion of other consumers; political situation; the number of services included in the package; fashion and finally promotion. The consumers also thought that it is not promotion that influences their repeat purchases but satisfaction with the package tour. They also stated that they pass on their opinion about the travel agent and its products to other people.

The consumers evaluated their attitude towards the travel agent as neutral and thought that there were no relations with the firm. This is not surprising in view of the fact that the travel agents considered the possibility of closer relations with the customers to be very limited because their aim was to get customers but not necessarily to keep them.

It should be noted that the above results represent the views of all the consumers surveyed as no significant differences in consumer opinions were identified in relation to the following independent variables: income, age, gender, family status, place of residence and education.

Towards Enhancing the Effectiveness of Promoting Package Tours in Poland

The results of the study into the effectiveness of promoting package tours by travel agents in Poland identified many differences in opinions between the travel agents and their consumers. The firms do not conduct marketing research and do not co-ordinate their promotional activities. They also do not make much effort to enhance the effectiveness of their promotion.

The primary study revealed important relationships and factors affecting the effectiveness of promoting package tours and allowed for the construction of a model for an effective promotion of package tours. Given the high dependence of the effectiveness of promoting

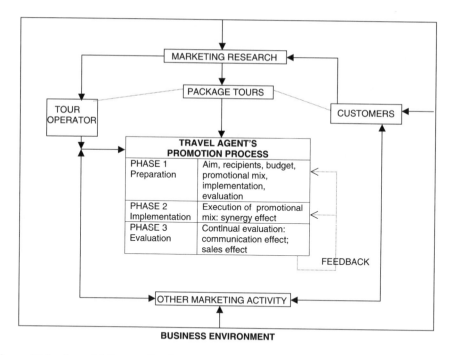

Figure 12.1: A model for an effective process of promoting package tours by travel agents.

package tours upon the activities of tour operators, the model assumes close co-operation between tour operators and travel agents in this process. The promotional process proposed in this model consists of three phases (Figure 12.1).

The first phase concerns the activities related to the preparation of the package tours using the results of marketing research. This is normally done by a tour operator but travel agents' input should be sought. Indeed, it is in the interest of the travel agent to seek ways of influencing the product design. Then the programme of promoting the products is prepared, which includes the identification of the aims of promotion, recipients, budget, promotional methods and tools, implementation and preliminary evaluation. Although much of this activity will depend upon promotional activities imposed by the tour operators, a specific promotional mix needs to be prepared by a travel agent that integrates the promotional programmes of all tour operators and the promotional needs of the travel agent and its consumers.

The second phase is called the implementation of the promotional programme. It refers to the execution of the promotional mix. Finally, the effectiveness of promoting package tours needs to be evaluated, which is the focus of the third phase in this model. In particular, the communication and the sales effect have to be estimated. The strengths and weaknesses of the promotional mix and individual promotional tools need to be identified. The results of this phase need to be considered and weaknesses addressed by introducing changes to the relevant components of the first and/or second phase of the promotional process.

All these activities must be co-ordinated and integrated with other marketing activities. Internal and external factors influencing the choices within the promotional process, particularly consumer needs, the behaviour and requirements of tour operators and activities of competitors, need to be considered.

It is expected that the proposed model of promoting package tours by travel agents will lead to improved business performance by the travel agent in terms of achieving the firm's aims, gaining positive financial results, and strengthening the market position of the firm.

Although the proposed model is theoretically simple, its application within the sector of travel agents, which is represented by the majority of small enterprises with a significant share of micro enterprises, may be quite challenging. The resources of the travel agents — including money, time, knowledge, skills, technology — as well as their limited influence upon the decisions made by tour operators, constitute potential barriers to the effective application of this model. On the other hand, however, making no efforts to enhance the effectiveness of promotional activities will not help travel agents in surviving in a highly competitive environment. This is particularly true in an environment where internet technology may significantly reduce demand for the services of the traditional travel agent. Application of this model may therefore require identification of the travel agents resource needs and encourage a search for more innovative ways of fulfilling these needs.

Conclusion

The evaluation of the effectiveness of promoting package tours by Polish travel agents showed that consumers are dissatisfied with the promotional activities pursued by the agents and generally think they are ineffective. The effectiveness of these activities can, however, be enhanced if the travel agents adopt an integrated and marketing approach towards promotion. Greater emphasis has to be placed upon building a base of loyal consumers who are willing to repurchase the agent's products and recommend them to other potential consumers. Promotional activities require improvements in the area of preparation of a promotional programme, its implementation and evaluation. Marketing research is crucial in undertaking such activities and so is an evaluation of the environmental factors. Co-operation between travel agents and tour operators is a pre-requisite for enhancing the effectiveness of promoting package tours by travel agents. Further research, however, needs to be undertaken in order to identify barriers to the successful application of the proposed model of promotional activities by travel agents.

References

Alejziak, A. (1999). *Turystyka w obliczu wyzwań XX wieku*. Krakow: Albis.
Dziennik Ustaw (1997). Ustawa o uslugach turystycznych, 28.08.1997, *Dziennik Ustaw*, No 3.
Mazurek-Lopacinska, K.(2000). *Strategia rozwoju turystyki w latach 2001–2006*. Wroclaw: AE.
Ministry of Economy (2006). *Centralna Ewidencja Organizatorow i Posrednikow Turystycznych*. Warsaw: Centrum Informacji Spoleczno-Gospodarczej Ministerstwa Gospodarki.
Pabian, A. (2002). Synergia miksów promocyjnych. *Marketing w praktyce*, *10*(4), 5–7.

Sliwinska, K. (1999). *Marketingowe instrumenty komunikowania sie firmy z rynkiem.* Katowice: SWSZZ.

Staszewska, J. (2004). Skutecznosc komunikacji marketingowej w systemie informacyjnym przedsiebiorstwa. In T. Kramer(Ed.), *Systemy komunikacji marketingowej* (pp. 101–108). Katowice: WSZMiJO.

The Institute of Tourism (2002). *Analiza rynku biur podrozy w Polsce, 2001.* Warsaw: The Institute of Tourism.

The Institute of Tourism (2005a). *Poland. tourism in figures 2004.* Warsaw: The Institute of Tourism.

The Institute of Tourism (2005b). *Foreign departures of Polish residents.* Warsaw: The Institute of Tourism.

Zawadzki, H.(2003). *Podróze polaków. Komunikat z badań. Instytut Turystyki.* Warszawa: Instytut Turystyki.

Chapter 13

Encouraging Enhanced Customer Relationship Management in Accommodation SMEs: The Case of Seville, Spain

Mario Castellanos-Verdugo, Mª de los Ángeles Oviedo-García and Nadine Veerapermal

Introduction

In the last few years, business competitiveness has risen as a consequence of economic globalization, growing economic integration, and market liberalization. Quality relationships in highly competitive sectors are considered a key element for business differentiation through which firms pursue a commitment to clients based on satisfaction, loyalty, and positive word of mouth.

The hotel industry is one of the most competitive economic sectors, as can be seen by the decreasing margins and the higher pressure that they face to offer more and better services. As a result, there is an increase of costs that needs to be controlled, as otherwise it would reduce the margins even more, adding to the pressure exerted on hotel managers.

One way of tackling this issue is by encouraging a continuous reselling pattern based on the premise that the cost of retaining an existing customer is much lower than that of acquiring a new one, as has been demonstrated by Reichheld and Sasser (1990). Thus, marketing efforts are more likely to be successful if they focus on customer retention (Sheth & Parvatiyar, 1995).

Customer retention is based on the quality of the relationship established with them, which is built on customers' evaluations and perceptions about the personal communication with the employees and their behavior. Therefore, relationship quality is one of the elements that can be used to cope up with the competition increase, as it is positively related with the matching between the customers' ideal preferences and the characteristics of the service provided.

The chapter starts with an outline of the relationship-marketing concept and how it might be articulated with accommodation small and medium sized enterprises (SMEs). Next, the characteristics of tourism activity as well as the hotel industry characteristics in Seville province (Spain) are analyzed. Then, we focus on empirical research that aims to analyze the differences between large- and small-hotel firms with regard to their customers' perception of the relationship quality. The results allow us to conclude with several policy implications for enhancing quality in accommodation SMEs.

Relationship Marketing

Among the most widely known definitions of relationship marketing is that of Gronroos (2000, p. 26), who establishes that relationship marketing is to "identify and establish, maintain and enhance, and when necessary terminate relationships with customers (and other parties) so that the objectives regarding economic and other variables of all parties are met. This is achieved through a mutual exchange and fulfillment of promises."

This definition, however, is neither unique nor universally accepted (Berry, 1983; Evans & Laskin, 1994; Morgan & Hunt, 1994). Each definition adds nuances and characteristic elements that contribute to shape the concept more precisely. While this diversity can provide the advantage of having a diverse set of perspectives, it can be somewhat confusing (Harker, 1999; Lindgreen, 2001).

Barnes (1997) notices that for a relationship to exist, both parties should mutually perceive its existence, and it should be characterized by a special status, based on some factors such as trust and commitment (Morgan & Hunt, 1994), which are associated with customer retention and profitability of the organization.

Recently, the limits between markets and industries started to blur as a consequence of the increase in market fragmentation, the shortening of the product life, and the rapid changes in customers' purchase pattern, who are becoming more and more sophisticated and knowledgeable. All these factors, along with the rise in market competition and continuous increase of the service sector's weight in the economy (Wong & Sohal, 2002), account for the importance that relationship marketing has gained. Under these circumstances, relationship-marketing strategies arise as a key issue to keep competitive advantage (Sharma, Tzokas, Saren, & Kyziridis, 1999).

Particularly in the service sector, relationship marketing is critical as it provides tangibility to the otherwise intangible services. Furthermore, relationship marketing in the service sector reduces the perceived risk and contributes to make customers define the decision-making criteria for service assessment. In this framework, the role of employees is of paramount importance, as they act as indispensable interfaces, insofar as the service cannot be rendered without their intervention (Bendapudi & Berry, 1997; Berry, 1980; Zeithaml, Berry, & Parasuraman, 1993).

One of the most remarkable dimensions of relationship marketing is the quality of the relationship, defined as a "bundle of intangible value which augments products or services and results in an expected interchange between buyers and sellers" (Wong & Sohal, 2002). It refers to the relationship's depth and general climate. That is to say, the relationship quality is the customers' perception of how the overall relationship meets their expectations, predictions, objectives, and wishes (Jarvelin & Lehtinen, 1996), and therefore it is a global impression that the customer has about the relationship as a whole, including different transactions.

As we stated earlier, relationship marketing goes beyond traditional marketing, known as transaction marketing, in that its goal is to build long-term relationships with valuable customers. Such relationships should be mutually profitable for both parties, and they are based on trust. In keeping up with Kim and Cha (2002), we understand that relationship marketing in the hotel industry is a set of marketing activities that attracts, maintains, and enhances relationships with customers that are profitable for both parties, with a focus on the retention of existing customers.

Owing to the growing interest in relationship marketing, many endeavors have been made to measure the relationship quality. Kim and Cha (2002), completing a previous study (Kim, Han, & Lee, 2001), propose a model of antecedents and consequences of the quality in the employee(customer relationship from the point of view of the latter. The model is graphically depicted in Figure 13.1, which includes the factor loads and the level of significance of each one of the proposed paths, resulting from Kim and Cha's (2002) work.

From the customer's perspective, the quality of the relationship is achieved through the employee's capability to reduce the perceived uncertainty. In this way, a high-quality relationship means that customer's trust in the service provider's future performance based on the satisfaction received from their previous experience. Relationship quality is a construct comprised of two indicators — trust and satisfaction. Trust is understood as the belief that those on whom we rely will meet our expectations (Shaw, 1997).

Satisfaction is the emotional response to the use of a product or service (Oliver, 1981), and it is a complex process, which includes both cognitive and affective processes, and psychological and physiological influences (Oh & Parks, 1997). Although traditionally

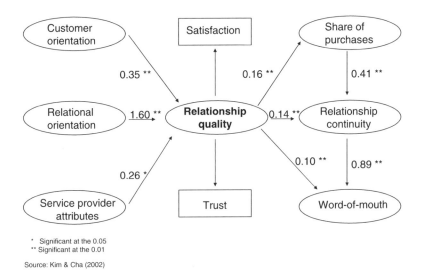

* Significant at the 0.05
** Significant at the 0.01

Source: Kim & Cha (2002)

Figure 13.1: Relationship quality model.

satisfaction was measured by comparing the individual's perception with his or her expectation of the service, it is now considered that the perception can be directly measured on the basis of service evaluation (Choi & Chu, 2001; Cronin & Taylor, 1992).

Kim and Cha (2002) propose three constructs as antecedents of the relationship quality. First is the customer orientation. Customer-oriented service providers render a service according to their commitment, putting the customer's interest first, and thus improving the organization's service and customer's satisfaction.

The second antecedent is the relationship orientation, that is, the trend of behavior aimed at cultivating the relationship between seller and buyer and ensuring its maintenance and growth with a favorable impact on the customers' opinion about the quality of the relationship (Crosby, Evans, & Cowles, 1990).

The service provider's attributes are the third antecedent of relationship quality. On each encounter with the service provider, through whatever means available (mail, telephone, in person, or through the Internet), the customer perceives an impression about the quality of the organization, and each encounter contributes to the overall satisfaction and the wish of maintaining the relationship in the future. Among the attributes of hotel service providers, the employees' appearance and experience is remarkable.

Succeeding at establishing and maintaining a quality relationship with customers yields various positive consequences for the organization. First, the quality of the relationship will be reflected in the market share because satisfied customers, being less sensitive to the price variable, are less likely to change providers, and more likely to spend higher sums than other customers by buying more frequently and in larger amounts and by purchasing additional products or services (Fornell, 1992; Griffin, 1995; Parasuraman, Berry, & Zeithmal, 1991).

The second type of consequence is the continuity of the relationship, that is, the parties' willingness to extend the cooperation or cooperation agreement over an undetermined period of time in the future (Heide & George, 1990).

Finally, the word of mouth, which is informal communication with other consumers about the ownership, use or characteristics of goods, services or employees; it stems from the building of relationships with customers (Beatty, Mayer, Coleman, Reynolds, & Lee, 1996; Griffin, 1995).

Tourism in Seville

The tourism sector in province of Seville experienced an increase of 13.4% in visitor numbers in 2004 compared with the previous year. Almost 66% were Spanish, while 34% came from abroad. Some 20% of the nearly 860,000 people visiting Seville came from the province; 15.4% came from other areas of Andalusia (mostly, from Cadiz and Malaga); and 26.4% came from other areas of Spain (Madrid in the first place, followed by Catalonia). Regarding foreign visits (38.2%), France, England, and Portugal were the main countries of origin, with Japanese (10.2%) and US people (5.4%) entering the ranking for the first time.

Of the total number of visitors, 462,737 spent the night at hotels in the province. Most of the accommodation demand in Seville is for hotel accommodation (68.4%), with hotels accommodating more than 80% of tourists in the surrounding province in year 2003.

Tourists who visited Seville in 2003 were very satisfied with the tourism offer of the province, qualifying it with 7.74 points. Still better results were achieved by the accommodation sector with a 7.91 points score on a scale from 1 to 10 (10 points being the maximum score). According to the survey on Hotel Occupancy carried out by the Spanish National Statistics Institute (INE), the number of visitors accommodated at hotels and boarding houses in Seville during April 2005 was 179,283, which amounts to an increase of 21.66% with regard to the same month of the previous year. The number of total travelers decreased by 4.69%, but the number of Spanish travelers increased by 53.57% in April.

Characteristics of the Hotel Industry

The accommodation sector has a number of characteristics that must be appreciated if measures to enhance quality are to be advocated successfully. These are summarized below.

First, the product offered is the rendering of a service that is nonstockable after being provided, although it can be stocked at some point of the production process (such as the cleaning material or the office stationery). Therefore once obtained, the product cannot be stocked for its subsequent sale because it expires immediately. Owing to the impossibility of stocking, the hotel is obliged to do its best to sell the whole production on a daily basis as any unsold material can be considered a loss. Besides, the service is often produced and consumed simultaneously, hence, the importance of the contact between the producer or service provider and the consumer. Thus, the way the staff of the hotel treats their guests is crucial and decisive for the customers' perception of quality and satisfaction. In contrast, the intangibility makes it more difficult to differentiate services in such a way that it is necessary to look for material aspects (palpable, tangibles) that the customer can associate with the service provided.

Second, the service cannot be transferred to the customer. On the contrary, for the service to be sold, the customer has to go to the service provision site.

The third notable feature is that production (the rooms) cannot possibly be increased in the short run, so the firm cannot cope up with demand peaks.

Fourth, hotels must offer a diversity of services in order to gain customers. But at the same time they must be flexible enough so as to accommodate themselves to a wide range of situations that are more or less predictable or to meet the different needs of the customers, such as laundry, ironing, gym, telephone, exchange, etc. (Musa-Alhasan & Sanchis-Palacio, 1993).

Finally, hotels' fixed costs (wages, advertising, depreciation of buildings, furniture and fittings, etc.) are much higher than variable costs. Fixed costs are costs that do not change in the short term, regardless of the changes in the occupancy rate of the hotel (Musa-Alhasan & Sanchis-Palacio, 1993). As a result, there is a very close relationship between the firm and customers in hotel service provision because the latter is present during the service preparation or rendering process. The concept of hotel service and product quality is also pivotal in view of the increase in market competition. In hotels, the quality depends on the staff's skills and capabilities as neither good facilities nor luxurious rooms are a guarantee of success on their own. Arguably, when it comes to buying a car, the customer is primarily interested in its technical specifications. When staying at a hotel, however, the technical quality is taken for granted based on the hotel category, with a guest's interest being drawn to the "human touches" (Musa-Alhasan & Sanchis-Palacio, 1993).

The Research Project

Taking into account the characteristics of the hotel industry in general, and of Seville's in particular, the quality of service is shaped as an essential element for competition. Yet, no empirical studies have addressed the antecedent variables and the consequences of the relationship quality of the hotel industry in Seville. This lack encouraged us to research customers' perceptions of relationship quality in accommodation sector in this town.

To assess the relationship quality, a 36-item questionnaire based on the model proposed by Kim and Cha (2002) was prepared, which was rendered into French, Spanish, and English and had the following three-part structure: the first part refers to the purpose of the visitors' stay in Seville; the second consists of the items addressing the relationship quality; finally, the third includes social and demographic issues of the surveyed individuals (see Table 13.1).

In the first stage of the research, we valued the goodness of the measuring scales of the different constructs for the population under study, with the purpose of ensuring that each set of items referred to a single underlying construct. We removed all the items that did not reach the required level of internal consistency through the Cronbach alpha (0.7), and those that did not prove the unidimensionality through the item(total correlation (0.3) (Nunnally, 1978; Nunnally & Bernstein, 1994).

The answers to the self-administered questionnaires were gathered at pubs and restaurants in Seville from both tourists and local people during the Easter holidays of 2005.

Our target population consists of overnight travelers accommodated in Seville; that is to say, hotel service users. According to the Monthly Report on the Tourism Outlook, which collects and synthesizes the information provided by the Hotel Occupancy Survey conducted by the INE, the number of visitors accommodated in Seville during April 2004 was 194,446. We chose this datum as population reference for our sample design because in 2004 the month coincided with the Easter celebration and, therefore, the number of guests in the hotels would be similar to that of the Easter 2005, held in March this year.

As the whole population could not be surveyed, a representative sample was selected. As a probabilistic sample, its theoretical size will depend on not only the selected sampling method but also the population variance, the level of reliability, and the maximum allowed error. Through a simple random design, the final sample consists of 384, with reliability level of 95% and allowed error of 5%. Four hundred questionnaires were distributed with 250 returned, 132 of which were removed because they were incomplete (response percentage of 29.5%). Therefore, the final sample was 118 valid questionnaires, which implies a sampling error of 9.02%.

Fifty-four per cent of the surveyed individuals were female, 43.6% were younger than 34, and 51.7% traveled with a companion. Regarding their origin, as expected, most of them come from other Spanish areas, mainly from Madrid, whereas the main countries of origin for tourists coming from abroad were France and Germany. The sample composition regarding the origin of tourists is similar to that of the INE.

Table 13.1: Item wording — relationship quality and scale reliability.

Construct (items)	Scale reliability (α)
Customer orientation	0.90
Understanding customer needs	0.87
A hotel employee is knowledgeable about customers' needs	
A hotel employee tries to understand the change of customers' needs	
Conflict resolution	0.88
A hotel employee deals with your inquiry and complaint courteously	
A hotel employee deals with your inquiry and complaint expeditiously	
A hotel employee resolves your inquiry or complaint even though these are not in his or her direct responsibility	
Relational orientation	0.70
Cooperative intention	0.68
A hotel employee treats you equally no matter how much you purchase	
A hotel employee helps you make a decision	
Contact intention	0.70
A hotel employee devotes time for you	
A hotel employee is in constant contact with you (phone, fax, e-mail, letter, etc.)	
You receive birthday card or presents from a hotel employee	
A hotel employee provides information about new events or package promotion programs	
Service providers' attributes	0.93
Expertise	0.87
A hotel employee has professional training and education about service	
A hotel employee demonstrates adequate knowledge about the hotel product and service	
A hotel employee shows interest in self-development to provide better service	
A hotel employee is competent in providing service	
Experience	0.86
A hotel employee seems to have a lot of experience	
A hotel employee seems to have appropriate past-career pattern	
Appearance	0.89
A hotel employee's appearance is professional	
A hotel employee is well dressed	
A hotel employee has a nice manner	
Relationship quality	0.92
Satisfaction	0.92
I think a service provider is favourable	
I am pleased with a hotel employee	

(Continued)

Table 13.1: (*Continued*)

Construct (items)	Scale reliability (α)
I am satisfied with hotel employees	
I am satisfied with hotel's overall products	
Trust	0.93
A hotel employee keeps promises	
A hotel employee is sincere	
A hotel employee is reliable	
A hotel employee is honest	
A hotel employee puts customers' interests first	
Share of purchase	0.71
Hotel usage frequency has increased	
I use other hotel services such as F&B outlets and catering	
Relationship continuity	0.73
I believe a hotel employee will provide better service in the future	
I will continue the relationship with this hotel	
I will visit this hotel again in the future	
Word-of-mouth	0.95
I want to recommend this hotel to others	
I want to tell other people about good things of this hotel	

Most individuals in the sample had a university degree (58.3%), 44.2% were employees, and 43.2% considered themselves as belonging to medium-high social class. They mainly came to Seville to attend special events. In this case, the special event is the Easter celebration, held from 21 to 27 March 2005 (29.9%). The second most common reason was to experience somewhere different (26.5%). The average stay of tourists in the city was 4.33 days. Regarding the type of accommodation, two-thirds chose a hotel, 26% a hostel, and only 12% went to a boarding house. The preferred hotel category is 4-star (45%), followed by 3-star (21%), and 1- or 2-star (9%).

Our first aim was to analyze the differences between large- and small-hotel firms with regard to their customers' perception of the relationship quality. Nevertheless, the analysis revealed that all the hotels chosen by our sample were SMEs.

For the purposes of this study, SMEs are defined as per the European Commission's definition, based on the number of employees. Thus, firms with less than 10 employees are called "micro," and those having between 10 and 49 employees are considered "small." Our interest in analyzing the differences between large and small enterprises was because of the growing awareness that the firm's size and the economic sector in which it operates condition the characteristics of the phenomenon under study, overcoming the traditional view of SMEs as scale versions of their larger counterparts (Andriotis, 2002; Friel, 1999; Morrison & Thomas, 1999; Thomas, 2000).

The finding that all the firms in our sample were small, regardless of their category, made us wonder whether the differences in service quality would be based more on the different categories of the hotels, and not on their size, as defined by the European Commission. Friel's (1999) work indicates that most of the firms operating in the tourism industry in the United Kingdom, in addition to applying marketing techniques in pricing, conduct some kind of research on consumers' needs, and formulate a marketing plan, at least in the short run. We aimed at determining whether or not the same thing would occur in the hotel industry of Seville with regard to customer relationship quality; and whether all accommodation SMEs would be able to manage relationship quality and earn the profits that arise from it, or, on the contrary, if there would be differences between hotels with regard to the customers' perception of the quality depending on the category.

In order to establish if there are significant differences between groups, we have used the ANOVA because it allows us to perform a significance test for the hypothesis that the averages of the groups are different. In ANOVA, we assess the variability among groups above the intragroup variability. Thus, the null hypothesis is that there are no significant differences according to the hotel category in the antecedent and consequence variables of relationship quality. The factor considered is the hotel category, with the following levels established: 4-star, 3-star, 1- or 2-star, and boarding house or hostel. The results of ANOVA are depicted in Table 13.2. The table only displays the items for which we have identified significant differences at a 0.05 level.

There are significant differences in customer orientation, relationship orientation, and service providers' attributes for the two relationship quality variables (satisfaction and trust) regarding the consequences in the market share and continuity of the relationship. Nevertheless, the ANOVA analysis only demonstrates that there are significant differences, but it does not show where they can be appreciated. *Post hoc* tests were performed to determine this. After applying the equality(inequality test for the population variance according to Levene test, either the Tukey or the Games-Howel test was applied accordingly.

With regard to conflict resolution, we can conclude that the best hotels according to customers' satisfaction are 4-star, followed by 1- and 2-star hotels, whereas 3-star hotels achieve very low values in this customer-oriented characteristic. In contrast, according to our results for the analysis of conflict resolution, boarding houses and hostels are the establishments with the smallest number of competences to solve conflicts, with 1- or 2-star hotels being on the top as far as conflict solving is concerned, even above 4-star hotels.

If we focus on the relationship orientation, we find that surprisingly, lower category hotels fulfill their customers' satisfaction more, and help them in making decisions. Furthermore, with regard to the intention of contact, once again 1- or 2-star hotels show better results, followed by -star hotels, three-star hotels, and finally, hostels and boarding houses. Four-star hotels are top of the ranking relating the service provider's attributes, and especially with regard to the staff's expertise and appearance, followed by one- or 2-star hotels.

In terms of the consequences of relationship quality, again it was surprising to find that the hotels that succeed better at building existing customers' loyalty are 1- or 2-star hotels and 4-star hotels. A similar phenomenon occurs with the continuity of the relationship, where 1- and 2-star hotels are ahead of 4-star ones from the customers' point of view, as they are more likely to continue the relationship with these hotels.

Table 13.2: Results of one-way ANOVA analysis.

Item	gl^a	F	p value
A hotel employee is knowledgeable about customers' needs	3	3.370	0.021
A hotel employee tries to understand the change of customers' needs	3	4.014	0.009
A hotel employee deals with your inquiry and complaint courteously	3	8.083	0.000
A hotel employee deals with your inquiry and complaint expeditiously	3	5.390	0.002
A hotel employee resolves your inquiry or complaint even though these are not in his or her direct responsibility	3	5.874	0.001
A hotel employee helps you make a decision	3	8.587	0.000
A hotel employee devotes time for you	3	3.693	0.014
A hotel employee is in constant contact with you (phone, fax, etc.)	3	3.192	0.027
You receive birthday card or presents from a hotel employee	3	2.843	0.042
A hotel employee has professional training and education about service	3	4.117	0.008
A hotel employee demonstrates adequate knowledge about the hotel product and service	3	2.793	0.044
A hotel employee shows interest in self-development to provide better service	3	3.797	0.012
I think a service provider is favourable	3	3.448	0.019
I am satisfied with hotel's overall products	3	3.335	0.022
A hotel employee is reliable	3	2.683	0.050
A hotel employee is competent in providing service	3	4.749	0.004
A hotel employee seems to have a lot of experience	3	4.770	0.004
A hotel employee's appearance is professional	3	6.993	0.000
A hotel employee is well dressed	3	13.208	0.000
A hotel employee has a nice manner	3	4.801	0.003
Hotel usage frequency has increased	3	5.170	0.002
I believe a hotel employee will provide better service in the future	3	3.762	0.013
I will continue the relationship with this hotel	3	5.679	0.001
I will visit this hotel again in the future	3	2.915	0.037
I want to tell other people about good things of this hotel	3	4.112	0.008

$^a gl$ means degrees of freedom

Conclusion

This chapter shows a surprising finding: the superiority of 1- and 2-star hotels compared to 3-star hotels, and even to 4-star hotels in certain cases, in some of the analyzed variables. This phenomenon can have several explanations. It can be due to the fact that 1- and

2-star hotels, being smaller in size (and therefore having fewer rooms), were able to establish a relationship with clients that was closer, more friendly, human, and efficient, with a better satisfaction of their needs (of whatever type) — thanks to a better knowledge of those needs. Another explanation can lie with the individual characteristics of the employees (their youth could make them more enthusiastic at seeking solutions to the possible problems of the customers; they can be more encouraged — thanks to a more personal contact with the guests, etc.).

This phenomenon can also be because of the characteristics of the customers, which may explain the differences in the perception of the quality relation. That is to say, user customers of lower category hotels could have lower expectations with regard to the relationship quality that they are going to receive from the service provider, and can therefore be pleased at receiving more than expected. The valuation that these customers will make of the relationship quality in this way should be more positive than under other situations where they would have had higher expectations.

Whatever the explanation may be — which needs to be identified in future analyses — it is clear that 3-star hotels are missing their opportunity to reach competitive advantage, as they fail at providing their customers with a suitable relationship quality, and thus they are positioned badly to compete, not only with higher category hotels, but also with those in a category immediately below them.

Besides, the results of our investigation allow us to applaud the relationship quality actions undertaken by 1- and 2-star hotels and 4-star hotels. The good results should encourage them to go on enhancing relationship with customers. In their future plans, they should strengthen their actions in the antecedent variables of relationship quality in order to achieve its expected advantages, which in our model are reflected in the consequence variables: market share, continuity of the relationship, and word-of-mouth communication.

Thus, the hotel industry in Seville displays significant differences in client-perceived quality. This finding is worth noting for two reasons: first, because it establishes differences between hotel categories in a variable that is important to enhance the sector's competitiveness, and second because it highlights those weaknesses that might be minimized in order to strengthen the hotel's future position in the market, regardless of their category.

The main implication of this research is its revelation of an urgent need for actions to improve customer relationship quality in 3-star hotels. In order to achieve improvement, it is necessary for public and private institutions in Seville to develop training programmes on customer relationship management. The Tourism Consortium of Seville and the Hotels Association of Seville and Province could usefully promote efforts for encouraging quality service in accommodation units. Moreover, benefits are likely to arise from encouraging accommodation SMEs, especially 3-star hotels, to obtain the quality brand "Calidad Turística Española" (Spanish Tourist Quality).

This research also brings into question the utility of the European Commission's distinction of firms according to size as far as the hospitality sector is concerned (Thomas, 1998). Within the hotel industry, that criterion has served to identify groups of firms with similar characteristics in a variable as important as the relationship quality from the point of view of the future competitiveness of firms in this sector. Thus, the European Commission's criterion classifies into the same category a group of companies that is too heterogeneous, at least with regard the accommodation firms in Seville.

References

Andriotis, K. (2002). Scale of hospitality firms and local economic development — evidence from Crete. *Tourism Management, 23*, 333–341.

Barnes, J. G. (1997). Closeness, strength, and satisfaction: Examining the nature of relationships between providers of financial services and their retail customers. *Psychology and Marketing, 14*, 765–790.

Beatty, S. E., Mayer, M., Coleman, J. E., Reynolds, K. E., & Lee, J. (1996). Customer-sales associate retail relationships. *Journal of Retailing, 72*, 223–247.

Bendapudi, N., & Berry, L. L. (1997). Customers' motivations for maintaining relationships with service providers. *Journal of Retailing, 1*, 15–37.

Berry, L. L. (1980). Sevices marketing is different. *Business, Atlanta, 30*, 24–34.

Berry, L. L. (1983). Relationship marketing. In L. L. Berry, L. K. Shostack, & G. D. Upah (Eds.), *Emerging perspectives on services marketing* (pp. 25–28). Chicago: American Marketing Association.

Choi, T. Y., & Chu, R. (2001). Determinants of hotel guests' satisfaction and repeat patronage in the Hong Kong hotel industry. *Hospitality Management, 20*, 277–297.

Cronin, J. J., & Taylor, S. A. (1992). Measuring service quality: A reexamination and extension. *Journal of Marketing, 56*, 55–68.

Crosby, L. A., Evans, K. R., & Cowles, D. (1990). Relationship quality in services selling: An interpersonal influence perspective. *Journal of Marketing, 54*, 68–81.

Evans, J. R., & Laskin, R. L. (1994). The relationship marketing process: A conceptualization and application. *Industrial Marketing Management, 23*, 439–452.

Fornell, C. (1992). A national customer satisfaction barometer: The Swedish experience. *Journal of Marketing, 55*, 1–21.

Friel, M. (1999). Marketing practice in small tourism and hospitality firms. *International Journal of Tourism Research, 1*, 97–109.

Griffin, J. (1995). *Customer loyalty: How to earn it, how to keep it.* New York: Lexington Books.

Gronroos, C. (2000). *Service management and marketing: A customer relationship management approach.* Chichester, UK: John Wiley & Sons.

Harker, M. J. (1999). Relationship marketing defined? An examination of current relationship marketing definitions. *Marketing Intelligence Planning, 17*, 13–20.

Heide, J. B., & George, J. (1990). Alliances in industrial purchasing: The determinants of joint action in buyer–seller relationship. *Journal of Marketing Research, 27*, 24–36.

Jarvelin, A., & Lehtinene, U. (1996). Relationship quality in business-to-business sevice context. In B. B. Edvardsson, S. W. Johnston, & E. E. Scheuing (Eds.), *QUIS 5 advancing service quality: A global perspective* (pp. 243–254). New York: Warwick Printing Company, Ltd.

Kim, W. G., & Cha, Y. (2002). Antecedents and consequences of relationship quality in hotel industry. *International Journal of Hospitality Management, 21*, 321–338.

Kim, W. G., Han, J. S., & Lee, E. (2001). Effects of relationship marketing on repeat purchase and word of mouth. *Journal of Hospitality & Tourism Research, 25*, 272–288.

Lam, T., & Zhang, H. (1999). Service quality of travel agents: The case of ravel agents in Hong Kong. *Tourism Management, 20*, 341–349.

Lindgreen, A. (2001). A framework for studying relationship marketing dyads. *Qualitative Market Research, 4*, 75–87.

Morgan, R. M., & Hunt, S. D. (1994). The commitment-trust theory of relationship marketing. *Journal of Marketing, 58*, 20–38.

Morrison, A., & Thomas, R. (1999). The future of small firms in the hospitality. *International Journal of Contemporary Hospitality Management, 11*, 148–154.

Musa-Alhasan, S. M., & Sanchis-Palacio, J. R. (1993). La determinación de los precios de alojamiento en la industria hotelera. *Estudios Turísticos, 117*, 49–60.

Nunnally, J. C. (1978). *Psychometric theory*. New York: McGraw-Hill.

Nunnally, J. C., & Bernstein, I. H. (1994). Psychometric theory (3rd ed.). New York: McGraw-Hill.

Oh, H., & Parks, S. C. (1997). Customer satisfaction and service quality: A critical review of the literature and research implications for the hospitality industry. *Hospitality Research Journal, 20*, 35–64.

Oliver, R. L. (1981). Measurement and evaluation of satisfaction processes in retail settings. *Journal of Retailing, 57*, 25–48.

Parasuraman, A., Berry, L. L., & Zeithmal, V. A. (1991). Understanding customer expectations of service. *Sloan Management Review, 32*, 29–38.

Reichheld, F., & Sasser, W. E. (1990). Zero defections: Quality comes to services. *Harvard Business Review, 68*, 105–111.

Sharma, A., Tzokas, N., Saren, M., & Kyziridis, P. (1999). Antecedents and consequences of relationship marketing: Insights form business service salespeople. *Industrial Marketing Management, 28*, 601–611.

Shaw, R. (1997). *Trust in balance: Building successful organizations on results, integrity, and concern*. San Francisco: Jossey-Bass.

Sheth, J. N., & Parvatiyar, A. (1995). Relationship marketing in customer markets antecedents and consequences. *Journal of the Academy of Marketing Science, 23*, 255–271.

Thomas, R. (1998). Small firms and the state. In R. Thomas(Ed.), *The management of small tourism and hospitality firms* (pp. 78–97). London: Cassell.

Thomas, R. (2000). Small firms in tourism industry: Some conceptual issues. *International Journal of Tourism Research, 2*, 345–353.

Wong, A., & Sohal, A. (2002). An examination of the relationship between trust, commitment and relationship quality. *International Journal of Retail and Distribution Management, 30*, 34–50.

Zeithaml, V. A., Berry, L. L., & Parasuraman, A. (1993). The nature and determinants of customer expectations service. *Academy of Marketing Science, 21*, 1–12.

Chapter 14

Motivation and Business Performance: A Case Study of Tourism SMEs in Norway

Hans Holmengen

Introduction

Conventionally, students were taught that profit maximisation was achieved when marginal income equalled marginal costs, i.e. producing one more unit would cause the cost to be higher than the income for the last unit produced and would, therefore, return less total net profits. For a variety of reasons this is not the case, especially for small tourism enterprises. First of all many would count visitors instead of money when making such calculations. This might be acceptable if revenue from travellers initiated some profit contribution, i.e. revenue minus variable costs. That for many practitioners the number of visitors was more important than money, however, is curious. Secondly, the owners' ways of acting rationally were in some cases totally absent. Even if the point of profit maximisation is a purely abstract notion, managers are expected to act cost efficiently and rationally. Empirically, this seemed not to be the case in small tourism enterprises. What was the real reason, or motivation, for running a tourism enterprise?

Researchers have discussed the problem of owner-managers' motivation for decades. They seem to agree that profit maximisation is not the main reason for running an enterprise; factors such as lifestyle are far more important. Others have, for some time, investigated the problems of measuring business performance (e.g. Eaglen, Lashley, & Thomas, 2000). Most business-performance measures are based on the theories of profit maximisation, i.e. the higher the financial measures, such as return on investment, the better the business performance. The aim of this chapter is to explore the nature of business performance and the motives for running a small tourism enterprise. By using regression analysis, the relationship between motives, motives implication on net profits and return on assets is examined. Based on the results, the use of the present business-performance measures is discussed.

Tourism in the New Europe
Copyright © 2007 by Elsevier Ltd.
All rights of reproduction in any form reserved.
ISBN: 0-08-044706-6

Definitions

'Revenues', 'cost' and 'profit' are important terms when measuring business performance. Thus financial as well as operational measures are commonly used. Wickham (2004, pp. 246–247) suggests the following measures of business performance:

> "*absolute financial performance* — e.g. sales, profits;
> *financial performance ratios* — e.g. profit margin, return on capital employed;
> *financial liquidity ratios* — e.g. dept cover, interest cover;
> *absolute stock market performance* — e.g. share price, market capitalisation;
> *stock market ratios* — e.g. earning per share, dividend yield;
> *market presence* — e.g. market share, market position;
> *growth* — e.g. increase in sales, increase in profits;
> *innovation* — e.g. rate of new product introduction;
> *customer assessment* — e.g. customer service level, customer rating"

Since Wickham deals with the challenges of entrepreneurs, measures like innovation and customer assessment are important. Appiah-Adu, Fyall, and Singh (1999) studied business performance in the airlines industry. As business-performance variables they used employee productivity, customer retention and return on investment.

One of their main hypotheses tested was that there is a significant relation between business performance (measured by the three expressions mentioned above) and marketing culture. What is important here are the arguments for the business-performance measures chosen. They argued that in industries where employees and customers are highly interactive, it is impossible to hide the organisation or the marketing culture. They argue that this is more significant in service industries than in goods-producing ones. In other words, business-performance measures may be adapted to industries and even to the purpose of the calculations. Most tourism production is cooperation between suppliers and consumers, and the product is consumed immediately.

Risk factor is one way of including several issues. Risk might be divided into three main parts: market risk, operational risk and financial risk. The sum of these is the overall risk or total risk for the enterprise or for the industry (White, Sondhi, & Fried, 2003). The disadvantage, however, is that it is rather difficult to calculate. For instance, market risk expresses the change in demand and, thus, the need for time series data is present.

Market risk is an expression of changes in demand over time (seasonal differences not included, i.e. changes are based on annual changes) and might be calculated as:

$$\frac{\text{Revenue}_t - \text{Revenue}_{t-1}}{\text{Revenue}_{t-1}}$$

Income from lodging in the city of Lillehammer varied between 2000 and 2004. As Table 14.1 shows, change in demand, measured by income, is rather low, i.e. the market risk is low. If demand variation is high, a dynamic cost structure is essential. If demand is more

Table 14.1: Income from lodging in Lillehammer in years 2000—2004.

	2004	**2003**	**2002**	**2001**	**2000**
Lodging income	131,677	118,912	125,142	126,932	133,399
Changes in per cent	0.107	−0.050	−0.014	−0.048	

Source: Statistikknett.com/oppland.

Table 14.2: Operational risk in Lillehammer.

	2004	**2003**	**2002**	**2001**	**2000**
Operational risk	,629	,656	,591	,584	,602

or less constant, managers can concentrate on cost efficiency. In other words, the higher the changes in demand the higher the market risk.

The operational risk reflects how the enterprise is operated. Most fixed costs exist whether there are changes in demand or not. In other words, demand does not influence fixed costs. Operational risk reflects the amount of fixed costs. A high percentage of fixed costs equals a high operational risk. That is, if there are only variable costs, there are no operational risks.

There are multiple ways of measuring operational risks (White, Sondhi, & Fried, 2003). One way is:

$$\frac{\text{Sum of fixed costs}}{\text{Income}}$$

To enable comparison, the costs, i.e. variable and fixed costs respectively, have to be treated equally in all enterprises. This assumption is hardly likely to be true. Therefore, other more reliable measures have to be found. As suggested in White, Sondhi and Fried (2003) operational risk might be calculated as:

$$\frac{\text{Fixed assets}}{\text{Total assets}}$$

They argue that fixed assets reflect the fixed costs (e.g. maintenance and depreciation). By using this measure, errors arising from separating fixed and variable costs wrongly are avoided. However, the problem of different value assessment remains.

Based on the latter formula, the operational risk of the hotel industry in Lillehammer is as contained in Table 14.2. Fixed assets amount to approximately 60% of the total assets. This indicates that the operational risk for the hotel industry is rather high. Skalpe (2001) suggests that the operational risk in the hotel industry is approximately double that of the food production sector.

Financial Risk

The financial risk factor reflects how total assets are financed. If interest-bearing debts are high, the financial risk is high. Interests influence net profits. Thus, a high rate of interest and high interest-bearing debts indicate less net profits.

The financial risk factor is calculated as follows:

Interest-bearing debts
    Total assets

Owing to high interest-bearing debts, the financial risk is high in the accommodation and beverage sectors. In the Lillehammer region, financial risk is 1.6 to 1.8 times higher than in the food sector.

Total Risk

While the market risk is low, there are high operational and financial risks suggesting that total risk is high for tourism SMEs in Lillehammer.

Return on investment is one important measure of business performance for several reasons: it is easy to calculate, it is comparable across industries, it gives owners an indication of how well invested capital is employed and, finally, it indicates effective (or otherwise) cost management. However, the disadvantages are clear. To compare figures from one business to another assumes that both enterprises apply the same principles of accounting. This might not be the case. Indeed, big differences are likely to appear due to different principles and tax-rule applications.

Return on investment is written as:

    Net income
Total owner's equity

Or in some cases:

    Net income
Total capital employed

This measure provides an expression of how well or how badly the enterprise is run. Total risk, expressed by changes in return on investment, expresses the sum of the other risk factors (see Figure 14.1). By using such figures, business owners are given information about their own business and the opportunity to compare their own business with competitors and the rest of the industry.

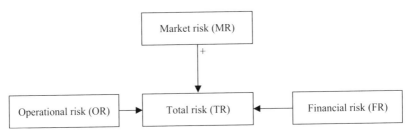

Figure 14.1: The relation between market-, operational-, financial- and total risk.

Small Business Owners

Researchers seem to agree that small business owners can be classified into two groups: that of the entrepreneurs and of 'ordinary' businesses, i.e. owner-managers (Beaver, 2002). The problem is that it is difficult to say when an enterprise changes from an entrepreneurial one to an "ordinary" one. Nevertheless, researchers seem to agree that the personality of the entrepreneur and a business owner differs. Motives for starting a business might be divided in two main groups: push factors and pull factors. Push factors, i.e. negative factors (Sundin og Holmquist in Spilling, 1998), are factors caused by situations like unemployment, debt and family crises. They are mainly financially motivated because the entrepreneur needs money.

The pull factors, or the positive ones, are those driven by the wish to utilise recourses, to take advantage of a situation discovered in the market or a market niche, or just the need to do something new or different. These are the self-development motivations. Or as described in Wickham (2004, p. 243): '. . . the achievement of personal intellectual and spiritual satisfaction and growth'.

The pull factors are:

> The financial rewards of entrepreneurship
> The freedom to work for oneself
> The sense of achievement to be gained from running one's own venture
> The freedom to pursue a personal innovation
> A desire to gain the social standing achieved by entrepreneurs (Wickham, 2004, p. 166)

But there are also some barriers that prevent entrepreneurship. These are factors such as risk, lack of capital, lack of competence and lack of suitable human resources. A venture is started as soon as the values of the pull factors are greater than the impediments. Thus, an entrepreneur is likely to be innovative, risk willing and tactical.

On the other hand, researchers seem to agree that an owner-manager's goals reflect the personal goals or motives of the owner-manager. Therefore, the business is likely to be an 'extension of his or her personality, intricately bound with family needs and desires' (Beaver, 2002, p. 42; Thomas, 2004).

Burns (1989) argued some time ago that motivations change over time. Owner-managers seem to be more concerned about their business goals, more policy-oriented and more strategic after some time. Such differences are likely to influence their way of managing and even their motives for being in business.

The Motives

Several researches have investigated people's reasons for running an enterprise. Why do they risk the money on projects that, according to statistics, have a 20% failure rate (Norwegian National Bureau of Statistics, 2005)? Why do they invest their time and knowledge in projects that make their working hours long and difficult? It is accepted that the focus on motivations and goals influences the way of thinking (and acting) in terms of business development (Dewhurst & Horobin, 1998). Thus, motives are likely to influence business-performance measures.

In order to reveal the motives of running a tourism enterprise in Norway a survey was executed. A total of 95 tourism enterprises in the eastern part of Norway were personally interviewed. Initially, 114 managers were invited to participate but 19 declined. The reasons for not participating were heterogeneous.

Based on the questionnaire employed by the STRATOS-group (Bamberger, 1994) adjusted to the conditions of Norway and to the tourism industry, 12 manifest variables were used in the questionnaire (Holmengen & Bredvold, 2003). These variables were:

- Having the pleasure of serving my guests
- Learning something new
- To control my working hour
- Making high profits
- Continue tradition
- To do a meaningful job
- To control my working situation
- Taking care and motivating my employees
- To test new ideas
- To control my everyday life
- Having interaction with my customers
- Influence on my future

The manifest variables were measured by a Likert scale, where 1 was 'not important' and 5 was 'very important'. Factor analyses were calculated in order to reveal the complex patterns of the multidimensional relationship (constructs) of the manifest variables (Hair, Anderson, Tatham, & Black, 1995). The following four constructs were revealed:
Lifestyle

- Having the pleasure of serving my guests
- Continue tradition
- Taking care and motivating my employees
- Having interaction with my customers
- Influence on my future

Self-development

- Learning something new
- To do a meaningful job
- To test new ideas

Control

- To control my working hour
- To control my working situation
- To control my everyday life

Profits

- Making high profits

A Principal Component Analysis was used. Varimax rotation and orthogonal axes were employed. The 70.2% of variation in the manifest variables is explained by the constructs. Chronbach Alphas are calculated for each construct and varies from 0.76 to 0.79.

Adding up every variable in their construct respectively, and then again dividing the sum by the number of variables in the construct, an index of each construct was calculated. The following indexes were revealed:

Table 14.3 shows 'self-development' was valued higher than any other construct. However, 'lifestyle' as well as 'control' was valued higher than the overall average (3.69). As expected, 'profits' had a low value. The motivation constructs shown above are likely to change over time; i.e. an entrepreneur, who has just started a business, is likely to have motivations different from someone who has been in business for some years. Such differences do not change suddenly, but slowly grow into different settings along with the needs of the enterprise.

By regressing age (measured from the point of time when tourism production started) of the enterprise (independent variable) and the motivations constructs (dependent variables), the changes in motivation constructs are revealed. Figure 14.2 shows the changes in motivation constructs over time.

Apart from 'lifestyle' and 'profits' (not significant) the estimates of 'control' and 'self-development' decrease as time passes. In other words 'control' as well as 'self-development' seem to have less importance in older enterprises than in the younger ones. This implies that managers after the entrepreneurial period are less concerned about these motivations, which

Table 14.3: Descriptive statistics of motivation factors ($n = 79-95$).

	N	Minimum	Maximum	Mean	Std. Deviation
Lifestyle	79	1.80	5.00	3.97[a]	0.6751
Self-development	94	2.00	5.00	4.22[a]	0.5673
Control	90	2.00	5.00	3.81[a]	0.7561
Profits	95	1.00	5.00	2.82[a]	1.1667

[a]Differences are significant on the 95% level.

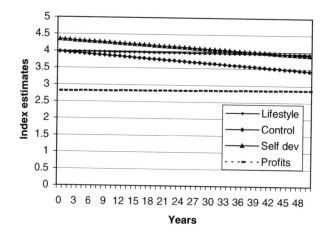

Figure 14.2: Motivation constructs vs. age of the enterprise — estimates.

again might be explained by the process of creating business routines that normally take place in an enterprise. The implication of this is that if motives influence business performance, the business-performance measures should differ accordingly. This might even be a reason for changing business-performance measures over time. This is, however, not the case. As mentioned previously, business-performance measures are normally based on profit maximisation principles.

During the entrepreneurial period it seems that control and self-development are the most distinctive motivations. Several authors confirm these findings (see e.g. Spilling, 1998).

Business Performance and Motivation

Dewhurst and Horobin (1998) developed a model explaining the relationship between commercial goals and strategies on the one hand and the lifestyle-oriented goals and strategies on the other. This is contained in Figure 14.3.

They argue that owner-managers supporting commercially oriented goals and at the same time implementing commercially oriented strategies are likely to be positioned close to point A. Conversely, owner-managers supporting lifestyle goals, and implementing lifestyle strategies are likely to be situated close to point B (Dewhurst & Horobin, 1998). Accepting the model as a simplification, it could be argued that when commercially oriented, commercially oriented business-performance measures are reflected positively. In other words, a successfully executed strategy is likely to reduce risk and thus perform well. On the other hand, when the leader is lifestyle-oriented, business-performance measures are likely to be less impressive.

However, as previously indicated, motives and goals change over time. Therefore, owner-managers are likely to be hovering between points A and B. At some times closer to A and at other times closer to B. The uncertainty of success of chosen strategy is rather

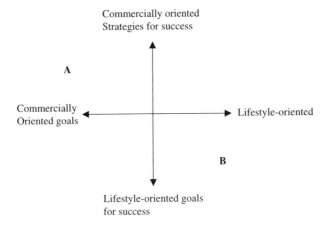

Figure 14.3: Model for owner-manager tendencies.

high, i.e. when measuring business performance, variables other than motives are likely to influence the results.

Regression Model

Risk as a measure of business performance has already been discussed. Return on investment is a measure of overall risk as well as a measure of how the enterprise is operated. As such it is a suitable measure of business performance. A multiple linear regression model is calculated as follows:

$$Y = ax_1 + bx_2 + cx_3 + dx_1 + \text{constant}$$

When Y = return on investments a, b, c and d are beta values of the independent variables respectively x_1 = lifestyle index x_2 = self-development index x_3 = control index x_4 = profit index
    The regression analyses revealed the following equation

$$Y = 0.01 \times x_1 - 0.16 \times x_2 + 0.13 \times x_3 + 0.01 \times x_4 + 0.06$$

x_2 (self-development) and x_3 (control) are significant on the 95% level. The 28.2% of variance (R^2) is explained.
    Lifestyle (x_1) and profit (x_4) are not significant, indicating that the betas 0.01 could just as well equal 0. On the other hand, the betas of self-development (x_2) and control (x_3) are significant. The implications are that when self-development is highly valued, the business-performance measure is less. The motive index control reflects the opposite. The result of a high valuation of control is a better business-performance result.

Implications for Policy

As argued previously, motivation factors are likely to change over time. As the enterprise matures, the owner-manager motives seem to change. From being control and self-development oriented at the beginning, they seem to become less important as time passes. However, the picture is more complicated than that.

Firstly, motivations for starting an enterprise are heterogeneous and complicated. Several dimensions have to be taken into consideration. For example, there might be some differences between entrepreneurs and other business starters. Investigating the differences between entrepreneurs and other business starters is not the subject of this chapter. Nevertheless, it is important to understand some main differences. Spilling, (1998) indicates that entrepreneurs tend to be more market oriented than other business starters. Entrepreneurs seem to be more 'self-development' oriented (i.e. test new ideas) than other starters. The control factor, however, seems to be less important among entrepreneurs. Such differences will of course influence the results revealed above. They are, however, not implemented in the present analyses.

Secondly the dimension of time and, thus, business development, is significant. The different stages of a business's lifetime are thoroughly described and discussed by several authors. The most typical classification is as described in Beaver (2002, p. 128):

> Birth, formation or existence. Here the firm is directly managed by the owner personally; a simple organic structure.
> Survival. This involves a more complex structure with some delegate tasks, supervised by owners
> Growth or take-off. Functional management has appeared and the owner is concerned with maintaining profitability and whether future growth and business development are personal.
> Maturity or consolidation. Here the firm acquires a more divisional management structure, with or without the original owner/entrepreneur.
> Resource, maturity, divestment or rejuvenation. Internal systems and complexity reveal a business concerned about obtaining the maximum return on investments and/or requiring re-organisation and rationalisation in order to re-invigorate the firm, its product portfolio and/or its management process.

In other words, as the enterprise grows older it seems that the focus is more and more on the enterprise, and less on the owner-manager. As the management of the venture becomes more professional, the personal motives of the entrepreneur or manager are less distinctive. This again indicates that business-performance measures should change accordingly, i.e. change from being motivation-oriented to becoming more financially oriented.

The linearity of these different stages has, however, been the subject of discussion for some time (e.g. Morrison, Rimmington, & Williams, 1999; Webster, 1998) with Storey (1994) arguing robustly that most enterprises do not want to grow bigger, even if the chance of failure is significantly higher for enterprises with no or negative growth.

Holmengen (1996) made similar observations in a survey of small tourism enterprises in the eastern part of Norway.

In Norway, to be granted loans or financial support from private or governmental financial institutions, financial business-performance measures are used to reach a judgment. Concepts such as return on investments, cash flow and equity share would represent typical criteria. 'Innovation Norway' is a governmental institution, which provides support for existing entrepreneurs and others starting a business. They will only support those with anticipated high returns. As a consequence, many applicants inflate such projected figures to qualify for support rather than providing for realistic expectations. Other means of measuring business performance could be used to better effect, such as knowledge, motivation and even the idea of the enterprise itself, perhaps then reducing the likelihood of rejecting otherwise valuable projects.

Conclusion

How to measure business performance is a subject of discussion among academicians as well as practitioners. So far, no one has developed a standard measure of business performance and thus, every researcher argues that the measures used in his or her work are the most significant. Due to the heterogeneous objectives of measuring business performance, the multiple ways of expressing it might well be justified. While some researchers take the macro perspective and others take the micro, the needs of different measures are obvious. In this chapter, it has been argued that if business performance is influenced by motives of running an enterprise, the use of risk measurements are adequate. By employing risk measurements like operational-, market- and financial-risk measures, the information is useful for example in strategic planning, marketing and budgeting.

Motives for running an enterprise are heterogeneous, and are not likely to be constant. In other words, motives change over time, and thus their influence on business performance also changes. Based on a set of manifest variables four constructs are developed. The constructs are 'lifestyle', 'self-development', 'control' and 'profits'. The importance of 'self-development' and 'control' seem to decrease, as the enterprise grows older.

Applying regression analyses, business performance is expressed by 'lifestyle', 'self-development', 'control' and 'profits' in the following way:

$$Y = 0.01 \times x_1 - 0.16 \times x_2 + 0.13 \times x_3 + 0.01 \times x_4 + 0.06$$

Only 'self-development' and 'control' are significant.

These findings are not well fitted to the facts that financial institutions are measuring the business performance by profit measures. As long as profits are less-important motives, business-performance measures should be adjusted accordingly. Such disparity is likely to lead to wrong conclusions. Good projects might be rejected while they should be accepted, and vice versa, weak projects might be accepted while they should be rejected.

References

Appiah-Adu, K., Fyall, A., & Singh, S. (1999). Marketing culture and business performance in the airline industry. *Journal of Travel and Tourism Marketing*, 8, 47—70.

Bamberger, I. (1994). *Product/market strategies of small and medium-sized enterprises*. Aldershot, UK: Avebury.

Beaver, G. (2002). *Small business, entrepreneurship and enterprise development*. Harlow, UK: Prentice Hall.

Dewhurst, P., & Horobin, H. (1998). Small business owners. In: R. Thomas, (Ed.), *The management of small tourism & hospitality firms*. London: Cassell.

Eaglen, A., Lashley, C., & Thomas, R. (2000). Modelling the benefits of training to business performance in leisure retailing. *Strategic Change*, 9(5), 311—325.

Hair, J. F., Anderson, R. E., Tatham, R. L., & Black, W. C. (1995). *Multivariate data analyses*. New Jersey: Prentice Hall.

Holmengen, II. (1996). Working paper 19/1996, Lillehammer: Lillehammer University College.

Holmengen, H., & Bredvold, R. (2003). Motives — The driving forces in achieving preferenced goals in tourism enterprises. ETCEEII Conference, Lappland, Finland.

Morrison, A., Rimmington, M., & Williams, C. (1999). Entrepreneurship in the hospitality, tourism and leisure industries. Oxford: Butterworth-Heinemann.

Skalpe, O. (2001). Oslo: Reiselivsbedriftenes landsforening.

Spilling, O. R. (1998). *Entreprenϯrskap pí norsk*. Bergen: Fagbokforlaget.

Stanworth, J., & Gray, C. (1991). *Bolton 20 years on: The small firm in 1990s*. London, UK: Chapman.

Storey, D. J. (1994). *Understanding the small business sector*. London, UK: Routledge.

Thomas, R. (Ed.) (2004). Small firms in tourism: International perspectives. Oxford, UK: Elsevier.

Verspagen, B. (2005). Innovation and economic growth. In J. Fagerberg, D. C. Mowery & R. R. Nelson (Eds.), *The oxford handbook of innovation*. Oxford, UK: Oxford University Press.

Webster, M. (1998). Strategies for growth. In R. Thomas(Ed.), *The management of small tourism and hospitality firms* (pp. 207—218). London, UK: Cassell.

White, G. I., Ashwinpaul, C. S., & Dov, F. (2003). *The analyses and use of financial statements*. New York: John Wiley & Sons.

Wickham, P. A. (2004). *Strategic entrepreneurship*. Harlow, UK: Prentice Hall.

Chapter 15

Tourism SMEs in an Aspirant Member State: Turkey

Sibel Mehter Aykın and Volkan Altıntaş

Introduction

Travel and tourism is one of the largest and fastest growing industries in Turkey, generating 1.5 million jobs and contributing approximately 11.8% to GDP (WTTC, undated: p. 34). Since the 1980s, tourism has been the focus of successive governments' policies to achieve export-led industrialisation. The Tourism Incentive Act of 1982 that gave generous incentives to tourism investment, has resulted in exceptionally rapid tourism growth in terms of volume, value and physical infrastructure. The tourism industry has developed further as Turkey has become more globally and economically integrated. Tourism-flows to Turkey are likely to increase as membership to the European Union (EU) approaches. Nevertheless, highly dominated by small- and medium-sized enterprises (SMEs), the fragile nature of the tourism industry needs special attention in order to cope with a number of problems, such as increased competition from Mediterranean destinations, continuing problems of organised crime and terrorist attacks and the financial problems in major tourist-generating markets (such as the moratorium by Russia and the recession in the EU). In this chapter, small- and medium-sized tourism enterprises in Turkey will be analysed with special emphasis on the accommodation sector. Following a profile of SMEs in tourism, development of the government policy on tourism and the allocation of tourism-investment funds will be explained within the context of National Development Plans (NDPs), and the changes incurred in the general incentive system as an outcome of the EU-membership process will be pointed out. Finally, the problems that hinder the development of the tourism industry will be addressed.

Overview of SMEs in Tourism

It is hard to find a common definition of SMEs in Turkey. As shown in Table 15.1, the criteria used to define the SMEs and the field of activity involved differ a great deal depending on

Table 15.1: Definition of SMEs by different institutions in Turkey.

Institution	Coverage of definition (field of activity)	Criteria	Micro enterprises	Small enterprises	Medium enterprises
KOSGEB	Manufacturing	Number of workers	–	1–50 workers	51–150 workers
Halkbank	Manufacturing, tourism, software	Number of workers	–	–	1–250 workers
		Fixed investment amount (€)	–	–	230,000 €
Undersecretariat of Treasury	Manufacturing, tourism, agriculture, education, health, software	Number of workers	1–9 workers	10–49 workers	50–250 workers
		Investment amount related to the Incentive Certificate for SMEs (€)	350,000 €	350.000 €	350.000 €
Undersecretariat of Foreign Trade	Manufacturing	Number of workers	–	–	1–200 workers
		Amount of fixed investment (€)	–	–	1,830,000 €

Source: KOBİ Stratejisi ve Eylem Planı, Kasım 2003: p. 18.

the tasks, resources and the customers of different institutions. For instance, the Small and Medium Size Industries Development and Support Administration (KOSGEB) and the Undersecretariat of Foreign Trade, ignoring the small- and medium-sized tourism enterprises, extend support only for SMEs in manufacturing industry. Whereas, there is still room for small- and medium-sized tourism enterprises in the definition of Halkbank and that of the Undersecretariat of Treasury. Nevertheless, the membership perspective of Turkey to the EU calls forth adoption of the definition envisaged in the Commission Recommendation 2003/361/EC of 6 May 2003 (ex Commission Recommendation 96/280/EC of 3 April 1996), which covers all fields of activities without discrimination.

The fact that enumeration of enterprises is carried out every 10 years, whereas the turnover frequency of businesses is quite high — 8.4 years on average (Yilmaz, 2003: p. 9) — and

Table 15.2: Distribution of SMEs by field of activity (2003).

Field of activity	Number of enterprises	(%)
Trade	794,744	46.19
Manufacturing industry	246,906	14.35
Construction	35,788	2.08
Hotel and catering	163,112	9.48
Transport	244,497	14.21
Social services	90,675	5.27
Others	144,876	8.42
Total	1,720,598	100

Source: Çolakoğlu, M. H. Avrupa Birliği'nin KOBİ Politikası Bilgilendirme Semineri. Antalya: 28.2.2005.

that SMEs are mostly associated with the manufacturing industry in Turkey, it is difficult to find comprehensive statistics on SMEs in tourism. As shown in Table 15.2, almost half of the total SMEs operate in the trade sector (46.19%), followed by manufacturing (14.35%) and transport (14.21%). The share of hotel and catering enterprises in total SMEs is 9.48%. It is ironic that the table does not cover figures on travel agencies, probably included in the 'others' item.

The following provides a picture of tourism undertakings in Turkey. A total of 1,130 investment-licenced and 2,240 operation-licenced accommodation establishments, of which distribution by types and classes are given in Table 15.3, exist in Turkey (TTIA, 2003: pp. 10–11). A total of 154 aircrafts, of which 80 are private sector air carriers and 74 are carriers of Turkish airlines, operate with a total of 28,299 seats (TTIA, 2003: p. 20). In total 236 investment-licenced yachts with a total of 2,645 beds and 1,058 operation-licenced yachts with a total of 9,234 beds are registered by the Ministry of Culture and Tourism (TTIA, 2003: p. 21), served by a total of 25 marinas, 8 of them being investment-licenced and 17 operation-licenced (TTIA, 2003: p. 22). A total of 4,487 travel agencies of different types including head office and branch offices operate in Turkey, as of 2003 (TTIA, 2003: p. 23).

The share of SMEs, including the service sector, amounts to 99.8% of all enterprises, contributing to 76.7% of the total employment in Turkey. The share of investment by SMEs in the overall investment amount is 38%. The SMEs realised 26.5% of the total value-added. The share of the SMEs in total export is 10% on average, while the share of SMEs in total bank credits is less than 5% (KOBİ Stratejisi ve Eylem Planı, 2003: p. 4).

Public Policy Landscape

Development of the Tourism Industry in 1960s and 1970s

Since the establishment of the State Planning Organisation (SPO) in 1961, the socio-economic life of Turkey has been directed by five-year NDPs, each setting the main

Table 15.3: Distribution of licenced accommodation establishments by types and classes (2003).

Accommodation establishments	Class	Investment-licenced		Operation-licenced	
		Number of establishments	Number of beds	Number of establishments	Number of beds
Hotels	5-star	94	61,989	160	94,694
	4-star	154	54,184	316	95,967
	3-star	262	39,200	540	83,065
	2-star	308	25,542	656	55,969
	1-star	71	3,465	129	7,256
Holiday villages	1st class	41	25,559	76	4,373
	2nd class	29	14,227	19	7,105
Motels	1st class	4	328	4	721
	2nd class	11	369	11	543
	motels	5	154	5	295
Special-licenced hotels		28	1,370	111	7,513
Apart hotels		–	–	87	9,027
Pensions		99	3,148	105	3,752
Campings		10	2,762	9	2,520
Inns		2	140	5	1,019
Golf facilities		669	2	488	–
Tourism complexes		5	8,929	2	891
Training and practice facilities		2	336	3	499
Thermal facilities		1	178	–	–
Service stations		1	54	–	–
Total		1,130	242,603	2,240	420,697

Source: Ministry of Culture and Tourism. Figures are taken from TTAI, 2003: pp. 10–11.
Note: At the end of 2003 around 30,000 beds are in operation with an investment licence. Together with operation-licenced beds, the total bed capacity in operation is 450,000.

principles, national goals, political priorities, strategies and tools, as well as the adminis-trative and legal framework to be adopted. Tourism has always been regarded as a prom-ising sector in NDPs that would contribute to the macro-economic goals, especially by combating unemployment and lowering foreign-trade deficits. However, in the 1960s and 1970s, tourism did not realise its full potential due to inadequate infrastructure and super-structure (Ist NDP (1963–1967), IInd NDP (1968–1972) and IIIrd NDP (1973–1977)). A total of 16,151 beds were registered in 165 acommodation facilities in 1966, rising to

56,044 beds in 511 accommodation facilities as of 1980 (http://www.tursab.org.tr/content/turkish/istatistikler/gostergeler/TESISYIL.asp). Tourist arrivals were only 198,000 people and tourism revenue was $7 million in 1963. Appreciating 5.5% and 45.5% respectively, over the last 17 years, the tourist arrivals rose to 1,288,000 people and tourism revenue up $326 million as of 1980 (http://www.tursab.org.tr/content/turkish/istatistikler/gostergeler/63TSTG.asp).

A Turning Point: Tourism Incentive Act and the Consecutive Developments

The 1980s mark the beginning of a new era in Turkey, when protectionist policies were abandoned for the sake of an open-market economy, known as '24 January Resolutions'. A number of new laws were put into effect, among which was the Tourism Incentive Act 2634 of 16 March 1982.

Based on the provisions of the Tourism Incentive Act, the Council of Ministers Decision no 85/10011 introduced the Resource Utilisation Support Premium (RUSP) that involved monetary support for tourism enterprises. RUSP had been allocated over equity capital and bed capacity on varying rates (7–20% until 1989 and 40% until 1991). In line with the principles and policies adopted in the former NDP that highlighted mass tourism, 91% of all Investment Incentive Documents issued for tourism invetments were backed by RUSP between 1985 and 1991 (Ataer, Erdemli, & Varışlı, 2003, p. 2; IVth NDP (1979–1983)). Consequently, the accommodation capacity reached 200,678 beds and the tourist arrivals 5,552,963 people, with an inrease in the tourism revenue up to $2654 million as shown in Table 15.4, overriding the goals and estimations put forth in the Vth National Development Plan (1985–1989).

Insufficient fund resources and problems encountered in the application of RUSP precipitated the adoption of other measures for funding tourism investments. In 1991, RUSP was replaced by the Credit backed by Resource Utilisation Support Fund (CRUSF) in line with the Council of Ministers Decision no 91/1468. The Turkish Development Bank was authorised to give credit with interest rates varying between 10% and 30% depending on the type and region of the investment, payable in four equal installments after a 2 years grace period (Ataer, Erdemli, & Varışlı, 2003: pp. 4–5). As shown in Table 15.4, 96 Investment Incentive Documents out of 256 were backed by CRUSF during 1991–1992, and as a result the accommodation capacity reached 219,940 beds, tourist arrivals 7,104,065 people and the tourism revenue $3639 million.

The Credit backed by Support Fund for Investments and Foreign Exchange Earning Services (CSFIFEES), allocated over fixed investments, was introduced by the Council of Ministers Decision no 92/2805 to replace CRUSF. Soon extended by Notification no 92/4, it was argued that the unfinished facilities having Investment Incentive Document could be financed by CSFIFEES provided that at least 40% of the investment had already been completed (Ataer, Erdemli, & Varışlı, 2003: pp. 5–6). Between 1992 and 1994, a total of 113 Investment Incentive Documents were backed by CSFIFEES, as shown in Table 15.4, causing the accommodation capacity to reach 265,136 beds, tourist arrivals of 6,695,705 people and the tourism revenue of $4321 million. However, figures realised between 1990 and 1994 were well below the rates estimated in the VIth NDP (1990–1994) due to the Gulf War and terrorist attacks in major tourist destinations in Turkey.

Table 15.4: Distribution of tourism-investment incentives, number of beds, tourist arrivals and tourism revenue by years.

Years	Council of ministers decisions	Total investment documents	Incentive documents backed by RUSP	Incentive documents backed by CRUSF	Incentive documents backed by CSF/FEES	Incentive documents backed by IIF for regional development	Amount of investment incentive certificates issued for tourism (million $)[b]	Number of beds (operation-licenced)[c]	Tourist arrivals[c]	Tourism revenue (million $)[c]
1985	85/10011	90	70	-	-	-	-	85,995	2,190,217	1,094
1986		195	170	-	-	-	-	92,129	2,397,282	950
1987		288	262	-	-	-	-	106,214	2,906,065	1,476
1988		463	444	-	-	-	-	122,306	4,265,197	2,355
1989		592	578	-	-	-	-	146,086	4,516,077	2,557
1990		138	137	-	-	-	-	173,227	5,397,748	3,225
1991	91/1468	141	79	59	-	-	366	200,678	5,552,963	2,654
1992	92/2805	115	2	37	36	-	257	219,940	7,104,065	3,639
1993		152	10	1	68	-	605	235,238	6,525,202	3,959
1994	94/6411	57	7	2	9	-	227	265,136	6,695,705	4,321
1995		137	4	2	-	-	452	286,463	7,726,886	4,957
1996		186	2	-	-	-	501	301,524	8,614,085	5,650
1997		284	1	-	-	-	1,025	313,298	9,689,004	7,002
1998	98/10755	244	-	-	-	4	820	314,215	9,752,697	7,177
1999		199	-	-	-	1	715	319,313	7,487,285	5,203
2000	2000/1721	154	-	-	-	23	520	325,168	10,428,153	7,636
2001		138	-	-	1	14[a]	345	368,819	11,618,969	8,090
2002		187	-	-	-	-	1,113	396,148	13,256,028	8,473
2003		257	-	-	-	-	1,820	420,697	14,029,558	9,676
Total		4017	1766	101	114	42+	-	-	-	-

Source: Statistics Institute of State (SIS), the Undersecretariat of Treasury. Figures are extracted from Ataer, Erdemli, Varışlı, 2003: pp. 2–9.
[a]As of first 6 months.
[b]Figures are taken from TTIA, 2003: p. 16.
[c]Figures regarding the period 1995–2003 are taken from the TTIA, 2003: pp. 2 & 8.

A New Perspective for Turkey: EU Membership

The relations between Turkey and the EU date back to 12 September 1963, when the Ankara Agreement creating an association was signed with the European Economic Community. The agreement envisioned three phases: a five-year preparation period, a transition period (two separate periods of 12 and 22 years as of 1973) and a final period. A Customs Union was planned to be completed by the end of the transition period. EU-Turkey relations gained a new dimension in 1993 when the Customs Union negotiations started. After two years of negotiations, the Association Council declared by Decision no 1/95 that the Customs Union between Turkey and the EU should take effect as of 1 January 1996 (for a full review see: www.deltur.cec.eu.int/ from which much of this section is drawn).

Following the second regular report by the European Commission on Turkey (October 1999), which recommended that Turkey should be provided with prospective membership; Turkey was given the status of a candidate country for EU membership at the Helsinki Summit (10–11 December 1999). Consequently, the Accession Partnership Document (APD), which integrated the priority areas under a single framework together with the financial support and the implementation conditions, was officially adopted by the EU Council on 8 March 2001. In the light of APD, the Turkish Government adopted the National Programme for the Adoption of the *Acquis* (NPAA) on 19 March 2001 that was soon revised in 2003 taking the latest developments into consideration. The NPAA sets forth a broad-range of agenda on political and economic reforms covering short- and medium-term targets. All the issues addressed in the APD as well as in the NPAA have been inserted in the NDPs of Turkey. Indeed, the harmonisation process of Turkish legislation with the EU *acquis* has been carried out since 1988 under the co-ordination of SPO following the membership application by Turkey in 1987, apart from the Ankara Agreement.

At the Brussels Summit (16-17 December 2004), the European Council decided to open accession talks with Turkey as of 3 October 2005, which formed another step forward in the integration process of Turkey with the EU. The screening process will start soon. For Turkey, the membership perspective entails adoption of the *acquis communautaire*, harmonisation of policies and raising the quality standards to European norms.

Latest Developments in the Tourism Industry

Beginning with the second half of 1990s, in line with the principles outlined in the VIIth NDP (1995–1999), investment incentives have been oriented towards regional development. It was argued that investments contributing to employment in the least-developed regions and eliminating regional development discrepancies would be supported by the state. In this context a number of Decisions and Notifications supplying credit from the Investment Incentive Fund (IIF) for regional development have been passed, such as Decision no 98/10755 and Notification no 99/1 designed for newly established facilities that have not formerly used credit allocated from IIF (followed by Decision no 2000/1821), and the Decision no 2000/1721 designed for unfinished facilities, for facilities not in operation and for facilities partially in operation due to insufficient capital (Ataer, Erdemli, & Varışlı, 2003, pp. 6–8). A total of 42 investments were backed by IIF for regional development as of June 2001 as shown in Table 15.4, and by the end of 2001, the accommodation capacity reached 368,819 beds, tourist arrivals were 11,618,969 people and the tourism revenue $8090 million.

The Council of Ministers Decision no 2000/1822 on State Aid for Investments by SMEs has been put into effect in line with the objectives defined in the VIIIth NDP (2000–2005) anticipating that 'depending upon the new trends in demand structure, development of the small size enterprises shall be given priority in the sector and they shall be evaluated within SME status' (VIIIth NDP (2000–2005): p. 189). New accommodation investments in the press other than the seashore between Çanakkale and İçel with 3 km hinterland and than the city center of Nevşehir, Ürgüp and Avanos, as well as renovation investments of the existing facilities have been covered by Decision no 2000/1822. Two Investment Incentive Documents in the least-developed regions and seven in the normal regions have been issued, and a total of 837,112,690,000TL credit has been allocated from IIF (Ataer, Erdemli, & Varışlı, 2003: p. 8).

Between 1985 and 2003, a total of 4,017 Investment Incentive Documents were issued: 2855 of them being allocated for establishment of completely new facilities, 600 for renovation of existing facilities, 243 for extension of facilities and 195 for unfinished facilities (Ataer, Erdemli, & Varışlı, 2003: p. 8). As of 2003, as shown in Table 15.4, a total of 257 investment documents were issued amounting to $1820 million and increasing the number of beds to 420,697. Tourism revenue increased to $9676 million, with 7,726,886 tourist arrivals by the end of 2003.

Tourism-Investment Incentives in Some EU Countries and Turkey

In Turkey, government spending on travel and tourism is less than the EU average, at 0.8% of total spend, compared to an average 4.2% (WTTC, undated: p. 7). However, new laws proposed in the year 2000, giving tourism priority status, has been an important step towards recognising the power of travel and tourism as an economic driver. The main legislation governing the tourism industry in terms of investment incentives and credit facilities are as follows:

Primary legislation on tourism is the *Tourism Incentive Act no 2634*. The aim of the Tourism Incentive Act is to take relevant measures that would help the tourism industry develop. It covers provisions regarding the procedures on determining the cultural and touristic conservation and development areas, as well as provisions regarding the incentives allocated for tourism undertakings. Tourism investments are provided with numerous incentives by a number of laws, provided that they have obtained either a Tourism Investment-Licence or Tourism Operation-Licence in accordance with the provisions of Tourism Incentive Act. The incentives envisaged in the Tourism Incentive Act include: allocation of public lands to investors on a long-term basis; provision of main infrastructure by the state; long-, medium- and short-term credit facilities for construction, furnishing and operations; preferential tariff rates for electricity, water and gas consumption; priorities for communication installation; and foreign personnel employment opportunity up to 20% of the total, in line with the Labour Law.

Council of Ministers Decision no 2002/4367 on State Aid for Investments forms the general incentive system for investments. The aim of the decision is to channelise savings towards investments of high value-added utilising high technologies in line with the targets put forth in the NDPs, with the norms of the EU and with the principles of other international agreements, in order to overcome the regional discrepancies, to create employment as well as to rise international competitive power. As a result of Decision no 2002/4367, Turkey has been divided into three regions: developed, normal and priority region in development, and the investments in different regions are provided with incentives accordingly. The investment incentives provided by the Decision no 2002/4367 involve exemption from customs and building societies fund, investment allowance, VAT exemption, exemption from taxes, duties, levies and charges and credit allocation. In order to benefit from any of these incentives, the investments should be granted a licence by the Undersecretariat of Treasury. To obtain the licence, the minimum amount of fixed-capital investment should be 200 billion TL for the priority region in development, and 400 billion TL for the other regions. Both investment and operation credits could be allocated from the general budget instead of the Investment Incentive Fund. Yet, the investments already supported in the context of Council of Ministers Decision no 2000/1822, explained below, could not be extended any further by Decision no 2002/4367. With Decision no 2002/4367, tourism is included among the priority sectors, thus the investment allowance applies at the rate of 100% for the tourism investments in all regions. Recently, the accommodation facilities were given the opportunity to enjoy electricity as a consequence of support facilitated by the amendment made to Decision no 2002/4367 by Decision no 2005/8680.

Council of Ministers Decision no 2000/1822 on State Aid for Investments by SMEs is the unique legislation in the field of SMEs. The aim of the Decision on State Aid for Investments by SMEs is to support businesses in line with the targets put forth in the NDPs, with the norms of the EU, as well as with the principles of other international agreements, in order to help them increase production, raise quality and standards so that they could gain competitive power and help them contribute to employment generation. The following activities are considered as investments by SMEs under Decision no 2000/1882:

1. Investments by the manufacturing or agricultural undertakings whose net value of total fixed assets (i.e. machinery and equipment, facilities and vehicles), excluding investments in land and building, do not exceed 400 billion TL.
2. Completely new investments in tourism (only the accommodation facilities) and modernising investments of the existing accommodation facilities.
3. Investments in the health industry, in the priority regions.
4. Investments in education in the priority regions and modernising investments in education in the normal and developed regions.
5. Investments by mining undertakings.
6. Investments in software development.

In order to benefit from the incentives developed for SMEs, the investments should obtain a Small- and Medium-Sized Enterprise Investment-Licence from the Undersecretariat of Treasury, together with the Tourism Investment- or Operation-Licence issued by the Ministry of Culture and Tourism in accordance with the provisions of the Tourism Incentive Act. The investment incentives provided by Decision no 2000/1822 involve exemption from customs and building societies fund, investment allowance, VAT exemption, exemption from taxes, duties, levies and charges, investment and operation credit allocated from the Fund. Tourism

Table 15.5: Tourism investment incentives in some EU countries and Turkey (2003).

Country	Non-repayable Cash Grants (as percentage of total investment)	Credits (as percentage of total investment)	Leasing Subsidy	Other
Portugal	20–70%	Up to 75%, 5–15 years term, 1–5 years grace period, interest rate 15–30% below market conditions	First year 30%, second year 15% of the lease expenditures	Special support to SMEs in the sector
Greece	25–40%	Up to 40%, long term, under the market interest rate	25–40% of the lease expenditures	Investment allowance up to 60–100%, 13$/day employment incentive for every new job for 18 months
Spain	20–50%	Up to 50%, 4–20 years term, 1/3 of it grace period	None	Personel training subsidy up to 50%, 40–60% exemption of social security premiums for every new job, special support for SMEs in the sector
Poland	15% 25% for superstructure, up to 50% for infrastructure	None	None	4,000 € employment incentive for every new job; 1,150 € personel training subsidy; investment allowance; 40–65% tax duties and local tax exemptions
Hungary	33–50% for thermal facilities, up to 25% for accommodation	None	None	3,000 € employment incentive for every new job; 50% investment allowance; regional tax exemptions
Turkey	None	None	None	Investment allowance, tax exemption on imported items, VAT exemption on local machinery and equipment, tax duties and charges exemption on local purchases

Source: TTIA, 2003, pp. 18–19.

is also included among the priority sectors under the Decision no 2000/1822, thus the investment allowance applies at the rate of 100% for the tourism investments in developed regions.

For the unclear issues in the Council of Ministers Decision no 2000/1822 on State Aid for Investments by SMEs, provisions of the Council of Ministers Decision no 2002/4367 on State Aid for Investments apply and investments are given the opportunity to benefit from incentives in the context of only one of these Decisions.

Some other laws, covering provisions common to the tourism industry, are briefly as follows: Tourism enterprises are exempted from real-estate tax for 5 years under the *Real Estate Tax Law no 1318*. In the context of the *Foreign Capital Encouragement Law no 6224*, the tourism industry has been fully open to foreign direct investments. Based on the Article 119 of the *Customs Law no 1615*, licenced companies are given the right to import materials much more easily. Further, travel agencies of a certain type and private Turkish airline companies, which have generated at least $1 million foreign exchange flow in the previous year, are given the opportunity to utilise credit from *Türk Eximbank* under the market interest rate (http://www.mugla_turizm.gov.tr/ilweb/sorular/Turizm%20Te%C5%9Fvikleri%20Nelerdir.doc).

Table 15.5 shows tourism-investment incentives in some EU countries and Turkey, as of 2003. According to the table, tourism-investment incentives in Turkey are limited with investment allowance, tax exemption on imported items, VAT exemption on local machinery and equipment and tax duties and charges exemption on local purchases, whereas some other EU member countries provide the industry with additional non-repayable cash grants, leasing subsidy and so on.

Problems Faced by the Tourism Industry

Despite the fact that the growth rate of the tourism industry in Turkey in terms of both tourist arrivals (7.4%) and tourism receipts (9.3%) is much higher than that of the world total (3.0% and 4.9% respectively) as of 2003 (WTO, taken from TTIA, 2003: p. 28), the tourism industry still faces a number of problems. Some of the problems identified by the Union of Chambers and Commodity Exchanges of Turkey (TOBB) and the cures suggested are discussed below.

Although the Tourism Incentive Act no 2634 contains numerous incentives for tourism investments as outlined above, most of the incentives have not been put into effect on the pretext that privatisation is at hand. Indeed, tourism undertakings have been hampered by a number of issues. For instance, not all the tourism enterprises are regarded as exporters. Only the licenced undertakings that generated the amount of foreign exchange determined by the Council of Ministers are considered as exporters and given the chance to benefit from export incentives. Similar difficulties apply to VAT exemptions. The highest VAT rate imposed on tourism is in Turkey (18%) as compared to the other competing countries in the Mediterranean Basin and the others (e.g. Portugal 5%, France 5.5%, Greece 8%, Luxembourg 3%, the Netherlands 6%). It has been argued that the tourism industry should enjoy export incentives and all the other incentives provided for in the Tourism Incentive Act, especially the preferential tariff rates for electricity, water and gas consumption

should be realised, and that the tourism industry should be given the opportunity to benefit from VAT exemption (TOBB, 2005: pp. 2–3).

The main means of transportation from tourist-generating markets to the Mediterranean
resorts is by air. Yet, Turkey has the highest fuel-oil prices among the Mediterranean
Countries, rising costs and underpining the competitiveness of the industry against rival
markets. Furthermore, the head tax imposed on private airlines carrying foreign visitors
are the highest as compared with other Mediterranean destinations. Another cost-rising
issue is the levies taken from foreign passive tourism, as the empty leg from Turkey to
abroad increases the cost of flights. In this sense, the fuel-oil prices should be reduced to
the level in Europe and the tour operators as well as the travel agents should be supported
by eliminating the exit levies, and the head tax should be either reduced or eliminated, at
least for the visitors from the EU, taking the membership-negotiations process into
account (TOBB, 2005: pp. 4–5).

The Municipalities are inclined to impose new taxes (e.g. accommodation tax) on the
tourism industry. Contrary to the wide belief that the tourism taxes are imposed on the
tourists themselves, who do not have voting rights in the host country, most are incurred
by enterprises. It is suggested that the accommodation tax introduced by the Municipality
Revenues Act should not be realised, or else, the tax collected should be redistributed to
the industry through tourism support services (TOBB, 2005: p. 6).

The marine sector is trapped by a number of issues. For instance, the harbour dues taken
in Turkey are the highest in the Mediterranean Basin. On the other hand, the motor-vehicle tax imposed on the marine vehicles contradicts with the equal treatment principle on
taxation envisaged in the Constitution and hinders the development of yacht tourism. In
this respect, the harbour dues should be reduced to the level in the competing destinations,
and the motor-vehicle tax imposed on the marine vehicles should be brought to an end
(TOBB, 2005: pp. 4–5).

Furthermore, it takes some 2 to 5 years to cut through the red tape of the investment
regulations and get especially the cruiser and yacht harbours established. For instance,
11 different ministries take part in the approval process of marina-construction plans.
Moreover, the procedure to issue the transit log, which enables yachts to enter and exit the
harbour, takes a long time, requiring the approval of a number of institutions. It is suggested that the 'round table' system in Italy should be adopted to eliminate the unneces-
sary bureaucratic procedures in investments, and that the transit log should be issued
electronically by a single institution, e.g. the Port Directorate (TOBB, 2005: pp. 2 & 4).

As a promising development, incentive instruments for investments by SMEs such as
credits, tax exemptions, investment deductions, VAT support and low-price energy have
been made available to help SMEs solve their problems on financing, employment, quality and standards. An SME Investments Partnership Company (KOBİ A.Ş.) has been
established under the leadership of TOBB, aiming at providing financial support and advi-
sory services for SMEs at the stages of start-up, development and enlargement. Within the
activities carried out by KOSGEB, consultancy services have been provided for SMEs in
the fields of investment, production, administration and marketing. With the help of the
Small and Medium Size Enterprises Information Network Project (KOBI-NET), electronic
commerce by SMEs has been encouraged. Thus, goods manufactured by SMEs have been
introduced to foreign markets and marketed online (VIIIth NDP (2001–2005): pp. 138–139).

However, neither of these developments covered SMEs in tourism as they have always been neglected in the policy-making process. Not until 2000 have tourism enterprises been recognised as SMEs. Acting selectively, the Council of Ministers resolved to grant the accommodation sector the status of SME by Decision 2000/1822 of 21 December 2000 as explanied above. Despite the fact that most of the travel agencies meet the criteria of SME defined by Commission Recommendation 2003/361/EC of 6 May 2003, they are not regarded as SMEs, nor are they given the opportunity to benefit from SME incentives. It is suggested that Decision no 2000/2822 should be realised to cover all sectors of the tourism industry as in the case of the EU (TOBB, 2005: p. 3).

Concluding Remarks

It is hard to find a common definition of SMEs in Turkey, which hinders compilation of comprehensive data. The share of hotel and catering enterprises in total SMEs has been estimated as 9.48%. There is no record on the share of other SMEs in tourism such as travel agencies, transport companies, catering firms etc. However, the membership perspective of Turkey to the EU calls forth adoption of the definition envisaged in the Commission Recommendation 2003/361/EC of 6 May 2003 that covers all fields of activities without discrimination.

Tourism has always been regarded as a promising sector in Turkey's NDP and would contribute to the macro-economic goals, especially by combating unemployment and lowering foreign trade deficits. Yet, until the Tourism Incentive Act was put in effect in 1982, the tourism industry could not realise its full potential. Based on the provisions of the Tourism Incentive Act, a number of investment incentives had been introduced in the course of time, among which were the Resource Utilisation Support Premium Credit backed by the Resource Utilisation Support Fund, Credit backed by the Support Fund for Investments and Foreign Exchange Earning Services, credit from the Investment Incentive Fund for regional development.

Turkey's prospective membership of the EU has provided a new momentum as it entails approximation of laws and policies, as well as raising standards to international norms. In this context, a number of new laws were proposed in 2000 and the incentive system in Turkey has been updated to include the tourism enterprises (only the accommodation sector) in the definiton of SME.

The existing tourism-investment incentives brought by a number of laws include exemption from customs and building societies fund, investment allowance, VAT exemption, exemption from taxes, duties, levies and charges, credit allocation under the market interest rate, tax exemption on real estate for 5 years, tax exemption on imported items and encouragement of foreign direct investments. As a reflection of the investment-incentive system on the tourism industry, a total of 257 Investment-Incentive Documents have been issued amounting $1820 million, rising the number of beds up to 420,697 and tourism revenue up to $9676 million with 7,726,886 tourist arrivals by the end of 2003.

Despite the fact that the growth rate of the tourism industry in Turkey in terms of both tourist arrivals and tourism receipts is much higher than that of the world total, the industry still faces a number of problems that undermine the competitive power of SMEs, e.g. high VAT rates and fuel-oil prices, various taxes and levies imposed on different sectors of the industry, bureaucratic procedures provided for in the investment regulations and definition of the SME, excluding travel agencies, transport firms, restaurants and the like. However, as Turkey adopts the *acquis communautaire*, the tourism industry is likely to make further progress towards approximation of its structure to the international norms and standards.

References

Ataer, M.U., Erdemli, S., Varışlı, A. (2003). *Turizm sektörüne sağlanan devlet yardımları.* Hazine Dergisi. Sayı: 16.

Bilgiç, M. (Ağustos 2002). KOBİ'lere Yönelik Finansal Destekler ve Yardimlar. KOSGEB: Finansman Destek Süreçleri Grubu.

Çolakoğlu, M. H. (2005). Avrupa Birliği'nin KOBİ Politikası Bilgilendirme Semineri. Antalya: 28.2.2005.

Devlet Planlama Teşkilatı (DPT). I. Beş Yıllık Kalkınma Planı (1963–1967). Ankara.

Devlet Planlama Teşkilatı (DPT). II. Beş Yıllık Kalkınma Planı (1968–1972). Ankara.

Devlet Planlama Teşkilatı (DPT). III. Beş Yıllık Kalkınma Planı (1973–1977). Ankara.

Devlet Planlama Teşkilatı (DPT). IV. Beş Yıllık Kalkınma Planı (1979–1983). Ankara.

Devlet Planlama Teşkilatı (DPT). V. Beş Yıllık Kalkınma Planı (1985–1989). Ankara.

Devlet Planlama Teşkilatı (DPT). VI. Beş Yıllık Kalkınma Planı (1990–1994). Ankara.

Devlet Planlama Teşkilatı (DPT). VII. Beş Yıllık Kalkınma Planı (1995–2000). Ankara.

Devlet Planlama Teşkilatı (DPT). Uzun Vadeli Strateji ve VIII. Beş Yıllık Kalkınma Planı (2001–2005). Ankara.

Duran M. (Ocak 2003). Yatırım Teşvik Politikaları ve Doğrudan Sermaye Yatırımları. Ankara: Hazine Müsteşarlığı Ekonomik Araştırmalar Genel Müdürlüğü. Araştırma ve İnceleme Dizisi No: 33.

Duran M. (Undated). Türkiye'de Yatırımlara Sağlanan Teşvikler ve Etkinliği. Ankara: Hazine Müsteşarlığı Ekonomik Araştırmalar Genel Müdürlüğü.

Yılmaz, F. (5 Aralık 2003). Türkiye'de Küçük ve Orta Boy İşletmeler. Ankara: İşbankası İktisadi Araştırmalar ve Planlama Müdürlüğü.

Commission Recommendation 2003/361/EC of 6 May 2003 concerning the definition of micro, small- and medium-sized enterprises (OJ L 124 of 20 May 2003).

Commission Recommendation 96/280/EC of 3 April 1996 concerning the definition of micro, small- and medium-sized enterprises (OJ L 107 of 30 April 1996).

16.3.1982 tarih ve 17635 sayılı Resmi Gazetede yayımlanan 2634 sayılı Turizm Teşvik Kanunu.

09.07.2002 tarih ve 24810 sayılı Resmi Gazetede yayımlanan 2002/4367 sayılı Yatırımlarda Devlet Yardımları Hakkında Karar.

22.04.2005 tarih ve 25794 sayılı Resmi Gazetede yayımlanan 2005/8680 sayılı Yatırımlarda Devlet Yardımları Hakkında Karar'da Değişiklik Yapılmasına Dair Karar.

30.07.2002 tarih ve 24831 sayılı Resmi Gazetede yayımlanan 2002/1 sayılı Yatırımlarda Devlet Yardımları Hakkında Kararın Uygulanmasına İlişkin Tebliğ.

Yatırımlarda Devlet Yardımları Hakkında 10.06.2002 tarihli ve 2002/4367 sayılı Kararın Uygulanmasına İlişkin 2002/1 sayılı Tebliğ'de Değişiklik Yapılmasına ilişkin Tebliğ (2005/1).

25.12.2000 tarih ve 24271 sayılı Resmi Gazetede yayımlanan 2000/2721 sayılı Yarım Kalmış ve İşletme Sermayesi Yetersizliği Nedeniyle İşletmeye Geçememiş veya Kısmen İşletmeye Geçmiş Yatırımların Ekonomiye Kazandırılmasına Dair Karar.

18.01.2001 tarih ve 24291 sayılı Resmi Gazetede yayımlanan 2001/1821 sayılı Yatırımlarda Devlet Yardımları ve Yatırımları Teşvik Fonu Hakkında Karar.

18.01.2001 tarih ve 24291 sayılı Resmi Gazetede yayımlanan 2001/1822 sayılı Küçük ve Orta Ölçekli İşletmelerin Yatırımlarında Devlet Yardımları Hakkında Karar.

18.022001 tarih ve 24322 sayılı Resmi Gazetede yayımlanan 2001/1 Nolu Küçük ve Orta Ölçekli İşletmelerin Yatırımlarında Devlet Yardımları Hakkında Kararın Uygulanmasına İlişkin Tebliğ.

The Turkish Tourism Investors Association (TTIA). (2003). Selected Data on Turkish Tourism.

Türkiye Odalar ve Borsalar Birliği (TOBB). "TOBB Turizm Sektör Kurulu Raporu", Türkiye Bölgesel ve Sektörel Ekonomi Şurası (5 Ocak 2005). Ankara.

World Travel and Tourism Council (WTTC). (Undated) TURKEY: The Impact of Travel and Tourism on Jobs and the Economy. London.

KOBİ Stratejisi ve Eylem Planı, Kasim 2003

Internet References

http://www.tursab.org.tr/content/turkish/istatistikler/gostergeler/63TSTG.asp
http://www.tursab.org.tr/content/turkish/istatistikler/gostergeler/TESISYIL.asp
http://www.mugla_turizm.gov.tr/ilweb/sorular/Turizm%20Te%C5%9Fvikleri%20Nelerdi r.doc

Chapter 16

Small Business in the Tourism and Hospitality Industry of Russia

Viktoria Saprunova

Introduction

In their attempts to respond to the individualisation and segmentation of demand as well as to the severe competition in the world tourism market, destinations and tourism enterprises have to provide a variety of tourist offerings and events on site. They are also required to have a clearly defined profile, authenticity and a unique market-positioning strategy so that they can attract their target groups. This calls for the development of such small tourism businesses, which are capable of developing various innovative, specialised and authentic products. The success of small tourism businesses is important in Russia, as they are often the main way to survive for a great part of the domestic population and they play a significant social role in the national economy.

Taking into account the significance of the small-business sector in the tourism industry of Russia, the chapter will consider (1) the factors stimulating the development of tourism SMEs; (2) the prevailing areas of small business activities in the Russian tourism and hospitality industry; (3) the key problems in the development of tourism SMEs in Russia, and (4) the support for small tourism enterprises in Russia. The chapter is based upon results of long-term market observation as well as interviews and surveys with tourism SME managers and employees that were undertaken by the author over the past 10 years.

Factors Stimulating the Development of Tourism SMEs

Background

Russia is a country with enormous potential for incoming and domestic tourism, which is very important for the successful development of many Russian regions. However, outgoing tourism prevails in the structure of the Russian tourism industry. Although only about 10% of the population of Russia are sufficiently affluent to go abroad on their holidays, it accounts for 14 million people. It is for this reason that Russia is considered one of the most important tourism generating markets in the world. The main reasons why wealthy Russians prefer to travel abroad rather than spend their holidays in Russia, and thereby support the development of domestic tourism, include the bad quality of domestic accommodation and service and the insufficient capacity of the Russian accommodation sector. The tourism infrastructure in most parts of Russia is underdeveloped or there is no infrastructure at all in some places of great natural attractions. The most-developed tourism regions are still, as it was in the Soviet times, only the Region of Moscow, the Region of St. Petersburg, the Golden Ring (a region of cosy ancient Russian towns situated near Moscow) and the Black Sea Region. This is mainly because the private sector of the economy was totally prohibited in the Soviet Union and all accommodation and tourism enterprises belonged to the public sector at that time. The tourism market was divided between three big state enterprises: Intourist, Sputnik and a tourist agency of the Soviet trade unions. Group excursions were the prevailing form of international incoming tourism.

The only sphere of private activity was accommodation in private houses and flats/apartments of the Soviet people. That kind of "business" was illegal but highly developed in the region of the Black Sea, which was the main recreation area for the whole Soviet Union. When Perestroika was declared in 1985, there were no tourism SMEs at all; no private small hotels, no catering enterprises, no fast food bistros – nothing except for private houses and flats to let in the Black Sea Region. It may be rather difficult for a foreigner to imagine that in the Soviet Union one could not find a private hotel or a restaurant near the highway while travelling by car. In the early 1990s, one could hardly find a hot-dog kiosk with water, coffee and fast food; not even in Moscow. Nowadays, 20 years later, SMEs form an important and successful sector of the new Russian economy. Although many changes have taken place and much has been achieved, there is still a lot to do and to improve in the area of supporting SME development in Russia.

Definition of Small Business Enterprise

Before the prevailing areas of SME activities and the SME support measures in Russia are considered, it is necessary to clarify what enterprises are regarded as "small business enterprises". This definition is essential from the point of state support and tax allowances. In the Russian Federation, the following guidelines are used to distinguish an enterprise as a small one.

Firstly, there is a *commercial restriction*: only private entrepreneurs and commercial organisations may be considered as small enterprises. Accordingly, non-commercial organisations, such as for example, institutions, consumers' co-operatives, public and religious organisations, funding bodies can not be regarded as small business enterprises.

Secondly, there is a *25%-share restriction*: an enterprise is considered as a small one only if the share of the shareholders listed below does not exceed 25% of the equity capital stated in the charter of the company. These shareholders include: the Russian Federation and subjects of the Russian Federation; public or religious organisations, funding bodies; one or more than one legal entities which are not small business enterprises.

Thirdly, there is a *staff number restriction*: the number of employees in a small enterprise may not exceed 50 persons in the hospitality industry and 100 persons in a transport enterprise (Federal Law, 1995).

All these restrictions relate to "small enterprises". As for "medium enterprises" there are no detailed and officially stated definitions of this concept in Russian law and normative acts.

The Need for the Development of Tourism SMEs in Russia

The deficit of the private tourist infrastructure in Russia makes this country rather attractive for foreign investors. This raises a question of whether Russia should let the well-known big international chains and concerns develop the core of the Russian tourist facilities and to implement the world quality standards or whether it should support the development of Russian tourism SMEs. Such a question is very current as many international enterprises are investing in Russia. In Moscow and St. Petersburg, for example there are many global expensive hotel brands, but very few small private-accommodation facilities of good quality and at moderate prices. It can be argued, however, that stimulating the development of the Russian tourism SMEs is essential for the reasons discussed below.

Today's tourism market is characterised by individualisation and the segmentation of demand, which is evident both in developed and developing countries. Tourism demand in developed countries, which are the most important suppliers of tourists for emerging destinations, tends to fall into smaller specialised segments. However, the evolution of tourist demand also occurs in emerging tourist countries. Indeed, in the early 1990s, Russian tourist demand was dominated by standard seaside holidays. Today the variety of holiday preferences among Russians is practically the same as in Europe. The evolution of demand of the affluent Russians follows that of the developed countries. For the destinations and tourism enterprises the individualisation and segmentation of demand means that they have to secure a variety of the offerings and events on site. Such a variety of experiences can be provided only through the engagement of many creative and distinctive domestic small enterprises.

Furthermore, the tourism market is facing tough competition. Globalisation can only escalate but not ease this tension. Under such circumstances, destinations are demanded to have a clearly defined and positioned profile and authenticity. Only in such a way, they are able to attract their target groups. The global chains of tourist enterprises such as hotels or restaurants are too internationalised and cannot always ensure the authentic experiences that particular regions offer. In Moscow, for example, there are McDonald's Restaurants, but the unique charm of the Moscow fast-food industry is created by the original domestic restaurants: "Mu-Mu", "Kroschka-Kartoschka" or "Elky-Palky".

The individualisation and segmentation of demand as well as the necessity to provide the variety of unique services and experiences at tourist destinations are the most important factors that require the development of tourism SMEs. Indeed, due to their flexibility, SMEs are able to offer innovative, specialised and authentic products that meet the requirements of both domestic and foreign clients and maintain the identity of the destination in the globalised world. This is one of the most important reasons why Russia should stimulate the development of the SME sector.

The regional variety of the vast country also makes it necessary to develop the SME sector in Russia. It seems impossible to create an effective tourism infrastructure in a short time within such a large geographical area only by the strength of big concerns and international chains. It is necessary to engage the indigenous population, who knows the domestic specifics, in the process of creating authentic tourist destinations to attract target consumer groups.

Another very important factor as to why Russia should stimulate the development of tourism SMEs is the poverty of the great part of the Russian population. Poverty is mainly caused by the centralised structure of the former Soviet economy; the economic and social transformation in Russia; the unfair redistribution of the wealth of the socialistic state wealth and of the national income; bureaucracy and corruption of the state structures and weakness of the democratic mechanisms. The Soviet socialist society was hated and is still being criticised both by developed capitalist countries and by Russians. Nowadays it is completely forgotten that this society had along with many weaknesses also an advantage: it ensured stability, equal rights and a minimal packet of social services to each citizen of the Soviet Union. The social function of the state was guaranteed by the so-called "social consumption funds". In the 1990s, these funds as well as the key assets of the Russian economy were misappropriated mostly by state officials during unfair privatisation. The main part of the population of Russia was deprived of that part of the common real estate that belonged to the Russian people. Under current conditions when the state is further destroying the system of social support (for example — the free health care and education systems) many people in Russia are becoming poorer. In such a situation their own business is for many people the only chance and opportunity to survive and thrive. This is another reason why the development of tourism SMEs should be stimulated.

Finally, SMEs can increase competition in the market. This is needed to keep prices at a reasonable level and enhance quality. In Russia, because of the shortage of lodges and hotels, accommodation is overpriced particularly in small towns where the price level in general is far lower than elsewhere. For example, in the small ancient town of Pereslavl Salesskij (situated about 130 km from Moscow) there has been only one hotel built during the Soviet times that offered services of a very poor quality. Close to this former state hotel, a new small one was constructed by private investors and according to Western standards. The price per night amounted to USD 60 while the former state hotel offered rooms at USD 20 per night (for reference: the average monthly salary of people in this town is about USD 200). Good-quality hotels are rare in Russian small towns, so nowadays the existing hoteliers can dictate their exclusive prices to the customer. The development of small private hotels and lodges could change this situation in the tourism market.

The above arguments indicate that in Russia the development of the SME sector can fulfil a very important function during the period of developing the tourism industry. In particular, it can contribute towards maintaining the authenticity of Russian tourist destinations, which is so much demanded by tourists. It can also help millions of Russians survive. It can increase competition in the market and secure the stability of society by forming the middle class and ensuring employment in underdeveloped regions of Russia.

Areas of SME Activities in the Russian Tourism Industry

Most tourism SMEs in Russia provide travel, accommodation and catering services. Furthermore, small enterprises are also very active in the provision of cultural attractions: private museums, folklore groups, festivals and other cultural events.

Tour Operators and Travel Agencies

The Russian tour operators and travel agencies sector is dominated by small enterprises. Among 6169 tour operators and travel agents registered in 2001 in Russia, 3089 (50.1%) enterprises employed 4–9 persons, 1872 (30.3%) enterprises — up to 3 persons, and 1208 (19.6%) — more than 10 persons (Tourinfo, 2001). Small tour operators are very creative and develop new routes and tours around Russia. The development of the "Big Ural Ring" in 2005 — a remarkable new tour route around the Ural Region — by three small enterprises from the Ural region is a good example of this. This region is very rich in unique natural resources, cultural attractions and mineral deposits such as salt, precious metals and precious stones. Since the reign of Peter the Great, the Ural Region was the "farriery" of Russian industry. Nowadays there are many interesting tourist attractions such as ancient towns, salt-mines (the seabed of the famous Permian sea), handicraft centres and unique industrial objects. In spite of all these attractions the Ural Region was not considered as "envisaging further development" because of the very poor tourism infrastructure.

Maybe only some people who visited the Urals could appreciate the courage and entrepreneurial spirit of the Big Ural Ring developers: no roads and very few accommodation and catering establishments. The road between two big cities of the Urals, Ekaterinburg and Perm, was so neglected that no bus excursions could be organised on it. In spite of all these difficulties those three small enterprises succeeded in looking for good tourist accommodation facilities for small groups and in offering a competitive tourist product in the Russian and world-tourism market.

There are many other similar examples of the creativeness and innovation of small enterprises within Russia, but unfortunately such initiatives and programmes are very badly positioned in the market and hardly known even in the domestic market not to mention the international market. The main problem of the small business is insufficient communication (for example no access to the Internet), no funds for advertising and promotion, and insufficient knowledge of foreign languages.

Small Hotels

Many places in Russia can offer unique natural, cultural and historic attractions but they are situated far away from big cities, have no accommodation facilities or have facilities of very poor quality. Because of the limited number of hotels, many Russian regions miss the opportunity of attracting tourists. The province of Vladimir (about 250 km from Moscow), for example, had to cancel the requests of foreign tour operators and lost in 2001 about 15,000 potential guests. Big investors are not interested in remote tourist regions but Russian SMEs are ready to invest money there. The sector of small private-quality hotels is on the rise in small towns of Russia such as Rostov Velikij or Uglitsch, Susdal. The hotel occupancy in such hotels reaches 80%.

The growing significance of what is called in Russia the "mini-hotels" (20–30 rooms) is evident from the fact that during the last 3 years an increasing number of tour operators have been including such hotels in their catalogues and offering them to their clients. Examples of such hotels can be found in the Black Sea Region where the unprofessional lodging business of the Soviet era has been transformed into civilised comfortable small mini-hotels.

Holiday Lets

There are two main directions in the development of SMEs in the holiday lets sector: as main holiday lodging, which are usually oriented towards the personalised needs of tourists (e.g. for nature or family tourism) and as additional lodging in popular tourism resorts with an undeveloped infrastructure.

In the Russian mountain Region of Adigeja (Northern Caucasus), for example, there is a whole village, which specialises in the business of main holiday lodgings. All 30 households of this village offer accommodation services. In the Soviet times, this settlement was a forestry enterprise but in the 1990s, it collapsed like many other state enterprises and the local employees were left without any ways to earn money and without any help. The inhabitants of the village recognised the tourism potential of the region and turned their houses into guest houses. The guests visit the village during all seasons and learn about it usually through private contacts as advertising is kept to minimum due to insufficient resources. In the first year of this initiative, one family served only 50 tourists. The best result during 8 years of operation was serving 400 visitors per family in a year. The prices for such services are lower than in neighbouring boarding houses and the quality of accommodation and food is often higher.

As for holiday lets as additional lodging, a typical example for Russia is the project of "Grandfather Frost" (Russian Santa-Claus) which has been implemented in *Velikij Ustyg*, situated 1000 km north of Moscow. This project is supported and promoted by the Moscow government. The small ancient town of Velikij Ustyg is declared the home of Grandfather Frost. As the tours to Grandfather Frost have been promoted very intensively, they attract many tourists. However, there is only accommodation capacity for a maximum of 500 persons daily and the quality of some of the accommodation facilities is very poor. One of the ways to solve the problem is the development of the existing private housing stock and to offer holiday lets for individual and group tourists.

Cultural Attractions

To create a new cultural attraction is not easy. Despite such constraints as limited financial resources or the economic transformation in Russia, such a task becomes even more difficult. Nevertheless, more and more private small entrepreneurs and enterprises are succeeding in doing so.

A very good example of creativity and risk-taking in the sector of small enterprises is a modest private museum in a small Russian town called Pereslavl-Salesskij. Pereslavl is an ancient Russian town, founded in 1152, situated some 130 km from Moscow, with 45,000 inhabitants. The town is rich in old churches, monasteries, museums and natural attractions and it is a part of the famous Golden Ring of Russia. Since June 2002, the family-owned "Iron museum" was added to the portfolio of visitor attractions in this town. The entrepreneur, a young man who worked at that time as an assistant in an art gallery together with his father, bought a burnt old house in the centre of the town and restored it with a start-up capital of only USD 1500. It now houses a private museum with a folk art gallery. A fine collection of ancient irons is exhibited there. The unique design of the exhibition, the old Russian household goods, fine souvenirs and the welcoming Russian spirit characterise this museum. This project is also very well positioned and promoted. The young man has proved that a private museum can be both a successful profitable enterprise and a museum performing the function of keeping and storing the treasures of folk culture for future generations. In 2003, the owner opened another museum, which is also very original and unique; the "Teapot museum".

A similar initiative is being carried out in the Susanino region, mentioned above. A local hunter is a very enthusiastic taxidermist. In a traditional wooden Russian peasant's house, called izba, he has recently developed a small nature museum in the village where he lives so that the children living there as well as the visitors could get to know the fauna of the surrounding forests. Furthermore he recorded the sounds of different animals and offers this "wild music" to his guests.

Folklore groups and ensembles are another cultural attraction. Folklore itself is the best and shortest way of communication between people. Family folklore groups and ensembles can become main attractions in small villages and remote areas. Tourists are very interested to be plunged into the original atmosphere of folk life at the destination. A farmer's household "Vosroshdenije" ("Revival") is an example of this. It is situated in the town of Pereslavl, which as stated before is a very ancient city. The household is founded by a husband and wife (a folklore teacher and a producer) who left Moscow, bought land near Pereslavl and a 100-years-old peasant's house. They decided to revive the traditions of a typical Russian lifestyle. In their old izba they offer some of the art of "get-together" — a Russian village tradition to assemble, to spin, to talk, to sing and to drink tea together. The tourists get to know this tradition, drink tea boiled in the samovar and can also see the old Russian-folk-music instruments, play these instruments and take part in a spontaneous formed folk-music band. This visitor attraction, the Iron Museum discussed earlier and the narrow-gauge railway can also be found in Pereslavl and make this town unique and distinctive among the range of other ancient towns within the Golden Ring region.

Catering

The Russian catering industry at the beginning of the 1990s was characterised by a few standard soviet state canteens and restaurants the number of which in Moscow (with more than 9 million inhabitants) for example did not exceeded 300. The variety and quality of the food offered was very poor. Ten years later, there are more then 6000 restaurants in the capital of Russia and their variety is similar to other big cities in the world. The pace of development is very high; while in 2001 there had been 36 Italian restaurants in Moscow, in 2004 this number increased by 75% and amounted to 63.

The catering sector is booming not only in Moscow but also in the other cities of Russia and near the roads. Mostly these are small private cafés and restaurants that offer ordinary services and meals. However, there are also some unique examples of creativeness and innovation among small private entrepreneurs. For example, on the road from Moscow to the Crimea, near the village of Saltiki, there is a remarkable, purpose-built resort New Saltiki which differs greatly from the other road catering establishments. It is situated near the city of Orel, about 400 km from Moscow. It is like a fabulous town, a peasant's farm and a small aqua park at the same time: funny statues of computer-game heroes, gnomes, pirates, animals, a stream, many bright-coloured flowers, they all create a good atmosphere. The initiator and creator of this restaurant and resort was a local businessman, who wanted to make a present to the people who are travelling on this road — "for the good of the peoples' soul". It was the main work of his life. He wanted to extend this rest area and to build a motel, and a pond for fishing but unfortunately the owner died in 2005 and so far nobody has taken over this initiative.

Key Problems in the Development of Tourism SMEs

SMEs are quite successful in many sectors of the Russian economy, mainly due to the following strengths of these enterprises:

- Product identity
- High potential for innovation and creativity
- Risk-taking
- Flexibility, market adaptation
- Fast decision-making
- Controllable internal-administration mechanisms
- Lower administrative costs
- Personalised services and products
- Hospitality
- Lower promotion costs due to direct contact with the target segments
- Relatively quick return on investment
- High ratio of capital turnover
- Easy accounting systems
- Stable and loyal customer base

When compared with large global firms, the key strength of SMEs is that they aim to benefit the society, particular the local community, and customers, which helps them compete in the market. On the contrary, the strengths of large enterprises are their image and status in the society, which enables them to secure the market-leader position. Large firms often try to adapt the society to their own rules of play, for example, to unify and to standardise the needs of people so that these needs can be satisfied with only one product (e.g. Coca-Cola or Hamburger). Large enterprises are therefore rather egoistic, dominating and overpowering while SMEs manifest themselves as collective, integrative and adaptive. SMEs help to diversify products and services, which is so needed in the tourism industry.

At the same time, however, Russian SMEs face a number of problems caused first of all by the weaknesses of small business, such as:

- A deficit of equity and limited investment capacity;
- High dependence on the despotism of the state authorities;
- Limited opportunities for employees to be educated and trained;
- Limited financial and human resources needed for marketing research and marketing measures;
- Limited resources for technical equipment and the implementation of latest technology;
- Disadvantages in purchasing goods and services needed for their own businesses;

- High seasonality (particularly in tourism);
- Low image of solvency;
- Practically no possibility to influence prices in the market.

Based on the weaknesses of Russian SMEs and on the results of market-information analyses the key problems of the current development of Russian tourism SMEs seem to be the following:

- Imperfection of the law: inefficient licensing regulations, over-centralisation of licensing functions, much confusion in the land law;
- Imperfection of the tax system in Russia: fewer tax benefits for SMEs and sectors with low-profit rates, such as tourism;
- Restricted access to financial and credit resources: interest rate for SMEs is 13–25% (in foreign currency), there are numerous pre-conditions for granting credits;
- Underdeveloped general infrastructure of the country: bad roads and travel facilities, shortage of accommodation facilities;
- No policy for co-ordination, customer information and purposeful promotion of the Russian tourism product in the domestic and international markets.

Support for Small Business Enterprises in Russia

There are two ways to improve the situation in the Russian-tourism industry and to support the courageous and creative small business sector in Russia: the top-down way and the bottom-up way.

Top-down support concerns state support, different measures of federal and regional authorities to stimulate the development of small enterprises. The state support in Russia currently occurs mainly through a range of normative acts, which regulate the legal status of and activity frames for tourism enterprises. Licensing and certification of tourism services, legal separation into tour operators and travel agencies and other ways of regulating the sector are (e.g. licensing taxes) are useful for the state but such measures may signify additional expenses and problems for the SME. What is needed is that the state does not fully control the tourism industry but creates an efficient legal framework and favourable economic conditions for the development of tourism SMEs. Given the weaknesses of SMEs mentioned above and results of interviews with tourism SME managers, various forms of state support for tourism SMEs are needed.

Firstly, tax remissions, full or partial exemption from taxes (during the first years after a SME is established) are needed. A good idea may be the establishment of "special economic tourism and recreation zones" as declared recently by Mr. J. Zhdanov, Chief of the Federal Agency for Management of Special Economic Zones, founded on July 22, 2005 (Zhdanov, 2006).

Investments of the state and local authorities in the development of infrastructure (roads, communication, municipal services) is also needed. There are only a couple of quality highways within the European territory of Russia. The farther one travels from Moscow the roads become worse and worse. The regions rich in natural and cultural attractions cannot develop their tourism under such conditions. Some of the stabilisation funds for stimulating the Russian economy could be used for this purpose.

The granting of mini-credits on preferential terms is another possibility. Deficit of floating assets is a common problem for SMEs. Even USD 300 granted as an initial investment, may be a great help for small businesses in many regions of Russia. In the Vologda region, for example, local authorities grant mini-credits to the owners who need to repair their private houses, which are intended to be offered as lodges to tourists. The most important thing is that such credits are granted quickly, without much paper work, at low rate or without charging interest. Nowadays there are some good examples for such banking activities in Russia: the KMB-Bank (Bank for crediting the small business) is granting mini- and micro credits for small enterprises. However, this support mostly is not offered by the Russian state. Among the shareholders of the KMB-bank which is specialising in crediting SMEs there are only foreign investors, such as the European Bank for Reconstruction and Development (EBRD) Bank and the Soros Economic Development.

Another way in which the state could support tourism SMEs is by the co-ordination of tourism activities. The forms of such co-ordination may be very different, including planning, conducting market research representation at exhibitions, inclusive promotion of the product, communication and booking services. In the province of Vologda, Kirillow region (700 km from Moscow to the north), for example, the local administration formed a state enterprise "Office for tourism and homecrafts". This enterprise disburdened the owners of the houses who are ready to receive tourists from any paper work and accounting, apart from the necessity to register themselves as private businesses. The "Office" develops local programs and organises the whole process of accommodation booking and payment by tourists. In this way, the administration helps the house owners to avoid many bureaucratic obstacles. All these activities make the work of SMEs easier in the house-letting sector and stimulate the development of incoming tourism in that remote region.

Information, education and training are needed. SMEs need to be kept informed about the latest state-of-the-art technologies and trends in tourism. SMEs often have no funds and no time to educate or to train their personnel and to implement new ideas and knowledge. The state can undertake partially this duty, for example in close co-operation with academic and scientific institutions.

One of the areas of state support that already benefited tourism SMEs was the simplification of accounting rules for this sector. The Russian accounting rules differ from the world standards and are very complicated and inefficient. Accounting in Russia is a very expensive and time-consuming activity. Nevertheless, small enterprises are entitled to have the so-called "simplified accounting and taxation system". The introduction of this system in Russia has significantly accelerated the establishment of new small enterprises.

As for bottom-up support, co-operation between SMEs is needed. The main purpose of such co-operation is "help for self-help". Working together, the small enterprises can overcome their weaknesses and gain additional advantages so that they are able to compete with larger firms. The purposes of co-operation may be very different, including creating and promoting common brand; development of complementary services; improving the quality of tourism services and products; raising the level of staff skills; co-ordination of marketing activities with the regional and national tourism authorities; collective purchasing and acquisition of funds.

The trend towards co-operation is evident among Russian tourism SMEs. The small enterprises are beginning to realise the advantages of co-operation and they are trying to follow this route for common success and development. A good example here is the "Small hotels of Baikal" partnership scheme started in 2005. It has brought together 12 small accommodation enterprises situated near the world famous Lake Baikal. The main tasks of the partnership are the development of a common brand, collective participation in exhibitions, popularisation of all-the-year-round recreation on Lake Baikal and an improvement in the quality and choice of tourism products and services in this region.

Conclusion

Development of tourism SMEs in Russia is a necessity and a pre-condition for the successful and sustainable revival of the economy. Tourism SMEs contribute to overcoming the centralised structure of the Soviet economy and to creating an opportunity for the improvement in standard of living and employment for thousands of people, particularly in underdeveloped regions of Russia. Tourism SMEs are an important factor for the stabilisation of the Russian economy and society as well. Since the stability of Russia is a very important international factor, so too is the stimulation of the Russian SME sector.

The tourism industry is a very important economic sector for the "new Russia" as it allows to use efficiently and in a sustainable manner the unique natural resources and the rich cultural traditions of this country and not to exhaust its raw resources such as mineral oil or gas. In tourism, the sector of SMEs ensures a great variety of the tourism product and plays a pivotal role in the development of new destinations. They form the profile of the destination and allow the positioning of the destination to the target audience.

The key problems of tourism SMEs development in Russia include insufficient state regulations, a deficit of financial and credit resources as well as the underdevelopment of the tourism infrastructure. To overcome these problems tourism SMEs need much support from the state. A good example of a successful "top–down" support is the simplification of the national accounting rules especially for SMEs. However, a more diverse range of support measures needs to be used if the tourism SMEs are to realise their potential. That is why the "bottom-up" support, that is co-operation of tourism SMEs as "help for self-help", is becoming increasingly important.

In general, in spite of some signs of further growth of the centralisation of the economy, the situation relating the development of tourism SMEs can be described as dynamic and forward-looking.

References

Federal Law. (1995). *On the state support for the small enterprises in the Russian Federation*, June 14, 1995, No. 88-FZ, Article 3, Clause1.

Tourinfo. (2001). *Russian Tourbusiness in Figures*, No. 37, p. 8.

Zhdanov, J. (2006). *Press release April 3, 2006*. Moscow: The Federal Agency for Management of Special Economic Zones.

Chapter 17

Small Firms in the New Europe: Key Issues, Conclusions and Recommendations

Marcjanna Augustyn and Rhodri Thomas

Introduction

The range of contributions to this volume provides an opportunity for comparing and contrasting the business environments, behaviour and practices of European tourism micro-enterprises and SMEs. This chapter reviews the key themes and issues that have been discussed, paying particular attention to similarities and differences of experiences of tourism SMEs in the established, new and candidate EU member states, as well as in the other European countries. As has been seen, some of the findings confirm what was already understood (or had long been suspected) while others challenge conventional wisdom. The implications for regional, national and European policy-makers and researchers are discussed towards the end of the chapter.

European Tourism SMEs: Key Features

In a recent review of a collection of international studies, Thomas (2004, p. 10) noted that "Lifestyle motivations predominate in the tourism sector but 'lifestyle' needs to be conceptualised in a manner that recognises the influence of sub-sector . . . national cultures . . . location . . . and domestic circumstances". This observation remains pertinent; if the term is to have any academic utility it needs to encompass a range of issues that incorporate motivations (they may be political, social or cultural) and lifestyle experiences. There is more to lifestyle businesses than noting that profit making or growth is not their primary objective (Lynch, Morrison, & Thomas, 2005). Holmengen's contribution provides additional evidence to support the idea that motivations for business ownership in tourism are not simply financial. His work points to an association between motives and levels of business performance.

The chapters that focus on Central and Eastern Europe suggest that the idea of lifestyle entrepreneurship has greater resonance in Western Europe. Indeed, the frequently severe economic conditions associated with the transition from the former command economies to market economies determined the relatively higher frequency of pursuing economic priorities by tourism SMEs in Central and Eastern Europe as compared with their Western European counterparts. Lebe notes that in Slovenia, tourism enterprises were set up with a view to either taking advantage of market situations or self-employment. In the case of Russia, Saprunova stresses that the development of entrepreneurship has been driven by poverty that occurred as a result of the economic transition. However, her chapter also illustrates that poverty has stimulated significant levels of creativeness and innovation in terms of product development on the part of Russian entrepreneurs.

The studies presented in this volume indicate that European tourism SMEs have high levels of failure, particularly in Central and Eastern European countries, that have only recently experienced privatisation. The novelty of market economies meant that many entrepreneurs possessed significantly lower levels of understanding of market processes and suffered when faced with the harsh discipline of market economies. These problems were fuelled by a significant growth in the creation of tourism SMEs by more experienced foreign investors attracted to Central and Eastern European countries.

Regardless of their specific location, all European tourism SMEs face some similar challenges, including fluctuations of demand, changing customer preferences, high staff turnover, low skills and knowledge levels, capacity constraints and poor productivity and profitability. In addition, the new and candidate EU member states experience rapidly changing business environments, particularly regarding the legislation and regulation that has had to be adjusted for the EU's requirements. Capital shortages, high interest rates, difficulties in obtaining bank loans, lack of systematic access to information and knowledge constitute the most acute barriers to the development of tourism SMEs in Central and Eastern Europe, which places them at a disadvantage as compared with Western European SMEs. In Russia, corruption, lack of access to the internet, insufficient knowledge of foreign languages and an inadequate tourism infrastructure constitute additional problems for tourism SMEs, particularly in remote tourist areas.

Support for Tourism SMEs

In March 2000, the European Council, held in Lisbon, claimed that in the following decade, measures should be introduced to enable Europe to become a modern, competitive, knowledge-based economy as the source of sustainable growth, job creation and greater social cohesion within Europe (Europa, 2006). Though there is a degree of vagueness about some of these concepts, a range of financial and non-financial policy interventions have been made, aimed at stimulating the growth and competitiveness of European SMEs in general and tourism SMEs in particular (European Commission, 2006). Examples of recent measures include the establishment of the Euro Info Centres (EIC) Network, SME policy development and the introduction of financial instruments such as the Start-up Scheme of the European Technology Facility, the SME Guarantee Facility and the Seed Capital Action (EC, 2000). Though presented as new, many of these interventions have a long tradition (for a review, including an assessment of the value of EICs see Thomas, 1998).

The importance of tourism SMEs has also been recognised by policy-makers at national levels. Several chapters within this volume discuss public sector support for tourism SMEs. The extent and the types of such support vary, however, from country to country. In their chapter concerning tourism SMEs in Turkey, Aykın and Altıntaş compared tourism investment incentives in some EU member states (established: Portugal, Greece, Spain and new: Poland and Hungary) and Turkey. They found that the variety of investment incentives is lowest in Turkey, while it is the greatest in Portugal, which offers non-repayable cash grants, credits, leasing subsidy and other incentives.

Measures introduced in the UK are examined by Matlay and Westhead (support for clusters of innovation), Leslie (schemes to promote environmental management in tourism enterprises) and Pheby (support offered by the Small Business Service, Business Links and Enterprise Agencies that includes free training in marketing, accounting, IT and writing business plans for anyone wishing to start their own business). In Finland, according to Komppula, the Theme Group on Rural Tourism was established with a view to developing a long-term rural tourism strategy and facilitating its implementation. There is also public funding available for the development of rural tourism supply at the local level. Priorities include the development of innovative products for attracting tourists in off-peak seasons, the establishment of hub-firms and networks supporting these development activities, and education and training projects.

According to Lebe, tourism SMEs have access to general support programmes that include incentives for women entrepreneurs, youth, education programmes for the long-term unemployed, and subsidised voucher consulting systems. Unlike Finland, where a raft of interventions have been devised to support rural development, the local and regional authorities in Slovenia have limited decision-making powers, which makes their schemes less effective.

By contrast, Slovakia has introduced Tourism Development Grant Schemes specifically aimed at promoting tourism SMEs. As Baláž points out, these programmes were supported by the EU-Phare Programme. Key projects that were supported included the development of tourism infrastructure, training and the establishment of tourism SME networks and partnerships. Apart from this initiative, Slovakian tourism SMEs also benefited from general financial and non-financial instruments, as discussed by Gúčik et al. The main financial instruments include credit and interest rate allowances, the provision of state guarantees, loans, non-refundable grants and the investment of risk capital companies. All schemes seem to have brought positive results in terms of investments, infrastructure improvement and job creation.

Other European countries also provide support for tourism SMEs, although the extent of this support is more limited. Holmengen, for example, referred to 'Innovation Norway', which is a government body that provides support for existing and new entrepreneurs and which supports only those which possess the potential for producing high returns. In Russia, as Saprunova explains, current support is limited to the simplification of accounting rules for the sector of small enterprises.

Tourism SMEs and Regional Development

Many chapters discuss the contribution of tourism SMEs to regional development. Particular attention has been given to the role of clustering of tourism SMEs (Mottiar & Ryan) and social enterprise (Pheby) in regional development and sustainability. Issues concerning rural tourism SMEs in Scotland, Finland and Russia were also discussed by Leslie, Komppula and Saprunova respectively. What are the major points of their considerations?

The need for collaboration and networking as a vehicle for enhancing the value of tourism to the local and/or regional economy has been stressed by several contributors. Mottiar and Ryan emphasise the importance of local formal and informal co-operation, Komppula suggests co-operation between tourism stakeholders that operate in rural areas, and Lebe advocates the need for the clustering of all tourism and tourism-related businesses into an integrated tourism product.

However, many destinations — particularly in areas less attractive to private business investment — suffer from insufficient development of the tourism product, which frequently leads to market failure, that is the inability of the market mechanism to meet the needs of consumers. Although the public sector can contribute to the reduction of the effects of market failure, Pheby argues that due to resource constraints the public sector may also fail to satisfy consumer needs. This is where Pheby sees the value of social enterprises which can close the gaps in destination supply by offering those services that the private and public sector are unwilling or incapable of supplying but that are essential in achieving tourist satisfaction.

Regional development through tourism requires taking into consideration the principles of sustainability and community involvement. Marciszewska and Staszewska stress the need for preserving the value of the unique and scarce resources that attract tourists. They emphasise that such approaches, while common in established tourism markets, are not frequently adopted in the new market economies where tourism enterprises are more concerned with pursuing short-term financial goals without due consideration of the negative social and environmental impacts that such attitudes frequently create. Within the context of Scottish rural tourism enterprises and the sustainability of their communities, Leslie found that the awareness of environmental management systems among tourism SMEs stimulates the application of such systems. However, the study undertaken by Marciszewska and Staszewska in Poland, indicates that the level of awareness of sustainability and environmental management issues was very low.

Marciszewska and Staszewska also found that their respondents pointed out the necessity for more active involvement of local communities and other tourism stakeholder representatives. Indeed, within the context of rural areas, Lebe argues that tourism SMEs are important providers of job opportunities for the local population. However, both Pheby and Saprunova draw attention to the possible tensions that may exist between tourists and the indigenous populations frequently. Pheby points to the possibility of locally-based social enterprises reducing such tensions as they ensure that most of the economic benefits arising from tourism are retained within their immediate area of operation.

In summary, the studies reinforced that the critical factors for successful development of tourism regions and the viability of tourism SMEs that operate within these regions; notably formal and informal co-operation, consideration of the principles of sustainability and community involvement. This applies to all European countries but tourism SMEs that operate in Western Europe seem to be more advanced in applying these principles than their Central and Eastern European counterparts.

Strategies for Achieving Sustainable Competitive Advantage

The growing competition in the tourism market requires that tourism SMEs employ appropriate strategies for gaining competitive advantage. Without such strategies, tourism SMEs may find it difficult to achieve their objectives, regardless of whether these objectives are economic, social or other. This volume has presented a range of strategic options open to tourism SMEs as well as examples of strategies and practices that some tourism SMEs have employed in order to achieve their goals. What are the strategies that the contributors have identified and could they be pursued by all tourism SMEs in all European countries?

Collaborative entrepreneurship through SME networks and strategic alliances, which often leads to the emergence of tourism clusters, has been advocated by almost all contributors. The concept of Virtual Teams of e-Entrepreneurs introduced by Matlay and Westhead is one of the most innovative and successful forms of collaborative entrepreneurship. Such teams usually operate in niche markets through internet trading and conduct joint national and Europe wide marketing campaigns. Matlay and Westhead argue that innovative new technologies enable the achievement of cost efficiency due to the proximity of the buyers and the sellers and high performance levels. Furthermore, they provide accessibility of team wide resources and training support. Virtual Teams of e-Entrepreneurs also facilitate effective collaboration between tourism SMEs in the Western and Central and Eastern Europe, which eases transfer of knowledge and best practice, particularly form Western to Central and Eastern Europe. Arguably, the transfer of knowledge and expertise between these two parts of Europe is essential if Europe is to compete in the global market. There are examples where such transfer is currently rather slow, as indicated in the chapter by Marciszewska and Staszewska within the context of the knowledge of sustainability issues among tourism SMEs in one of Poland's regions, Pomerania.

The creative application of technology is also seen as an important marketing tool, both in terms of product design, distribution of tourism products, promotion and relationship marketing, as discussed by Staszewska et al. within the context of Polish travel agents and by Castellanos-Verdugo et al. within the context of Spanish hotels.

Other strategies also prove to be effective in attaining the objectives of tourism SMEs. Differentiation by focussing on niche market segments was advocated by Matlay and Westhead within the context of Pan European Virtual Teams. It was also promoted by Gúčik et al. within the context of hotel industry in Slovakia, by Leslie within the context of rural tourism in Scotland and by Pheby within the context of UK tourism social enterprises. Similar strategies were suggested by Saprunova for Russian small businesses. She called for the development of innovative, specialised and authentic tourism products that would enable the adoption of a unique market positioning strategy capable of attracting niche market segments.

However, Marciszewska and Staszewska emphasise that not all strategies lead to sustainable development and pursuing some of them may damage the natural, social and cultural resources that primarily attract tourists to a destination. While it could be argued that environmental management is a good strategy for attaining competitive advantage, Leslie's findings question this assumption and suggest that customers awareness of the firm's environmental management may not necessarily influence their purchasing choice.

Some of the above are consistent with Dale and Robinson's considerations concerning the strategic imperatives for tourism SMEs. It should be noted, however, that what works for one tourism SME may not work for another and the choice of a strategy should follow a detailed analysis of the external and internal business environment, including the consideration of the firm's resources, capabilities and its strategic objectives.

Implications for Policy-Makers, Managers and Researchers

The comparative analysis of the results of the studies presented in this volume enables us to identify the major implications for public policy-makers at regional, national and European levels and for managers of tourism SMEs. It also provides a platform for specifying a future research agenda.

Policy Implications

As indicated throughout the volume, European tourism SMEs face a number of challenges. In order to reduce these difficulties, the public sector offers a wide range of measures that are aimed at creating favourable conditions for the development of tourism SMEs. Nevertheless, the studies presented in this volume have uncovered possibilities for introducing further supportive measures that could enhance the competitiveness and sustainable development of tourism SMEs. These instruments may differ from country to country depending on their political systems, the type of measures currently in place and the importance of the tourism industry to the development of specific economies and regions. While some of these measures will be more effective if they are decided and implemented at regional level, others may require the involvement of national or European bodies.

One of the spheres that require support is the continuous enhancement of knowledge and skills of the managers and employees of tourism SMEs. The specific areas of focus and the means by which such support is delivered will differ depending on the local needs of tourism SMEs. For example, the findings of the study by Castellanos-Verdugo et al. indicate that there is a need for training in the field of customer relationship management and service quality for managers and employees of 3-star hotels in Seville, Spain. Similarly, Staszewska et al. indicate the need for developing expertise in customer relationship management within the context of travel agencies that operate in Silesia in Poland. In contrast, Marciszewska and Staszewska indicate the need for developing knowledge and skills in the area of sustainability and environmental management among tourism SMEs in the region of Pomerania in Poland.

A case is often made for audits of the skills and knowledge needs of tourism SMEs at the local or regional level. The identification of such needs might be accompanied by an analysis of the preferences of tourism SMEs concerning the ways in which such skills and knowledge could be enhanced. In practice, however, such approaches make assumptions about the manner in which SMEs learn and engage with public sector agencies which are, generally, not borne out by the evidence (Morrison, 2003; Thomas & Long, 2001). Although provision of training is the most frequent way in which the public sector supports the development of knowledge and skills, this is not the only vehicle for attaining such a goal. Indeed, experience indicates that the engagement of tourism SMEs in training programmes is low, even if they are offered free of charge. It is, therefore, necessary to consider other, more innovative means by which knowledge and skills of tourism SMEs could be enhanced and how the public sector could support these initiatives. Several studies presented in this volume indicate alternative areas of public sector support for knowledge transfer and skills development among tourism SMEs. For example, the public sector could introduce measures that facilitate collaboration among tourism SMEs in the form of Virtual Teams as discussed by Matlay and Westhead. Subsidised specialised business advice services — as indicated by Pheby — or encouragement of networking among tourism SMEs at regional, national or international levels — as stressed in several chapters throughout the volume — might also be considered.

Apart from the enhancement of knowledge and skills, other measures are also required to stimulate the competitiveness of tourism destinations. Indeed, there is a symbiotic relationship between the performance of a tourism destination and the viability of destination tourism SMEs. Mottiar and Ryan indicate the need for such support within the context of Irish tourism industrial districts. It should be noted, however, that other countries, for example the UK, have already undertaken various measures aimed at enhancing the competitiveness of tourism destinations (Augustyn, 2004). The UK clustering policy fosters the development of cross-sectoral networks and stimulates knowledge transfers. It has the potential, therefore, for addressing some of the problems that Leslie and Komppula identified in relation to SMEs that operate within rural tourism destinations. Although support for the development of tourism clusters in the UK is a relatively new phenomenon and the effectiveness of such a policy remains to be assessed, other countries could consider the introduction of similar support measures with a view to enhancing the competitiveness of their tourism regions. In Central and Eastern Europe, and particularly in Russia, as indicated by Saprunova, there is also an urgent need for the development of the infrastructure which requires the support from the public sector and which currently constitutes a serious barrier to the development of tourism destinations and the viability of tourism SMEs.

Although the performance of many tourism SMEs depends partly upon the success of the destinations within which they operate, tourism SMEs compete among themselves. Their capability and ability to select strategies that will enable them to gain competitive advantage over their rivals is important. Where owner-managers do not possess an appropriate understanding of the market and the business environment within which they operate, a case can be made for introducing support by the state.

Several contributors within this volume raised the problem of inadequate statistical information concerning tourism SMEs and tourism demand, particularly in Central and Eastern European countries (e.g., Baláž; Saprunova; Staszewska et al.) and in Turkey (Aykın & Altıntaş). Similar difficulties concern specific areas of tourism SME operation, for example rural tourism in Finland (Komppula) or social enterprises in the UK (Pheby). Several Central and Eastern European countries also face a language barrier that prevents them from accessing some of the information that is available in foreign languages only. Much work can therefore be done within this area and such work could be further supported by the public sector at all levels as well as by professional bodies. Central to these efforts is further support for research and development activities that are needed both at the regional, national and European levels.

The studies presented in this volume indicate the need for introducing financial incentives for the development of the sector of tourism SMEs particularly in Central and Eastern European countries as well as where tourism entrepreneurship needs to be encouraged (e.g. rural areas). However, Pheby notes that dependence upon grant finance may discourage entrepreneurial or innovative activity. It is, therefore, essential that the criteria for awarding grants and other financial incentives foster entrepreneurial culture and innovation so that the firms that receive such support are sustainable.

Given the changing environment within which European tourism SMEs operate, a continuous search for improved ways and means of facilitating the development of tourism SMEs is necessary if the measures are to retain their currency and the resources invested in supporting the tourism SME sector are to be well spent. This requires establishing good communication and co-ordination channels between all tourism stakeholders and across all levels of tourism SMEs operation or influence.

Managerial Implications

For many commentators, there is no doubt that a well-designed policy and a set of support measures can significantly contribute to creating an environment conducive to developing European tourism SMEs and fostering their entrepreneurship and innovation (though the evidence base is sometimes less than explicit). However, to compete effectively in a market that is frequently characterised by oversupply, individual enterprises need to develop and implement strategies that can confer competitive advantage. A range of strategic options from which tourism SMEs can choose has been discussed within this volume. It is the creative combination of these strategies and the firm's resources that enable tourism enterprises to achieve their long-term goals (Augustyn & Pheby, 2005).

The main problem for tourism SMEs in Central and Eastern Europe is, however, the preoccupation with achieving short-term financial goals. Consequently, they pay little attention to service quality, customer satisfaction and customer retention (as illustrated by Staszewska et al.), or to sustainability (as indicated by Marciszewska & Staszewska). This requires a significant shift in business philosophies and attitudes but such a shift is necessary if tourism SMEs in Central and Eastern Europe are to compete effectively in European and global markets. While the public sector may be able to offer support, only individual enterprises themselves are able to change their strategies and business practices in such a way that they are more oriented towards satisfying the needs of customers and other stakeholders.

Considering that the success of many tourism SMEs depends upon the success of a tourism destination within which they operate, the active involvement of tourism SMEs in destination wide co-operative and collaborative initiatives is necessary. An appreciation of the benefits that destination wide collaborative initiatives may bring is crucial in fostering collaborative attitudes and engagement among managers of tourism SMEs.

Research Implications

The issues discussed in the preceding sixteen chapters of this volume indicate a number of implications for further research, some of which are outlined below.

Firstly, the concept of Virtual Teams of e-Entrepreneurship discussed by Matlay and Westhead opens a range of research questions that need to be answered. For example, what is the extent to which other European tourism SMEs engage in such collaborative work? What are the barriers to a wider engagement in such initiatives? What are the advantages and disadvantages of participation in Virtual Teams? What are the factors that determine the success of Virtual Teams of e-Entrepreneurship? Addressing these questions would greatly enhance our understanding of this new concept.

Another important area of future research concerns Holmengen's discussion of motivations for running tourism businesses. Understanding the lived experiences and motivations of micro businesses and how and why they change in different parts of Europe would be valuable. The relationship between the motives for running a business and the entrepreneurial behaviour and/or engagement in collaborative initiatives on the part of owner-managers would also provide a greater understanding of the behaviour of tourism SMEs. Attempting to gain some understanding in the context of informal, as well as formal, economic activity would be particularly welcome because there has been such little research on this matter to date, yet — anecdotally at least — informalisation is endemic in the tourism sector.

The work of Mottiar and Ryan also stimulates a range of research questions. For example, how can tourism industrial districts be identified? Where do they exist? What are the inter-firm relations within industrial districts? How are these relations formed? What are the similarities and differences between tourism industrial districts, tourism clusters and tourism destinations? Which concept can best stimulate the prosperity of tourism SMEs and the regions within which they operate? Finding answers to these questions may help in creating the conditions that are more favourable for the development of tourism SMEs.

It has been accepted for some time that strategic frameworks developed for larger enterprises do not fit comfortably into a small business context. Dale and Robinson indicate that there is a need for SME specific research work concerning the development of human resources, the impact of labour migration on the tourism economy, approaches to managing change and innovation and factors that foster a more intrapreneurial culture.

While it could be argued that the employment of environmental strategies can help tourism SMEs achieve competitive advantage, Leslie's findings question this assumption and suggest that customers' awareness of the firm's environmental management may not necessarily influence their purchasing choice. Further studies into this area are needed. Perhaps more importantly, however, is the need to continue with research that finds ways of influencing the business practices of SMEs so that they are consistent with the principles of sustainable tourism.

Pheby argues that social enterprises may play a significant role in enhancing the competitiveness and sustainability of tourism destinations and thus making tourism SMEs that operate within these areas more viable. However, he stresses that no studies have been undertaken to assess whether this ownership model can provide a useful contribution towards economic development within the tourism industry in the UK and Europe. Further studies are, therefore, required.

The impacts of the recent accession of the ten new EU member states upon the economic performance of European tourism SMEs and upon the structure of the European tourism industry are worthy of investigating. This may provide some insights into the possible consequences of the future enlargement of the EU for the European tourism industry.

Studies concerning the impact of globalisation and trends in international tourism upon European tourism SMEs are also needed, as they may uncover new areas of support that is required to ensure the competitiveness of European tourism SMEs.

As this volume has shown, research into policies affecting tourism SMEs in the 'New Europe' and studies of their business practices are being undertaken in many parts of the continent. Inevitably there are areas of relative strength and elsewhere knowledge is almost non-existent. The collective challenge for researchers is to use the insights afforded by this book as a platform for future inquiry.

References

Augustyn, M.M. (2004). *Advantage West Midlands tourism and leisure cluster as a strategy for sustainable development.* Unpublished paper presented at the International Conference on "Networking and Partnerships in Destination and Development Management", organised by ATLAS, Naples, Italy, April.

Augustyn, M.M., & Pheby, J. (2005). Capability-based growth: The case of UK tourism SMEs.' In E. Jones & C. Haven-Tang (Eds.), *Tourism-SMEs, service quality and destination competitiveness* (pp. 87–107). Wallingford, Oxfordshire, UK: CABI.

EC. (2000). Council Decision of 20 December 2000 on a multiannual programme for enterprise and entrepreneurship, and in particular for small and medium-sized enterprises (SMEs) (2001–2005). *Official Journal of the European Communities 2000/819/EC.*

Europa. (2006). *The European Charter for small enterprises.* Online http://europa.eu.int/comm/enterprise/enterprise_policy/charter/index_en.htm (last updated: 02/02/06, accessed 09/03/06).

European Commission. (2006). The *acquis* of the European Union under the management of DG Enterprise and Industry. List of measures (The 'Pink Book'). *EC Enterprise and Industry Publications.*

Lynch, P., Morrison, A., & Thomas, R. (2005). *Lifestyle labels and concepts.* ATLAS Annual Conference, Barcelona, Catalonia, November.

Morrison, A. (2003). SME management and leadership development: Market reorientation. *Journal of Management Development, 22*(9), 796–808.

Thomas, R. (1998). Small firms and the state. In R. Thomas (Ed.), *The management of small tourism and hospitality firms* (pp. 78–97). London, UK: Cassell.

Thomas, R. (2004). International perspectives on small firms in tourism: A synthesis. In R. Thomas (Ed.), *Small firms in tourism: International perspectives* (pp. 1-12). Oxford, UK: Elsevier.

Thomas, R, & Long. J. (2001). Tourism and economic regeneration: The role of skills development. *International Journal of Tourism Research, 3*(3), 229–240.

Author Index

Subject Index